THE

Bliss

EXPERIMENT

THE

Bliss

EXPERIMENT

28 Days to Personal Transformation

Sean Meshorer

ATRIA BOOKS

NEW YORK   LONDON   TORONTO   SYDNEY   NEW DELHI

You will find tags (like the one shown above) throughout this book, and you can use them to access enhanced digital content. To do so, simply download the free app at gettag.mobi. Then hold your phone's camera a few inches away from the tag and enjoy what comes next. You can also visit youtube.com/seanmeshorer to watch these videos. If you access video content through a mobile device, message and data rates may apply.

ATRIA BOOKS
A Division of Simon & Schuster, Inc.
1230 Avenue of the Americas
New York, NY 10020

As this book is based on personal experiences from the past, events have been compressed and some dialogue approximated. Names and distinguishing details have been changed.

First Atria Books hardcover edition May 2012

ATRIA BOOKS and colophon are trademarks of Simon & Schuster, Inc.

For information about special discounts for bulk purchases,
please contact Simon & Schuster Special Sales
at 1-866-506-1949 or business@simonandschuster.com.

The Simon & Schuster Speakers Bureau can bring authors to your live event. For more information or to book an event, contact the Simon & Schuster Speakers Bureau at 1-866-248-3049 or visit our website at www.simonspeakers.com.

Designed by Ruth Lee-Mui

Manufactured in the United States of America

10   9   8   7   6   5   4   3   2   1

Library of Congress Cataloging-in-Publication Data

Meshorer, Sean.
    The bliss experiment : 28 days to personal transformation / Sean Meshorer. — 1st ed.
        p. cm.
    1. Happiness. 2. Meaning (Psychology). 3. Self-actualization (Psychology). I. Title.
    BF575.H27.M47 2012
    158—dc23
                                                                                    2011040917

ISBN 978-1-4516-4211-7
ISBN 978-1-4516-4213-1 (ebook)

*To Brook for her support and understanding,
to my mom for her support without always understanding,
and above all, to Paramhansa Yogananda
for helping me to discover the bliss within.*

CONTENTS

VIDEO TABLE OF CONTENTS

Orienting Ourselves Toward Bliss

The concepts in this book are both a challenge and a promise that I extend to you, the reader. If you give these ideas and practices just twenty-eight days of concentrated and dedicated attention, you can remarkably improve your happiness, understanding of life's true purpose, and spiritual progress—guaranteed.

What's the catch? Just one: you actually have to *do* it with full attention and energy.

How can I make such a bold claim? It's simple: the ideas and practices in this book have been proven to work, time and again, with thousands of people from all backgrounds and levels of experience. It worked for me, it worked for them, and it can work for you too.

This book is based upon a class series that I created and teach throughout the Los Angeles area. Over the years, as a spiritual teacher, minister, counselor, and friend, I've encountered countless people who want to find happiness, meaning, truth, and spiritual inspiration. It is from that yearning that the idea for the course was hatched.

I've seen this program work for every imaginable personality, age, religion, or life experience. Initially, even I was surprised by just how much participants improved their happiness and spiritual awareness in so little time. It scarcely seemed possible, especially since it took me several *years* of hard work to make noticeable progress in my own life. In hindsight, I realize that my slowness was due primarily to the fact that I began by stumbling in the dark, trying to figure out too much on my own, without the benefit of clear guidance from someone who had already blazed the trail. Had I found something like this book when I first started, I could have saved myself years of confusion, false starts, and outright suffering.

In support of this claim is an amazing fact: the course that I teach—the basis of this book—comes with an unusual promise. Anyone who does not experience a noticeable improvement within a month can receive a full refund. To date, not a single person has *ever* requested his or her money back.

Why Bliss?

For as long as I can remember, I've been driven to understand the paradoxes of modern society. We have a higher standard of living, access to previously unimaginable luxuries, and more ways than ever before to instantaneously fulfill every desire and pleasure. Yet antidepressants are among the most prescribed drugs in the world. Most of us spend the bulk of our waking hours at work, yet a majority of workers report dissatisfaction with their jobs. Even as our material lives get easier with each generation, stress-related illnesses are skyrocketing. Anger and anxiety are ascendant. As our celebrity-obsessed consumer culture bombards us with images and fantasies of the "good life," materialism contributes to increasing social inequality and environmental catastrophe by encouraging relentless consumption. On the whole, we're wealthier than ever, yet we are now more deeply in debt—as individuals and nations—than ever. Though we desperately search for solutions, by every objective measure, our reported levels of well-being are actually declining.

In part, our difficulties have increased because the traditional solutions are faltering. Utopian political and social ideologies of both the left and the right have been largely discredited or seen as the angry vestige of extreme cultural warriors. We are now less likely than ever to find solace in formal religions. The latest studies call into question whether antidepressants and other pharmaceuticals even work at all. Modern psychology is more than one hundred years old, yet its promise of a "cure" for what ails us remains more elusive than ever.

It would be insincere to pretend that I'm merely a disinterested spectator to the personal and planetary problems we face. More than twenty years ago, I began my own personal quest for meaning, truth, and happiness. I needed to understand the "meaning of life" not merely out of intellectual curiosity but also because I was desperate to pull myself out of the depths of anxiety and depression that were drowning me. I didn't know if it was possible to find enduring meaning and truth yet still be happy in my discovery. It was a tremendous risk. I wanted to find both meaning *and* happiness but wasn't at all sure that they coexisted. I feared that if I ever did figure out the meaning of life, I would discover that it was one big bummer.

My problem—*our* universal problem—was this: we all want to be happy, we want to lead meaningful lives, and we want to know truth. All three qualities—happiness, meaning, and truth—are equally important. One without the others isn't enough. After all, what use is "happiness" if we also feel that life is ultimately meaningless? Who among us would be content to be "happy" but also know that we are deeply deluded or fundamentally ignorant? On the other hand, what could be more miserable than discovering the "truth" that life is meaningless or joyless?

My personal quest became an existential gamble, with my very life used as the betting currency. This book is what I discovered after a long, sometimes painful quest.

Eternal Truth

For something to be both meaningful and true, it must be enduringly so. To take just one obvious example, either God exists or doesn't. It's impossible for God to exist for some but not others. We can each choose to *believe*, or not, that God exists, but ultimately, either the believer or the nonbeliever is wrong. It's the same with physics: whether we "believe" in gravity or not is irrelevant; we are all equally subject to it no matter what we profess.

Because truth is enduring, I made a concerted effort to stay open to the differing approaches and experiences of a wide range of people, cultures, and eras. There is no reason to think that only a small group of people in one period of time has cornered the market on truth. From the ancient civilizations of India, to twentieth-century French philosophy, to the latest breakthroughs in science, I've tried to cast as wide a net as possible.

Early in my quest, I discovered the happy news that there indeed exists what has been termed a "perennial philosophy": every epoch, religion, and culture has discovered and expressed the same truths over and over again. From Cicero of ancient Rome, to Saint Augustine of the early Christian

Church, to the medieval Islamic philosopher Abu Nasr al-Farabi, to the anonymous authors of the Hindu Upanishads, there is a tremendous consistency of thought and experience.

In current times, especially in the West, one of many new expressions of universal truth has reappeared in the guise of what's being called "positive psychology." As most of its proponents admit freely, the vast majority of the ideas and research projects are cribbed from the universal, thousands-year-old teachings of perennial philosophy.

Which isn't to say that positive psychology hasn't made a contribution. Wonderfully, scientists have found new ways to prove—or at least legitimize—the validity of certain slivers of the perennial philosophy, employing only the most rigorous and mainstream scientific techniques. In the process, they've assisted in the reintroduction and acceptance of long-known truths into scientific discourse. The downside is that they've singled out only the most easily verifiable components of universal truth, having little choice but to ignore those aspects that don't reduce easily to a laboratory setting. In so doing, less important ideas and practices have been stripped of context and overemphasized, while the most important aspects have been inadvertently marginalized. This has led to a new kind of fragmentation and confusion.

My own life project is to find, understand, experience, and then assemble *all* the pieces of the puzzle—for others and myself. My hope, then, is that here we'll find an understanding of the practices and attitudes necessary for self-realization as presented by every major religion, philosophical tradition, and, now, science as well. Because the very aim of human striving—bliss itself—is a unitive state of unbroken oneness, it requires the acknowledgement and understanding of the complete picture. When we stitch together the ancient and contemporary, Eastern and Western, scientific and spiritual, and practical and mystical into one unified whole, a thrilling picture of human potential emerges, one that instantly satisfies our deepest yearning for happiness, meaning, and truth.

What Is Bliss?

There exists within us all a pure state of bliss that, in fact, turns out to be the solution to *everything*. Bliss is where happiness, meaning, and truth converge.

I don't make this claim lightly. As we will see, everything—and I do mean *everything*—boils down to our (sometimes subconscious) pursuit of bliss. We pursue money or relationships because we think they'll make us happy. We pursue our vocation, our hobbies, and our life's passions because we feel they are deeply meaningful to us. We explore science, religion, and philosophical inquiry because we want to know the truth of our existence. Bliss is the universal place that these intersect, where all questions are answered, where every fulfillment is attained.

Bliss is found in every religion but does not require a specific religion in order to know it. Bliss is the ultimate state of consciousness that every religion holds as its highest goal and achievement, though each uses different terminology to explain it. Whether we are Christian or Hindu, Jewish or Muslim, Buddhist or atheist, Wiccan or animist, Taoist or Native American, we all strive for bliss.

Bliss is an innate state of inner joy. It is constant, undisturbed by outward gain or loss. We all have the capacity for it, no matter our age, background, physical or mental disabilities, ethnicity, gender, or religion. External circumstances, whether positive or negative, happy or sad, do not affect it. It is a state of unity, transcendence, completeness, knowingness, wholeness, and uplifted consciousness; it is a feeling of oneness and connection with all of creation. Bliss is never boring; it feels ever new, expansive, and infinite. When bliss appears, one instantly recognizes it as the most central of all truths. Bliss is the eternal, forever unchanging reality that permeates the universe.

My spiritual teacher, Paramhansa Yogananda, explained that while in bliss, our "consciousness perceives all motion and change of life, from the circling of the stars to the fall of a sparrow and the whirling of the smallest electron . . . solids melt into liquids, liquids into gaseous states, these into energy, and energy into cosmic consciousness. [The blissful person] lifts the four veils of solids, liquids, gases, and energy, and finds the Spirit, face to face. He sees the objective universe and subjective universe meet in Spirit. His expanded material self mixes with the greater spiritual Self and knows their unity."

We will learn much more about bliss as this book progresses. Chapter 22, "The Nature of Bliss," contains a much expanded description and explanation.

The Secret to Finding Bliss

This begs the question, How come more of us don't know about or haven't experienced bliss?

First, it should be noted that many of us *do* sometimes have glimpses of bliss, but as quickly as those glimpses come, they vanish. We usually don't fully understand what we've experienced or how to reproduce it—or even whether it *can* be reproduced.

The root problem is that we are looking in the wrong places. Happiness, meaning, and truth can never come from externalities such as luxury goods, celebrity, social engineering, psychoanalysis, political systems, or even through professing superficial belief in religious dogmas. We look for them everywhere except the one place they truly reside: inside ourselves.

It gets worse: when we look in the wrong places for happiness, meaning, and truth, we create unintended consequences that often carry us further away from our goal. The sensory portion of our nervous system, which gives us the miraculous abilities to see, hear, touch, taste, and smell, is also responsible for gradually leading us off course, most especially when these faculties are misused and misunderstood. We become so infatuated with the countless combinations of sense pleasures and worldly possibilities that we lose sight of even the capacity for experiencing the infinite bliss within.

The secret to finding bliss is simple: it is a process of reversing our orientation inwardly instead of outwardly, of removing and revealing. We must strip away our expectations and learned beliefs that external conditions can truly satisfy us. Instead we must learn to identify, appreciate, and tap into the reservoir of supersatisfaction that is already extant inside us, requiring no external environment, situation, or circumstance whatsoever.

We must put aside much of what we think we know and who we think we are by identifying our misconceptions, errors, and false beliefs that block access to genuine happiness and understanding. The challenge is that the layers of falsity run deep. Not only is our external world a trap, but so, too, are our own minds. It is only by uncovering the calm, clear space that dwells deep inside us that we can then see how to reliably tap into the bliss experience awaiting us all.

Put another way, bliss is the process of peeling away the darkness to reveal the beautiful light underneath.

Unearthing the Raw Diamond of Bliss

One of the best ways to understand what I mean is to visualize a raw, uncut diamond. Have you ever seen one? If not, its salient feature is that it looks nothing at all like the highly coveted sparkly rocks that we set in our jewelry. Uncut diamonds are dark, dusty, and often encrusted with other minerals that obscure their true nature. They often appear rough and either blandly colorless or pale, without any noticeable luminosity or exuberance. In fact, they are so ordinary looking that, famously, Brazilian gold miners in the eighteenth century threw away a fortune in unrecognized diamonds while they were panning for gold.

In reality, as we know, raw diamonds are anything but ordinary. They are the most valuable substance in the world. We don't, however, see this until we first dig them out of the earth, remove the excess dirt and debris, then chisel away the outer layers of mineral encrustation, precisely trim the facets in just the right way, and then, finally, meticulously polish it to perfection. Only after all these steps does the most brilliant and enduring substance on the planet make its appearance.

Bliss is like that diamond: all this time, lying quietly dormant inside us, is a sparkling reservoir of infinite bliss. Too often, though, we overlook it, even throw it away, as we mistakenly search for something else of much lesser value.

Much conspires against us, tricking us into wrong directions. Our sensory pleasures and worldly desires continually misdirect our attention. Money, sex, fame, beauty, power—all elaborate ruses that only misguide us. So too are we trapped by ruminating about the past or worrying about the future. Negative or harmful environments of our choosing undermine our best intentions. Our own minds often work against us: whether by distracting us with an endless procession of fleeting and ultimately meaningless thoughts or emotions, or by distorting ultimate reality beyond all recognition.

Not only do all of these forms of outward focus distract us from noticing the raw bliss diamond within, every time we follow our sensory pleasures or look for happiness outside ourselves we further obscure our hidden treasure. Our external focus creates new layers of dirt and grime, further obscuring our bliss diamond and setting us back. By the time most of us figure out that we've been looking for happiness, meaning, and truth in all the wrong places, we've created a monumental excavation project for ourselves—and that's *if* we can even figure out where to start digging.

Bliss requires continually stripping away false layer after false layer until finally the glorious, invaluable diamond inside us is revealed, and we realize that bliss is, eternally, our own highest and deepest nature. It is that which remains after everything external and fleeting disappears.

Three Levels of Consciousness

Throughout this book, we'll make reference to three different states of consciousness. Our level of consciousness directly correlates to our experience of bliss. The three states are (1) subconsciousness, (2) everyday waking consciousness, and (3) superconsciousness.

Everyday waking consciousness needs the least explanation. It's the state you're in right now (hopefully) as you read this book. It's our normal state of consciousness most of the time, when we aren't sleeping.

The subconscious mind is a repository for the thoughts, impressions, and feelings that are passed on to it by our conscious mind. It's like a giant underground storage facility that automatically and indiscriminately accumulates a disorganized assortment of *stuff*—positive and negative—over a lifetime (perhaps many lifetimes if you believe in reincarnation). It tends not to have a well-organized retrieval system. Instead it pretty much just tosses things down there in a heap. I visualize our subconscious minds as the mental equivalent of hoarders; those people who compulsively accumulate every possession they come across, regardless of whether it's priceless or worthless. However, unlike out-of-control physical hoarders, who are relatively rare, we *all* suffer from mental hoarding.

This isn't to say that our subconscious minds are useless or mostly negative. Far from it: they store all kinds of helpful thoughts and memories. For example, our subconscious holds our habit patterns, including a long list of laborsaving shortcuts (like the ability to tie our shoes or drive a car). Were it not for this mechanism, our conscious minds would be so overwhelmed with mundane tasks that we would have no time for anything else, including higher-order pursuits. Life would become intolerably rote and dreary. The problem is that the subconscious is quite indiscriminate. It also stores lots of crappy things: terrible memories, bad habits, deep-seated anxieties, fears, and delusions. All of which hold enormous power over us, often subtly influencing our decisions without our realizing it.

The third state of consciousness—superconsciousness—is experienced so rarely that many people don't even know it exists. If consciousness is everyday waking reality, and subconsciousness is our subterranean repository of thoughts, feelings, memories, and habits, then superconsciousness is an exalted state of heightened awareness that can be thought of as "above and beyond" our regular waking consciousness. Its main attribute is bliss. In fact, it can be said that we must be in a state of superconsciousness in order to feel bliss; therefore, *to be in superconsciousness is to experience bliss.* If we remain in only the state of everyday waking reality, the best we can experience is what I term "everyday happiness." This is why bliss exists on an entirely different octave and is of a different category altogether than happiness.

Superconsciousness is not something that we produce in our brains. Rather it is something we tune into, just as a radio receives sound waves from the air around us and transmits them into audible frequencies. Superconsciousness is not an altered state. It's a pure state of unfiltered, unalloyed consciousness. If anything, it would be more appropriate to think of subconsciousness and waking consciousness as the altered states. They take pure superconsciousness and down-convert them through the prisms of ego, limitations, ignorance, and negative emotions into something lesser.

The Course of This Book

This book can be thought of as a course in two senses. First, it is a series of lessons organized into twenty-eight chapters. Each chapter can be thought of as relatively self-contained. Only one main topic is discussed at a time, almost always accompanied by a specific exercise, or "Bliss Experiment."

This book is also a course in the sense that it is a path that we will walk together, leading to our final destination of bliss consciousness.

Each chapter represents a step along our journey. These are the steps necessary for us to discover where to begin digging for our bliss diamond; how to peel away the layers of useless detritus; how to liberate our bliss diamond in just the right way, in harmony with its natural facets and fault lines; and, finally, how to polish that bliss diamond into a sparkling beacon that will not only glisten within us but also shine light onto the world around us.

The Nature of the Experiment

We've looked at the "bliss" aspect of this book. Also in the title is the word *experiment*. What do I mean by that?

Genuine spirituality is scientific. Sometimes this means the very specific sense of actual laboratory experiments carried out by degreed professionals publishing in prestigious journals. While important to know and reference whenever possible, that is my secondary meaning.

Primarily, spirituality should be scientific in the sense that it does not require dogmatic belief but is provable and reproducible. That is to say, you should never just take my word for it. I want you to personally experience these practices and truths for yourself. Our "laboratory" is inside our own minds and bodies. Each practice in this book is a set of guidelines for how you can conduct your own Bliss Experiment, observing and experiencing the results inside your body-mind lab.

Ultimately, there is only one way to discover happiness, meaning, and truth: by doing these practices for yourself and seeing what happens. This is how I got to where I am, by personally doing each and every practice recommended in this book and assessing the results it had in my mind and consciousness. In my personal journey, I've actually tried many, many practices *not* found in this book. I stopped doing the ones that didn't work or didn't make sense for me. I've always felt that it does great violence to ourselves to continue doing things that we don't believe in or even know outright don't work. The moment a practice is failing you (as opposed to you merely failing to do the practice), it should be discontinued.

How to Use This Book

As a starting point, I recommend moving at the pace of one chapter and its related exercise(s) per day, although of course you can move faster or slower. It's important, however, to give yourself enough time to really absorb the lessons and practices of each chapter.

If you feel that one chapter per day is too fast, especially because you really want to delve deeply into some of the practices before moving on, you might consider one chapter per week—or even per month. Conversely, you might find that one chapter per day is too slow. Learn at whatever pace feels right for you. But until you have a clearer sense of that, for now, I recommend starting with the idea of one chapter per day for twenty-eight days, a pace that has proven effective for a wide range of people.

I cannot stress enough that this book is not intended as "pure philosophy" or a bunch of abstract new-age ideas randomly thrown together. This program is serious, proven, and practical; it's a hands-on resource for personal transformation.

That said, I don't want to give you false impression that this is a bunch of hard work and that you must "put your shoulder to the grindstone" or "grin and bear it," or anything like that. The great thing about practicing happiness and bliss is that by definition it should be enjoyable—even outright fun. The mind-set behind finding happiness, meaning, and bliss is *not at all* like what you might have experienced when dieting or trying an exercise regimen: "I know it's going to be grueling, but think how worthwhile it will be in the end" is not the approach we take here.

The wonderful thing is that you'll discover it's just the opposite. The further you go and the deeper you practice, the lighter, happier, freer, and more joyful you'll feel. The whole point is that you'll actually be *happy* to do this!

Most of the chapters follow the same general format, containing four main sections: the story, the science, the spirit, and the experiment.

The Story

Each chapter opens with a true story based upon real people, real conversations, and real experiences. However, I've changed names and identifying details in order to protect their privacy. The stories have been culled from years of teaching, counseling, or interacting with the many thousands of people I've been fortunate enough to know. My hope is that each story will help you to immediately understand and relate to the specific issue or topic that we'll be exploring in that chapter. They also give you a wide range of people's experiences to draw from, many of which are drastically different from my own.

The Science

I realize that some of you may not be interested in the scientific research that either directly proves or at least points to the conclusions and practices I'm advocating. While I've tried hard to keep this section short and readily understandable, if you find yourself disinterested, you have my permission to skim or skip these sections.

If you're anything like me, though, you'll find a quick tour through the science of each topic interesting and valuable. There's a tremendous body of mainstream scientific research that supports, even proves, the validity of the ideas and practices recommended in these pages. Our spirituality should be as harmonious and consistent with the full scope of human knowledge and experience as possible. Furthermore, since this book contains a series of spiritual experiments for you to practice, it made sense to include an overview of the most relevant research. In many cases, you'll discover that not only are my claims provable in your own body-mind laboratory, but they've also been proven in traditional scientific laboratories.

That said, by no means do I claim—or even *want* to claim—that science "proves" everything we discuss regarding spirit. One of the great abuses of science is the dogmatic claim that it's the *only* way we can know truth. Science is only one tool, among many, that we have available to us. Science cannot penetrate the ultimate mysteries of our existence. God, metaphysics—even love—can't be proven in a laboratory. I have separated science and spirit into discrete sections precisely so that we remain aware of the boundaries between them.

I apologize in advance if you find my presentation of scientific research too brief or simplistic. Please understand that this book is intended for a wide audience; not everyone has the same scientific literacy or degree of interest. If you want to delve deeper into the scientific aspects of what I'm presenting, an extensive bibliography is published on the companion website to this book, theblissexperiment.com.

The Spirit

Here we venture beyond the realm of science and into the deeper realms of philosophy, religion, consciousness, and transcendent understanding. This is the core of each topic, where we examine fully the subject at hand, interpret and extend the scientific research, and try to gain both a deeper and broader understanding and perspective. I hope it is where you'll discover new ways of looking at yourself and our world. I'll delineate both the philosophical reasons for our approach and how you can apply it to everyday life.

It's important to understand what I mean by "spirit" and "spirituality." Here's what spirituality means to me:

- the sacred sensation that the world itself is miraculous, and crucially connected to and revealing of our essential being, and is therefore deserving of our concentrated, reverent attention;
- to wonder and marvel at the mystery of existence, and to feel awe in the face of the Infinite;
- the inner-directed *practice* of self-transcendence;
- the direct search for happiness, meaning, and truth, and the willingness to go *wherever that journey leads*.

We'll explore this in greater detail later. For now, let me highlight one point: spirituality is the fusion of the practical and the mystical. Many people mistakenly believe that spirituality is airy-fairy, vague, even hippy-dippy-trippy. Granted, there is a profoundly mystical element to it—or *should* be, if it's truly practiced and experienced. *Mystical* doesn't mean unclear or ungrounded, it means beyond the scope of our ordinary, everyday language to elucidate easily. The experiences themselves are very much grounded in the fabric of reality itself. Spirituality isn't just mystical, it's concrete, practical, and encompasses *all* aspects of daily living. It's not something that happens *to* us, it's a process in which we consciously, actively participate. Spirituality is the practice of inhabiting everyday life with exalted consciousness.

The Experiment

Although this is often the shortest of the four sections, in many ways, it is the most important. Happiness, meaning, and bliss come to us primarily through activity and practice; they can't be discovered solely through intellectual cogitation. From a certain perspective, it could even be said that the other three sections are presented in order to convince you that the practices are worth doing. On the other hand, you needn't do every practice. Not everyone resonates with, understands, or even needs all of them. Try as many as possible at least once but then feel free to focus on those you most need or gravitate toward most strongly.

Here's a tip: You may want to keep your own "Bliss Journal" as you work through this book. You don't have to buy anything special. Either use your existing journal if you have one, buy an inexpensive notebook, or use your computer, tablet, or smart phone. There you can write down your answers to some of the exercises, note key ideas that call out to you, chart your progress, and generally have a central repository for your Bliss Experiment.

Online

Finally, through the miracle of modern technology and the innovative thinking of my publisher, many chapters end with a Microsoft Tag. If you point your smart phone at this tag and take a picture, your phone will play a video filled with supplementary information and demonstrations. (More information about how to do this can be found at the front of this book.) If you don't want to watch it on your phone or tablet computer, there is also a website address that you can surf to on your main computer.

You will also find expanded talks on a particular topic, demonstrations, worksheets, interviews with people, music, helpful hints, answers to frequently asked questions, and many other resources. In addition, there is an online community in which you can also find and interact with other like-minded souls conducting their own Bliss Experiments. All of this bonus material is available to you absolutely free on my website. Most of us learn best by combining the written word with visual images and auditory explanation. I strongly encourage you to take advantage.

Nonlinear Progress

The analogy of bliss as a raw, uncut, and unrecognizable diamond that we must slowly but surely unearth by peeling away layer after layer of rock is useful but limited in one important sense.

While diamond mining in the real world occurs in a set order, the reality of bliss is that *all* of these steps can happen in any order, or even simultaneously. Some of us have all of the different layers possible between bliss and us. Others have already stripped away a few layers before we found this book—or never had them in the first place. Furthermore, our search for bliss need not be quite so structured or linear. In the real world, you can't actually polish a diamond until long after one you've completed all the intervening steps of finding the right place to drill, and so on. When it comes to bliss, however, it's entirely possible to practice the experiments in chapters 2 and 24 simultaneously.

It's also possible that you'll discover you're already doing or have already mastered one of the later steps, while still having quite a bit of room for improvement on an earlier one. As but one example, you could have a significant desire for material wealth (discussed in chapter 2) while taking up the practice of meditation (chapter 24) or having already forgiven those who have harmed you in the past (chapter 8).

Each of us is unique. We all walk slightly different pathways to bliss. Our journeys include the same basic elements but never in quite the same order or manifested in quite the same way, just as we each have unique fingerprints and DNA.

Thus, while I've tried to present the chapter topics in a logical sequence, beginning with that which is furthest away from bliss and then slowly introducing those understandings that draw us closer, once you've read through and absorbed the book once, you are free to continue working with it in whatever order works for you.

Measuring Your Experiment

While I promise you that if you actually do your Bliss Experiments over the next twenty-eight days or whatever pace you choose, it's important to see this as a lifetime process. It is unlikely that you will completely master each of the concepts and practices in this book in a single day, or even a week, or a month, or a year. That's neither expected nor required. Be gentle with yourself, see it as a process, and, above all, don't get discouraged if your life isn't 100 percent "solved and perfect" right away.

The yardstick for success is improvement, not perfection. Do you feel like, overall, things are going in the right direction for you? Even if at first improvement seems relatively minor, keep going. The more you do it, the more you internalize these concepts and practices, the better and better it gets, and the happier and more blissful you'll feel.

Change can be difficult to detect in the short term. Just as it's nearly impossible to notice your hair grow from one day to the next, it can be equally difficult to notice your internal growth. Over time, however, clear improvements will emerge.

If you decide to keep a Bliss Journal, you'll be able to read back a week, a month, or a year. That can help you appreciate your progress more concretely. Whether you do or don't keep a journal, most likely you'll also begin to notice the change in your everyday moods, feelings, and internal dialogue. Or you might not even notice it yourself, but someone will comment, "You seem happier or more peaceful." Or you may notice that your reactions to things that used to anger or depress you have lessened or been transformed entirely. Standing in the grocery line, driving, interacting with your partner or family, in the workplace—every day, we are given dozens of situations that can act as a mirror.

A key theme throughout this book is increasing our awareness, especially of our motivations, our reactions, and ourselves. Ultimately, cultivating that inner awareness—which will be discussed in depth later—is the key to measuring our Bliss Experiment. If we take the time to pay attention to ourselves, we might be surprised by how much we've changed.

My Story, Your Story

The depth of our despair measures what capability and height of claim we have to hope.
—Thomas Carlyle, Scottish essayist and historian (1795–1881)

Few people have found more ways to be unhappy than I have. Not long ago, while leading a seminar, I described some of the challenges I've brought upon myself, only to realize that a few of the more empathetic people in the audience were crying. One woman had such a look of concern on her face, she was obviously wondering if I ought to be put on a suicide watch. Though appreciated, she needn't have felt that concern, for by then I was able to relate my stories calmly, joyfully, even humorously. I was long past the immediate suffering and well into reaping the benefits of the solutions I have discovered.

I've come to realize that once people see you at the front of a hall, delivering a lecture or teaching a class, or providing counseling, they tend to idealize you. Or they act as if you just dropped from the sky, filled with timeless wisdom. Or worse: some kind of perfected being. I like to remind people that I too have a story and a journey—one still unfolding—and that we are not so different. Wherever you are right now, whatever you've been through or are going through, chances are I've been there myself. It's this painful truth that allows me to feel comfortable writing this book. I've earned it the hard way: by learning from one dumb mistake after another.

From a nearly fatal accidental drug overdose, to a heart problem, to paralyzing anxiety and depression, to battling severe and ongoing chronic pain, I've not always led an easy life. While my sufferings might seem terrifying, even insurmountable to some, I can now rattle them off without feeling even the slightest twinge of sadness. It's as if they happened to a different person, and in a way, that's true: years ago, I *was* a different person. The person I am now has a far deeper understanding of the nature of pain, suffering, happiness, and bliss than I did before I went through these trials. I am grateful for my sufferings, for each of them has taught me valuable lessons that have helped me to achieve greater—and deeper—levels of genuine happiness than I ever imagined possible.

It may be helpful to share some of my story now, before proceeding to the heart of the book, so that you know that the attitudes and practices I am proposing are neither theoretical nor feel-good fantasies but authentic, proven techniques that will work for you regardless of your background or circumstance.

In the Beginning

I've always been philosophically inclined. By eighth grade, I was already consumed with finding answers to life's Big Questions: Why are we here? What is the purpose to life? What constitutes a good life? Does God exist? In high school, as an amusing jab toward my predilection for weighty conversation, I was voted "Biggest Pseudo-Intellectual" of my graduating class. Raised in a mostly secular Jewish home in a suburb of Cleveland, Ohio, I attended a well-known private school. I spent most of sixth and seventh grades immersed in the standard pursuits of young adolescents: acting cool and trying to be popular. I engaged in all the usual boyhood ways of achieving this: acting tough, talking about people behind their backs, and sucking up to the "in-group" leaders. I was slowly working my way up the social ladder—until the eighth grade, when it all went disastrously wrong.

One day I came to school, and the "cool kids"—my supposed friends—had turned on me. Seemingly overnight, I went from "in" to "out." My erstwhile friends began tormenting me. They refused to talk to me, unless hurling insults; tried physically bullying me (not usually successfully, since I was an accomplished wrestler and no pushover); placed threatening notes in my locker; and actively discouraged other kids from speaking to me. Since it was a small school, there was no escaping their persecution.

Everyone knew about it, even the teachers. It was like a suburban version of *Lord of the Flies*.

At the time, I was devastated. What could be worse for a thirteen-year-old boy? I tried to get back into their good graces but made no progress. The harder I pushed, the worse it became. I briefly contemplated suicide.

Not long after the ostracism started one of my few remaining friends—and, it so happens, my second cousin—was diagnosed with terminal stomach cancer. Ian was fourteen. I still vividly recall visiting him at Rainbow Babies & Children's Hospital in Cleveland the night they came to fit him for his first wig. The chemotherapy had left him weak and emaciated; most of his hair had already fallen out. I watched as the wig specialist shaved off the remaining strands, put a wig on his head, and tried to style it to match his real hair as best as possible.

Ian was not only a friend but also a family member. We shared a similar background, attended the same school, and even looked a lot alike. I couldn't help but wonder why this was happening to him and not to me. Especially since he was a nicer kid than I was. There seemed no rhyme or reason for it. Watching Ian battle cancer and then die not long after made me more reflective and more determined than ever to understand the meaning and purpose of my life.

Though still somber and contemplative from Ian's death, I gradually discovered the benefits of being expelled from the so-called cool group. For most of eighth and ninth grades, I was a social pariah, which meant that I had little to do on evenings or weekends. While other kids were hanging out, chatting on the phone, or going to parties, I stayed home, mostly alone. I began reading voraciously, watching independent films, thinking and exploring my inner self for the first time. My father had an extensive library that included many of the great works of literature, philosophy, art, and culture, and I read them all.

Even though by tenth grade my social life had mostly recovered and I had a good group of new friends—though by and large not the same ones as before—I had developed a true love of reading. Throughout high school, I worked my way through the Western canon of Great Books, eventually delving deeply into philosophy, social science, and psychology. I also began reading Buddhist and Taoist literature, and dabbled in Zen Buddhist meditation. I recall a group of us at a teacher's house, himself a philosopher, being surprised that I was able to hold an in-depth discussion with him about Austrian philosopher Ludwig Wittgenstein's *Tractatus Logico-Philosophicus*.

Prior to being ostracized, one of my best friends was Davey, a boy who was clearly much smarter than I was. Davey seemed destined for Harvard University. Unfortunately, his years of popularity took their toll on his ambition and intellectual development. He stopped studying and started partying. He ended up at a college far below his capabilities. It was a similar story with virtually all of my former friends. My seemingly random excommunication from that shallow and destructive peer group proved nothing short of a blessing. That was the first time I realized that suffering could lead to a positive outcome—but it wouldn't be the last.

My Philosophy of Despair

From my first day at Stanford University, I knew I wanted to be a philosophy major. I even hoped to make that my career. The freedom and lifestyle of a university professor combined with the opportunity to muse on the meaning of life full time seemed an unbeatable combination. I discovered quickly that many of my philosophy professors also held positions and taught classes in the Religious Studies Department. And, of course, many of the Asian "philosophies" such as Confucianism, Taoism, and Buddhism were never formally distinct from "religion." The two departments offered a joint-degree program; thus, my original interest in philosophy quickly branched out to include religious studies as well.

My professors encouraged me to study anthropology, sociology, and psychology in addition to the standard philosophy and religion coursework. My first two years at Stanford were thrilling. My fellow philosophy and religious studies friends and I had an unshakeable sense that we were really "getting to the bottom" of life's meanings and mysteries. We felt we were quickly acquiring a unique insight into "truth" and often pitied students who were wasting their time studying trivial subjects such as medicine, engineering, English, economics, and political science.

Despite feeling more certain than ever that my intellectual understanding was expanding, midway through my sophomore year, my personal life was collapsing. At first I didn't see the connection. It was only after disaster struck that I realized just how badly I had been drifting off course.

Though my studies were varied on the surface, I gravitated toward a group of professors that had a most particular and unified viewpoint. Brilliant as they were, they mostly shared a bleak, or at least deeply conflicted, outlook. While they were endlessly fascinated by the different philosophies and belief systems concocted by philosophers and religious leaders through the centuries, their own personal beliefs clustered around the existential. Many were either borderline or even full-blown alcoholics. Few, if any, had clear spiritual beliefs; in fact, just about all of them were atheists or agnostics—and if any of them weren't, they kept it a tightly guarded secret. It was an atmosphere in which the great philosophers and religions were discussed and analyzed but also frequently scorned and discredited, or at least kept at a safe, academic distance.

I drifted more and more deeply into reading and admiring existential and deconstructivist philosophers and psychologists. When one of my professors introduced me to Ernest Becker's Pulitzer Prize–winning work on religion and psychology, *The Denial of Death*, I felt a jolt of electricity as I read it. Additional heavy doses of Kierkegaard, Heidegger, Sartre, Nietzsche, Weber, Durkheim, Freud, Derrida, and more, left me feeling simultaneously powerful in my newfound "understanding" and increasingly uneasy in my soul. As "philosophers," many of us, myself included, felt implicitly that our "deep" understanding of the human condition set us above others—but also lent us a depressing air of exclusive sadness.

Many of my friends were drinking and partying, often while also strongly interested in making money, achieving success, or becoming famous. Among my circle of professors and fellow philosophy students, there was a prevailing attitude of "think hard, drink hard," meaning that we all agreed that the more one thought about life, the more necessary it was to have a good, stiff drink as often as possible. Thus, I indulged in copious amounts of alcohol and drugs—the only way that I could see to cope with the misery of our human condition.

I increasingly felt alone and isolated, particularly because I was sure that I now possessed special insight into humanity that others simply didn't have. My arrogance bred contempt for those who didn't know what I thought I knew. I didn't realize then what I would learn much later: true wisdom never isolates, it unifies. Wisdom is harmonious and blissful, not divisive and alienating. But you couldn't tell that to me then.

My own mood and attitude had deteriorated so much that midway through my sophomore year, my roommate and best friend, who was premed (and, thus, outside of my philosophy circle of friends and professors), actually moved out of our shared dorm rooms. I was difficult to live with, my attitude worsening with every passing month. I had a college friend, who was a great guy and good friend but also happened to be a drug dealer and an infamous campus wild man. (Years later, we had a brief reunion on the streets of San Francisco; he was wearing a court-monitored tracking ankle bracelet due to an assault conviction.) Since high school, I had dabbled in drugs, mostly marijuana and the psychedelics. Slowly but surely, my drug use increased. By the end of my sophomore year, I was regularly smoking weed, ingesting mushrooms and ecstasy, plus drinking more than ever.

A Trip to the Emergency Room

It all came crashing down in the spring of my sophomore year, during the wildest party at Stanford: the Exotic Erotic Ball, which was hosted by the very on-campus house in which I lived. Partygoers dress as scantily as they dare, get as high as possible, and generally have as much hedonistic "fun" as they can take.

Despite my escalating drug use, I had never experienced any kind of negative reaction. No matter how much I drank or how many drugs I ingested, I was always fine. The night of the Exotic Erotic, most of the residents of my house—the party hosts—prepared for the big night by taking ecstasy. My drug-dealing friend had the responsibility of scoring the ecstasy for fifty of us. We took turns snorting it in lines off a mirror. After the others had taken theirs, my roommate and I looked down and realized that we had extra—he must have miscalculated his order, because there was still a huge pile of it left. We looked at each other like kids in a candy store, quickly snorting up all of the leftovers, excited that we had hit the mother lode. As the night progressed, I ingested every intoxicant I could find: alcohol, of course, but also nitrous oxide (whip-its), and marijuana, and probably some other things I can't even remember.

A group of us were sitting in a circle in my room—which was part of a security-controlled VIP area—passing around a bong. I'll never forget that moment: as the first hit went deep into my lungs, I could almost see the smoke cloud rising up my body. When it hit my brain, I completely lost it. Ecstasy is a strange drug: half hallucinogen, half speed. The amphetamine in it speeds up your heart; and I had a double or triple dose in me. Marijuana also increases heart rate. The combination, aided by booze and nitrous, caused my body and mind to lose control. My heart started pounding like it was going to explode. My entire body was agitated and twitching. I couldn't stop moving. Worse, my mind was racing like never before. Endless thoughts, images, fears, anxieties, and negative emotions cascaded through my head, as if a dam had broken. I became terrified that I was going to have a heart attack and die on the spot or go completely insane.

I was in such bad shape that I knew I had to get to an emergency room as quick as possible. I grabbed a friend of mine and pleaded with her to drive me to Stanford Hospital.

After a few minutes in the waiting room, a nurse came to check me out. I told her about all the drugs I had taken, and she took my pulse on the spot. I was quickly escorted to the trauma area. She double-checked my pulse, listened to my heart, took my blood pressure, and then told me that my heart rate was well over two hundred beats per minute. She immediately hooked me up to an intravenous line and administered several medications, including something to prevent a stroke. Later she told me I had in fact been in grave danger of stroking out at any moment. She also gave me something to counteract all the speed and stimulants in my system, plus I had to drink liquefied charcoal to absorb any remaining alcohol in my stomach.

The entire time, my mind was racing. An unstoppable cycle of fear and anxiety had been triggered in my brain. I realized how alone and scared I was. I was terrified of dying. I began doing a life review. Or rather, my mind forced a life review upon me, since, frankly, I was just hoping to make it stop. It was as if I could see the house of cards that I had constructed for myself crashing to the ground. My sense of self was shattered. I realized that my ego, which I had carefully built up, was, in fact, fragile and false. I came face to face with my fear of death, my extreme loneliness and isolation, my creeping suspicion that life had no meaning, and a general feeling that I had been deceiving myself. I'd thought that my philosophy studies were leading me closer to the truth—that I knew something that others did not; that I had cracked the meaning of life—and then, in just one night, it became clear that I had in fact hit a dead end. If *this* was the meaning of life, it was bleak, cold, desperate, and hardly worth living.

After I was discharged from the hospital the following morning, I pretended at first that nothing had changed. When people asked me what happened, I said it was no big deal. I didn't want to talk about it. I even tried to keep partying. But a curious thing happened: every time I took a hit from a bong or even drank some alcohol, I would have intense flashbacks to that night in the emergency room. My heart would start racing. My mind lost all control. I instantly relived the hell of my overdose, both physically and mentally. Finally, I realized that this was something I had to face. I couldn't pretend that nothing happened and that everything would return to "normal."

My Bad Streak Continues

My suffering was far from over; in fact, it was just beginning. That summer, after returning home from Stanford, I was in bad shape. My heart kept feeling like it was racing, skipping beats, and generally behaving erratically. My parents took me to see a heart specialist at the Cleveland Clinic—the top-ranked cardiology center in the US. The cardiologist diagnosed me with a severe irregular heartbeat—which I was certain resulted from my drug overdose—and told me that I needed a pacemaker right away or I might have a heart attack.

In my already fragile state of mind, this news exploded like a bomb. I was more afraid than ever. I thought that every second could be my last. Just to be sure, though, my doctor retested me. I had to wear a portable electrocardiogram device called a Holter monitor three different times over the span of a week. The monitor recorded every beat of my heart for twenty-four hours. I was completely overcome with anxiety virtually every minute of every day. I grew more and more depressed. I was so afraid that I was going to die that I even began sleeping in my parents' bedroom.

Though I was far from a religious person—a committed atheist, in fact—I remember speaking with a close family friend who was also a medical doctor in charge of wellness programs for Progressive Insurance. He gave me an informal second opinion while I waited for the final tests to come back and for an appointment to have my pacemaker surgically implanted. I don't remember his medical advice but I remember how we ended our phone conversation. He suggested that I concentrate on the following prayer:

> Grant me the serenity
> To accept the things I cannot change,
> Courage to change the things I can,
> And wisdom to know the difference.

I didn't recognize it at the time but learned later that it was a version of the Serenity Prayer widely used by spiritual seekers and in recovery programs. It was new to me; I studied philosophy and religion, I didn't *practice* them. Since I was desperate and seemingly bereft of options, and because a genuine MD—not some self-help quack—suggested it, I decided to try repeating it to myself. I didn't know the first thing about formal prayer, but I did begin saying the words over and over again in my mind as I was lying around or as I went through my daily activities.

My First Miracle?

Something amazing happened. At my next cardiology appointment, after I had worn the Holter monitor a second time, the doctor told me that the Cleveland Clinic had made a mistake. Apparently the recording from the first test must have been switched with someone else's, because on the second test, he could no longer find any trace of the heart problem. The cardiologist explained that it was impossible for my heart to be so damaged in the first test and then perfectly fine in the next. Although there was no proof that another patient's results had been mistakenly assigned to me, he couldn't think of any other explanation. A subsequent Holter test confirmed that my heart rate was indeed normal. Nevertheless, it took me months, filled with fear and anxiety, before I eventually came to trust that I was no longer on the brink of cardiac arrest.

In hindsight, I can't help but wonder. After all, I did go to the emergency room that night of the Exotic Erotic Ball. There was no doubt that my heart was in a danger zone and I was at risk for a stroke. Weeks later, I went to get those tests at the Cleveland Clinic because I could *feel* something wrong in my chest. It seemed clear that my heart was genuinely skipping beats; it's a pretty unmistakable feeling. The fact is that the only thing that changed between my first and second tests was learning and repeating the Serenity Prayer—and the slight opening to spirit that it represented.

No Miracles for My Dad

Whether the disappearance of my heart difficulties was a mistake or a gift, one thing it was not was the end of my trials. Just weeks after my ordeal at Cleveland Clinic, my father was diagnosed with mesothelioma, a lethal form of lung cancer. He was diagnosed in July, and on Christmas Eve, he died. I was scheduled to go to Australia's Great Barrier Reef in September as part of my junior year abroad. I was going to study anthropology, Aboriginal culture, and marine biology, among other things, which I saw as an extension of my philosophical education. Plus, it was a great excuse to hang out in the sun, go scuba diving, and drink Australian beer, all for school credit!

The five months from my father's diagnosis until his death were grueling, intensified not only by my own personal struggles but also because of my father's mental and spiritual suffering. He tried but largely failed to come to terms with his impending mortality. I won't belabor it here, but suffice to say that his cancer diagnosis unearthed a lifetime of anger, fear, disappointment, and disillusionment, some of which was taken out on my mother, my sister, and me. His death, and the drama around it, magnified and worsened my own fears, anxiety, and depression.

A Change of Direction

With the cancellation of my semester abroad at the Great Barrier Reef and unable to leave Cleveland while my father was dying, I had a lot of free time. My reading practices shifted dramatically. I stopped studying existential philosophy. I started taking a yoga class and learned Transcendental Meditation—a practice that both of my parents had learned years prior but had long since abandoned. I started reading a variety of different firsthand accounts from practitioners of Eastern religions, as well as books exploring the intersection of, conflicts between, and possible resolutions of scientific and theological issues.

As I was warming up for a yoga class one day, my teacher asked me if I had ever read *Autobiography of a Yogi*. I had never heard of it. She urged me to read it but didn't say much else. The next day, I bought a copy and began working my way through it. The effect was electrifying. I didn't really believe it, but, still, there was just something about it, and about the author, Paramhansa Yogananda, that I found exhilarating. Yogananda, who was the first Indian spiritual teacher to permanently move to the West and the progenitor of the yoga and meditation practices now part of mainstream American culture, was either completely insane or someone who had personally experienced spiritual truth at the highest level. He wasn't just talking about or analyzing various philosophies or religions, or merely proposing theoretical constructs, he was claiming to live it, to experience it immediately and directly. It was a completely different approach than anything I had encountered. I was determined to find out whether he was a genius or insane.

After my father died, I didn't feel ready to return to Stanford. I decided to become a certified yoga teacher—not because I was interested in teaching yoga, but because it was a good reason to spend extended time at a retreat facility, "away from it all," and to heal from everything that had happened to me over the past eight months. I thought of it as a replacement for my cancelled junior year abroad. Mostly, though, it was driven by a growing sense, fueled by reading *Autobiography of a Yogi*, that the best way to understand the Eastern religions was to actually practice them, not just study them.

I ended up going to a Northern California spiritual retreat in the foot-hills of the Sierra Nevada Mountains. The guest retreat was part of a much larger community spread over nearly one thousand acres. It is a modern, Americanized variation on the ashrams of India and based on the ancient principles of Yoga and Vedanta, which are the practical and philosophical branches of Hinduism, respectively. Virtually everyone who lives there is a meditator and a disciple of Paramhansa Yogananda. I spent about eight weeks there, first completing a yoga teacher certification course, then stay-ing on for a work-study program. Within six weeks of arriving, I took a discipleship vow to Yogananda, who is my guru, or spiritual teacher. It was a profoundly moving and life-changing experience.

Yogananda was born in India in 1893. From a young age he was trained to bring India's ancient science of self-realization to the West. Before coming to America, he was ordained in the 1,200-year-old swami order founded in the ninth century, and given the name Paramhansa Yogananda. In Sanskrit *param* is defined as "highest," and *hansa* as "swan." The sacred white swan is a symbol of spiritual discrimination. Yogananda means liter-ally, "one who achieves bliss *(ananda)* through the practice of yoga." In 1920, he became the first yoga master to permanently relocate to America. In 1946, he published what has become a spiritual classic and one of the best-loved books of the twentieth century, *Autobiography of a Yogi*. In ad-dition, Yogananda established headquarters for a worldwide work, wrote a number of books and study courses, gave lectures to tens of thousands in most major cities across the US, and trained numerous disciples. He was the first Hindu ever invited to the White House, by Calvin Coolidge, and he personally initiated Mahatma Gandhi into Kriya Yoga, his most advanced technique of meditation. He lived in the US until his death in 1952. Yogananda's primary message to the West highlighted the unity of all religions, the importance of personal spiritual practice, and the essential harmony between science and religion.

Despite a generally uplifting and eye-opening stint at the retreat, I was still anxious, confused, and depressed. However, the difference was that I now saw a glimmer of light. Though I had taken just a few tenta-tive steps down the road of discovery—not nearly enough to know what I would find—I felt increasingly confident that there was something *to* find.

I returned to Stanford and completed my degree, though I now avoided the more extreme existentialist-focused classes that I previously sought and relished. Within six months of graduation, with my completed degree in philosophy and religious studies in hand, I decided to move back to the spiritual community. At the time, I had no plan. I didn't think I was making a permanent decision or that my life had taken any kind of irrevocable turn. I was just taking the next step in front of me; the one that felt right for that moment in time.

That was close to twenty years ago.

In the intervening years, while living full-time in the ashram community, meditating daily, and learning how to integrate a complete range of spiritual practices and attitudes into daily living, I worked in a natural foods store, then in an independent bookstore as a book buyer, and as an event promoter. In 1998, a disciple of Paramhansa Yogananda asked me to be the president and publisher of a book publishing and media company, Crystal Clarity Publishers. I spent more than nine years running the company, publishing spiritual books and producing relaxation and world music albums. Most amazingly for me, I was now the publisher of many of Paramhansa Yogananda's books, including the original 1946 edition of *Autobiography of a Yogi*, the very book that had set my life on this course. On that dark day that I first picked up a copy of *Autobiography*, it never occurred to me that I would one day devote my life to publishing, selling, marketing, and supporting one of the best-selling and most important books in the history of publishing. For me, it was not only a sacred privilege but also a miracle.

A New Kind of Suffering

Alas, my life didn't stop at that moment; no permanent paradise was attained. About seven years ago, I was confronted with one of my biggest challenges yet: severe, disabling, and incurable chronic pain.

After a Monday of playing sports and exercising—weight training, running, soccer, and volleyball, capped with yoga postures—I woke up the next morning with extreme pain on the right side of my back and in my right hip. I thought at first that I was merely experiencing muscular soreness or that, at worst, one of my spinal vertebrae was temporarily out of alignment. I went to my chiropractor, thinking that a quick adjustment would fix it. After some X-rays and a couple more visits to a second chiropractor, my concerns escalated. The adjustments weren't helping, and my pain was increasing.

I sought the top specialists in the country from Stanford Hospital, UCSF Medical Center, Johns Hopkins Hospital, and more. For the first two years, I was repeatedly misdiagnosed, including by some of the finest doctors in the United States. I also visited every kind of holistic practitioner you can imagine: acupuncturists, chiropractors, bodywork specialists, homeopaths, energy healers, medical intuitives, physical therapists, and practitioners of Alexander technique, Ayurvedic medicine, prolotherapy, biofeedback, guided visualizations, and countless others. After enduring a couple of misdiagnoses and undergoing nearly a dozen invasive medical procedures—including corticosteroid injections, countless blood tests, MRIs and CT scans, radio-frequency neurotomies, blood tests, and a test called a discogram (which was apparently so horrifying that one of the observing doctors in the surgical suite actually passed out while watching), it was finally determined that I have a rare and severely painful condition called sacroiliac joint dysfunction.

The sacroiliac joint is what connects the base of our spine, the sacrum, to our pelvis. Virtually every movement, including sitting, walking, and even sleeping, creates irritation, and inflammation. Imagine walking around with a permanently torn anterior cruciate ligament (ACL) in your knee or a torn rotator cuff in your shoulder; only in my case, there is no known surgery to fix it, and we actually use our SI joints much more than a knee or shoulder. There is virtually no form of body movement or positioning that doesn't involve or impact the SI joint. Once severely damaged, it is difficult to treat and completely incurable.

I was now virtually bedridden, working through not just the severe pain itself but also a paralyzing array of side effects from a multitude of medications that were sometimes worse than the pain itself. I could no longer sit for long periods of time, concentrate well, or work effectively. I lost almost all functionality. I could sleep only on my left side. Driving a car, flying, or even sitting at a desk was excruciating. For two years, I seldom left the house unless it was to go to a doctor or wellness practitioner.

As it became clear that no cure was forthcoming, and my mental distress increased, I enrolled in two different programs at interdisciplinary pain clinics. First I commuted to one in San Francisco, then switched to a more effective program closer to home. Pain clinics make little attempt to cure pain. They are intended only for those who have already tried every possible medical procedure and are now facing a lifetime of chronic pain. They focus on teaching coping mechanisms, improving our understanding of how pain works, and offering a multitude of techniques and practices designed to help patients restore functionality despite being in constant pain. I was assigned a team that included a medical doctor specializing in pain management; a pain psychologist, who taught me biofeedback and coping mechanisms; a physical therapist; and a wellness practitioner who taught visualizations and other complementary practices. Working together, combined with implementing many of the practices in this book, in an intensive monthslong program and daily attention, I eventually regained most of my functionality.

As helpful as the program was, for seven years now, my body continues to experience severe pain twenty-four hours a day without cessation. I even hurt while I sleep. It is an omnipresent part of my life now.

Few people can imagine what it's like to live in chronic pain. It's very different from both the everyday aches and pains that we all experience and even from acute pain. As terrible as acute pain can be, it eventually fades or disappears altogether. Severe chronic pain is different. It's always present, whether you're awake or asleep, working or relaxing, sitting or standing. (Yes, I feel it even as I type this sentence.) When you are confronted with something from which you know there is no escape, *ever*, probably not even for an hour, or even a minute, day after day, week after week, month after month, year after year, it can gnaw at you unless you make a concerted effort to work with it.

In a sense, lifelong chronic pain is a creation of modern medicine. Prior to modern times, people with my level of pain usually died, often very quickly. Studies have shown that severe, untreated chronic pain frequently leads to multiple organ failure. Without intervention, our bodies simply shut down. It's our body's last recourse.

The first two or three years of my injury were dark times. Despite my years of spiritual practice, despite living in an ashram, I still struggled mightily. Nothing had prepared me for this. Not only was the pain frequently unbearable and the medication side effects paralyzing but also, even worse, I confess that for a long while, my mental outlook left much to be desired. I experienced many genuine moments of despair. I was still in my early thirties, and it felt like my life and future were lost. My job was gone, my enjoyment of life was gone, my relationships were strained and limited—even my ability to meditate was severely compromised. In a different way, my mental and spiritual suffering was as high as it had been years ago when I went through my near-death experience and subsequent depression.

Countless doctors, healers, friends, family, and especially my fiancée, Brook, have helped me tremendously, each in his or her own way. But above all, it was the remembrance, return to, and deepening of the attitudes, practices, and techniques outlined in this book that made the greatest contribution. Not for the first time, they saved my life.

It took some time, but ultimately I was able to make critical shifts in my understanding of this illness, gaining real insight into the difference between pain and suffering. They are not the same, as we'll discuss later. I came to accept what was happening to my body, to see it as a positive catalyst for deepening my understanding and prodding me toward new levels of spiritual growth. As I stopped resisting and started accepting, I quickly regained functionality. Unlike my experience with the irregular heartbeat, this time I didn't have a miraculous physical healing; instead it was a mental and spiritual miracle.

Much more than most of us realize, our destiny is in our own hands, no matter our outward circumstances.

I am living proof of that.

Your Story

Recently, after hearing my story, a young woman asked me, "Do you think it was necessary to go through all that suffering in order to get where you are?" She was still in her twenties, and I felt her concern: she hadn't yet experienced a lot of personal suffering. I could see her mind wondering if that was necessary; if somehow "God" (or whatever you want to call it) *needed* us to suffer first.

I replied, "No, I don't think that I *needed* to suffer that much; it's more that I wasn't sensitive and open enough sooner. If I had been, I could have spared myself a lot of trouble." In other words, neither God nor our "Highest Self" nor anyone else wants, let alone requires, us to suffer just for the sake of finding our purpose or the hidden wellspring of bliss within. It's more that we usually don't figure out to look inside ourselves until *after* our outer world reveals itself to be less than fulfilling.

We all have our stories of pain and suffering, to greater or lesser degrees. As a minister and spiritual teacher who works with thousands of people each year, I am fully aware that as difficult as some events have been for me, they are no worse than countless others are. Quite frankly, when I reflect upon the enormous suffering that occurs every day, my own experiences are middling at worst. My intention behind telling you my story, then, isn't to claim that my challenges are worse than yours are. I've led neither an easy life nor a horrific one.

My point is: precisely because my experiences are no different from yours, there is every reason to believe that what has worked for me will work for you. I'm not special in any way. And what you'll learn in this book doesn't require any special background, skills, understanding, or life experience. It worked for me. It's worked for thousands of people that I've personally met. It *will* work for you.

None of us indefinitely escapes pain, tribulation, and death. But we can learn the difference between pain and suffering, how to overcome our tests and difficulties, and most of all, find a deep resevoir of bliss inside ourselves that nothing—not even the worst imaginable outward circumstances—can disrupt or obscure.

We are all interconnected in ways that we usually miss or don't understand. We don't always see it or consciously experience it, but the connection *is* there. So, too, we are far more similar than different. Ultimately, the specifics of my story don't matter all that much. We are living the same story, in six billion unique variations. The details change from life to life, but the underlying experience and potential are the same. Ultimately, my story is your story. And your story is my story. We are on the same journey, leading to the same place, though we each discover it in our own way, at our own pace.

As you will see, we all have within us a remarkable, even infinite, capacity for lasting joy. We just have to learn how to access it.

PART 1

Not This, Not That

Though we all share the same innate impulse to find happiness, meaning, and truth, knowing how or where to find them is not so easy. We want to find our diamond of bliss, but life doesn't appear to come with a treasure map where X marks the spot. Yes, there are religious Scriptures and self-help books available, but which ones? Whose interpretation? They hardly seem clear and straightforward. Our parents, teachers, or religious leaders offer their wisdom, some of it quite good, but we know that most of them have their own limitations and imperfections.

Though we get whatever help we can, we're mostly left to find our way via trial and error—lots and lots of trials, which mostly end in errors. We go digging here and there for happiness, but even when we seemingly hit a dry hole, we're never quite sure. Did we not dig deeply enough? Did we quit too soon? Are we mostly in the ballpark, just a few feet or inches off course? It's no wonder that life sometimes feels scary, confusing, disappointing—even depressing.

Because few of us have been given the right tools to uncover bliss or are certain of the best place to look, it's only natural that we begin our journey by searching in the most superficial and obvious spots. We're surrounded and constantly exposed to wealth and material objects, drugs, sex, romance, celebrities, beauty, myriad forms of power, and so on. It makes sense to try these avenues first.

Unfortunately, as many of us have discovered, these turn out not to be the solution for which we've been searching. The good news, however, is that the ways in which these things fall short of meeting our deepest needs provide us with tremendous insight, offering us our first clues as to the *right* place to dig.

CHAPTER 1

From Pleasure to Bliss:
The Happiness Scale

Do not look for rest in any pleasure, because you were not created for pleasure: You were created for spiritual JOY. And if you
do not know the difference between pleasure and spiritual joy,
you have not yet begun to live.
—*Thomas Merton, American contemplative monk (1915–68)*

Let's begin by surveying our landscape and orienting ourselves in it. By
doing so, we can understand the larger framework in which we begin our
journey to finding bliss.

Happiness, meaning, and truth can mean different things to different
people. Happiness in particular has several different components. The different types of happiness are:

- numbness,
- pleasure,
- relief (false happiness),
- everyday happiness, and
- bliss.

I find it helpful to think of these five aspects of happiness not as discrete
experiences—each inhabiting its own little world—but rather as varying
degrees of the same impulse; different states of consciousness on the same
continuum. The most important level of all, bliss, is not only the least

understood but also so seldom experienced that most of us don't even realize it exists. Our entire human journey can be thought of as the adventure from one end of the happiness scale to the other: from pleasure to bliss.

The better we can understand each of these components and how they relate to one another, the greater our clarity of mind and ability to navigate our journey toward bliss successfully.

The Story

Jane came to my classes because she was intrigued by the idea that she could learn to consciously induce what had been a lifetime of apparently random moments of deep bliss, often followed by feelings of despair as they dissolved. From a young age, she experienced jaw-dropping moments of awe; it felt like her everyday world fell away, revealing a field of pure awareness in which she could see not only herself but also see how she was connected to every atom of creation. Sometimes this revelatory moment would be accompanied by an intense wave of energy that started at the base of her spine and swept its way up her body to the top of her head. The feeling was so intense that she felt like her mind and body couldn't possibly contain it, that she might burst apart.

As quickly as these experiences came, they vanished. Jane tried talking to her Protestant minister about them, but he seemed alarmed by the confession. He thought she might need a doctor. She once confided in a devout Catholic friend of hers, only to be told that she might be possessed by something "satanic." Eventually she stopped discussing it and even came to resent these "attacks" as frightening and confusing intrusions.

Jane's adult life grew increasingly hedonistic. She spent most of her free time dating, partying, going to concerts, and engaging in a moderate amount of drinking and drug usage. Although she occasionally went to church or read spiritual books, mostly she felt this was a waste of time. None of the conventionally religious teachers or followers she knew had ever helped her or really seemed to offer much in the way of deep understanding.

After our first class together, Jane walked up to me, excited. She told me that for years she had been wondering what, exactly, was happening to her. From my description, she was now sure that she had been experiencing a "wave of bliss." More importantly, she was thrilled to hear that it was indeed possible to learn how to more consciously harness and work with these experiences.

I had Jane complete the Happiness Scale exercise at the end of this chapter. Afterward, we discussed the results. It was clear that while Jane would occasionally have these incredible feelings of awe and connection, she spent most of her daily life working, dating, partying, and occasionally doing some volunteer work for an environmental group. She admitted that she spent the bulk of her time pursuing pleasures and, from time to time, a bit of everyday happiness. She had little experience with any kind of spiritual practice or discipline, including meditation, although she had been to a few yoga classes. She didn't regularly spend time with people who were actively developing their spiritual lives.

At first Jane was a little defensive. She didn't see what possible connection there could be between how she spent her time and the randomness of these blissful experiences. She pointed out that she had been experiencing these moments of bliss since childhood, long before her life had turned hedonistic. She also observed that the relative frequency of her bliss experiences never particularly diminished as an adult, despite her hard-partying ways.

Notwithstanding her initial resistance, as the weeks went by, Jane made an effort to spend less time pursuing pleasure and more time consciously practicing the techniques explained in this book. Two months after completing my class, Jane emailed me with exciting news: she'd had another bliss experience, only this time she was able to work with it, go deeper into it, and experience it more fully than ever before. She didn't feel confused or depressed afterward. For the first time, she felt as if she knew what she was doing and where she was going. She knew that she has a long way to go, but she was also happier than ever before and more certain of her spiritual potential than she'd ever thought possible.

The Spirit

As mentioned, there are five types, or degrees, of happiness, which I have arranged on a progressive scale (see illustration on the following page):

numbness, pleasure, false happiness, everyday happiness, and bliss. The lowest form of happiness is numbness; the highest is bliss. Understanding these levels and where we are concentrating most of our time and effort is essential to discovering bliss.

The Happiness Scale

Numbness | Pleasure | False Happiness | Everyday Happiness | Bliss

---

Let's go through the scale, from left to right.

Numbness

It may seem odd that numbness is on this scale at all. What does numbness have to do with happiness? Well, for many of us, being numb represents a positive step forward. Sometimes we are in so much pain—physically, mentally, or spiritually—that feeling nothing is an improvement. This is one reason that we abuse alcohol and drugs, or why some people continually watch television or play video games. These are ways of distracting us, even if only tenuously or intermittently.

After a year or so of being in intense chronic pain, I finally had to quit my publishing job. When not shuttling from one doctor to the next, I spent most of my time at home, often unable to get out of bed. The pain was excruciating and relentless, twenty-four hours per day. During those dark days, though I tried to do whatever spiritual practices I could, I inevitably found myself spending a lot of my time surfing the Internet, watching lots of DVDs (I've never had television, cable, or satellite TV in my adult life), and consulting with my doctors to find medications that could relieve, or at least lessen, the agony I felt. Distracting myself in this way was a form of numbness. If I hadn't previously experienced bliss, I might have believed that this was as close to happiness as I was capable.

One needn't be only in physical pain to strive for the comparative happiness of being anesthetized. Countless people who have suffered through physical, sexual, or emotional abuse also resort to all kinds of numbing tactics—*anything* to blot out the pain. Virtually all alcoholics and drug addicts can attest to this being one of the original motivations for their substance abuse.

Pleasure

Once we discover successful numbing techniques, we often feel emboldened enough to add a little pleasure to our numbness. As appealing as numbness may be in contrast to pain, none of us considers it a good long-term strategy. We all want to feel something, to be *alive*. Thus, we begin pursuing, perhaps cautiously at first, activities that help us break through our barriers. Easy pleasures such as sex, shopping, eating, travel, or otherwise pampering the body are a logical next step. In addition, certain drugs such as GHB (gamma hydroxybutyrate), cocaine, and ecstasy are used more for pleasure enhancement than for numbing. At least these activities allow us to *feel* something, however primitive or rudimentary those feelings might be.

Unfortunately, as we'll explore in depth over the next few chapters, seeking pleasure is not a successful long-term happiness strategy. Physiologically, our body has clear limits to how much pleasure we can enjoy before it lapses back first into numbness, then even into full-blown agony. What is true physically is doubly true spiritually. Not only is pleasure fleeting, too much of it irrevocably leads to severely negative consequences.

Pleasure moves over us like a wave. For a wave to crest, it requires an equal-sized trough, or depression, just before and after that peak. Every wave is really a set: one peak and one trough. So it is with the waves of pleasure. The wave comes, gives us a temporary peak experience or excitement, then recedes, leaving an equally severe depression in its wake. The higher the peak, the lower the trough. It's a fact that applies equally to physics and spirituality.

False Happiness

There's an old joke: "Why do I keep hitting myself with a hammer?" Answer: "Because it feels so good when I stop!"

False happiness is that feeling we experience when we have *temporarily* fulfilled our desires. It's akin to the relief we feel after having scratched an itch that was driving us crazy. Imagine pinching your arm as hard as possible. Now release it. "Aaahhh, that feels better!" we might sigh. "Thank goodness *that's* over with!" This is often what we feel in that moment when we have fulfilled a particularly intense desire, whether for a shiny new car, in sex, or whenever any kind of longing is fulfilled.

There's a moment, often fleeting, when we feel satiated. Our most recent desire has been fulfilled, but our minds haven't yet concocted the next desire to take its place. If we are unaware of the falsity of this kind of happiness, we might even mistake it for contentment. Really, though, we are merely experiencing the calm before the storm; our next wave of desires is quietly gathering force. Usually we don't have to wait long before the next tsunami of desire comes crashing through our consciousness.

Everyday Happiness

What I call everyday happiness is a genuine type of happiness; a legitimate and important stepping-stone on the way to bliss. This is the type of happiness that most psychologists—particularly those in the positive-psychology movement—dwell upon as our final goal. Working on those practices, activities, and states of being that bring us to everyday happiness is a good thing. Finding everyday happiness involves a variety of positive traits, including gratitude, optimism, serving others, experiencing a sense of connection with the world around us, and having at least a small sense of purpose or meaning. From a physiological level, we can even say that being happy in an everyday sense requires achieving "balanced brain chemistry." If we were to perform a brain scan or draw blood on someone who was happy in this sense, we would very likely find the "right" regions of their brain lit up, or their balance of the mood-regulating brain chemicals serotonin, norepinephrine, endorphins, and other brain chemicals were "just right."

Pursuing strategies that raise our level of everyday happiness is essential to finding the bliss within. Often, until we have located this deeper level of bliss, everyday happiness is the best we can do—and that's certainly good enough to keep us going. But ultimately, this kind of happiness isn't anywhere near enough. In fact, it's so woefully incomplete that those who trick themselves into being satisfied with everyday happiness eventually discover that even this can feel hollow.

It's here that we introduce a radical departure from most psychologists and self-help authors. What they won't tell you—*can't* tell you because they haven't experienced it themselves or studied it in a laboratory—is that there is something far beyond everyday happiness. Each of us has within us the capacity for infinite, ever-new, all-encompassing bliss.

Bliss

Bliss is the only true, permanent form of happiness. Everyday happiness is subject to fluctuation; even positive psychologists warn that we can't experience everyday happiness *all* of the time.

We covered a basic explanation of bliss in the preface. We'll continually explore and expand our understanding of bliss as we progress through each chapter, topic, and practice. Bliss is also the direct and exclusive focus of chapters 22 through 26. One of the principal qualities of bliss is that it surpasses the capacity of our human languages to fully capture and express. As such, one of the best ways to advance our understanding is not through formal definitions but as an unfolding revelation that comes into clearer focus as we relate it to the full range of our challenges and experiences. For now, then, I'll add only this:

Bliss is like white light. Just as pure light is the totality of all color, bliss is the conglomeration of all positive qualities. When seen through the prism of spiritual awareness, the subcomponents of bliss are joy, unconditional love, inner peace, power, connectedness, awe, and wisdom. Bliss cannot even be *attained*, really. The soul simply realizes that bliss simply *is*. It is what remains after everything external and fleeting disappears.

Comparing and Contrasting

We can already start to see how very different bliss is from pleasure or everyday happiness. Pleasure is based on the senses. For example, we cannot imagine feeling pleasure without the ability to see, hear, touch, taste, or smell. One can feel bliss even if all five senses were impaired. People may describe certain feelings of relief as "blissful," but, in fact, it is only an emotional release and therefore superficial. Bliss is *not* an emotion, for our emotions fluctuate constantly and are usually triggered by changes in circumstance. Happiness in the regular sense is also outer directed. While it may include higher-order fulfillments such as warm relationships or serving others, it stills requires external situations and relationships to reach fruition. Bliss doesn't require any kind of outer relationship with the world— not even a positive one. You could be locked in a box, devoid of all human contact, and still experience it.

Another crucial difference: happiness can be pursued; there are concrete steps we can take to feel happier. Happiness, to some extent, requires *action* on our part. Bliss, on the other hand, is a state of *being*. Accessing the bliss within us requires nonaction, of learning how to *be* rather than to *do*. It is about stripping away all that is *not bliss*.

A True Story

Nine hundred years ago, during the Sukhothai period in Thailand, a ten-foot-high statue of a seated Buddha was cast in solid gold. The statue weighed over five and a half tons, the largest of its kind in the world. Today you can see it on display at Wat Traimit (Temple of the Golden Buddha) in Bangkok. The gleaming, beautiful, and powerful statue captivates and inspires all who approach it. The statue, however, was found only in the 1950s. The true story of how it disappeared and was eventually rediscovered is as fascinating as the work itself.

When the Burmese invaded Thailand in the late eighteenth century, Buddhist monks covered it in plaster in order to conceal and protect it from the invaders. Only a few people knew that it was made from solid gold. When these monks died, the secret was lost. In 1957 the temple housing the Buddha statue needed renovation. While the apparently worthless plaster statue was being moved to a new temple in Bangkok, it slipped from a crane and fell into the mud. A temple monk, who had dreamed that the statue was divinely inspired, went to visit it. Through a crack in the plaster, he saw a glint of gold and soon discovered that the statue was solid gold.

We, too, are made of the solid gold of spirit. Our underlying nature is pure bliss. However, after years of mistakes and neglect, we have forgotten that beneath our surface lies an abundant reservoir of bliss. And like that plaster-covered statue, discovering this is not so much a process of building and adding but of stripping away all that impedes us. Once we peel away our frayed and dull surface, we experience the gleaming bliss of our pure being. All of the bliss that we could ever need is already inside us, just waiting to come to the surface.

Heading in the Right Direction

Few of us dedicate all of our time to pursuing or experiencing just one of the main types of happiness: numbness, pleasure, everyday happiness, or bliss. For most of us, our lives are a mixture of all four, with occasional moments of false happiness occurring between desires. To a degree, this is understandable and acceptable. We needn't spend *all* of our time pursuing only bliss. Most of us aren't ready for that kind of single-minded dedication.

The short-term goal is to ensure that we spend at least a portion of our time in the everyday happiness and bliss spectrums of the Happiness Scale. Just bringing these into our consciousness even a little more than they are right now can engender enormous, positive change. Once we've had even a little experience of bliss, we'll naturally gravitate toward it anyway.

Using the example of my own life, as already mentioned, there have been many times when I was in such excruciating physical pain that I was entirely content just to find a way to feel nothing; to achieve a kind of numbness. In addition, there are also many small pleasures I enjoy, such as having a great meal at a top-flight restaurant. It's difficult for most of us to live entirely at the bliss end of this scale. The point is to ensure that we are at least spending *some* of our time digging for bliss. If we make a conscious, regular commitment to do this, we will naturally find ourselves living on the bliss end of the spectrum with greater frequency and consistency.

But it should be a natural, organic process. It cannot be forced. If we force ourselves too far outside of what is real for us at the moment, or beyond our current spiritual capabilities, then we set ourselves up not only for disappointment and disillusionment but also for a terrible rebound effect in which we may find ourselves more deeply enmeshed in the pursuits of numbness and pleasure than ever. Be gentle and patient with yourself: concentrate on uncovering the bliss within only as it feels natural to do so.

The Experiment: Balancing Your Happiness Scale

Note: You can perform this exercise by either writing or drawing your observations in your Bliss Journal or by mentally tabulating your results.

1. Review the Happiness Scale on page 24. Think about all of your life's activities over the recent past.
2. Approximately what percentage of your time, thoughts, or efforts have you spent pursuing numbness, pleasure, everyday happiness, and bliss? Assign a percentage to each. (Note: False Happiness is not usually something that we directly pursue. It's more of an accidental way-station, a place in which we briefly find ourselves when one desire has been satiated but our minds haven't yet created a new one in its place. It's not a state that we should consciously choose. As such, we won't include False Happiness as part of this exercise.)
3. As you reflect upon it, do you feel that you might be spending too much time in one area, particularly at the numbness or pleasure end of the scale? Does it feel like you're allocating the right amount of time—for you—to each pursuit?
4. Do you want to change how much time you allocate to achieving everyday happiness or bliss?
5. What is the right percentage of time or energy allocations for you? For example, you might feel guided to spend 25 percent of your time on each of the four. Or you might spend 25 percent on bliss, 50 percent on everyday happiness, and 12.5 percent each on numbness and pleasure? Come up with a distribution that feels intuitively right for you. You may alter it later.

Online

Scan the Microsoft Tag above to view a brief video, "Bliss and Superconsciousness," or go to youtube.com/seanmeshorer.

CHAPTER 2

Why We Fail at Being Happy

I can think of nothing less pleasurable than a life devoted to pleasure.

—John D. Rockefeller, American oil magnate
and philanthropist (1839–1937)

Now that we have an overview of the types of happiness and where they fall on the Happiness Scale, it's time to look specifically at the most common happiness strategies. By examining these approaches—ones that we *all* try at one time or another—we will further refine our understanding of where they fall on the scale and why we so often fail at finding happiness, meaning, and truth.

The most common false solutions turn out to have a great deal in common: they are all external. As it turns out, we *have* been given a treasure map to find the hidden bliss diamond. The difficulty is that instead of being somewhere outside of us, it's hidden in the one place we never think to look: deep within ourselves.

The Story

I've known Betty for nearly twenty years. During that time, I've watched her try out innumerable personas, careers, relationships, hobbies, and even religions. Betty grew up in a famous family, though she isn't famous herself. Not only did she experience fame up close but also the enormous wealth that comes with it. Betty's family, to their credit, placed a strong emphasis on academic and career achievement. She wasn't allowed to coast upon the successes of others, and although she was destined to be wealthy via her inheritance, she didn't behave at all like a "trust-fund brat."

Betty worked hard, went to an Ivy League school—her parents were dynamic movers and shakers in academia and business—and was expected to find her own career. Though much was expected of Betty, her parents were not strict. She was given plenty of space to go through her "punk phase," her "jock phase," and her "religious phase" without much familial interference.

Betty also had a procession of love affairs, with both men and women, some of which had an almost dangerous intensity to them. She was given ample leeway to explore her creative side as she trained in painting, music, and poetry. Since her family wasn't perfect—no family is—she also had lots of psychotherapy along the way.

Yet until recently, Betty was still restless and unhappy. For a long time, she couldn't understand why. Though we are friends, I never felt in a position to offer much advice or direction. Mostly I watched from a respectful distance, supporting her in whatever small ways I could.

In the last few years, without my help or suggestions, Betty stumbled across many of the same solutions that I offer in this book. Though I largely found them through the help of my spiritual teacher, Paramhansa Yogananda, Betty found hers through an entirely different teacher and path. But the core principles and practices are almost exactly the same.

Not long ago, Betty reflected to me, "I kept looking outside myself. I had access to all these amazing experiences, and I just kept burning through them, figuring that if I tried enough things, eventually I'd hit upon just the perfect one. But it never happened."

The Science

In recent years, science has helped us to understand some of the physiological reasons that external events fail to satisfy us. All forms of pleasure are ultimately processed and experienced through our nervous systems. A soft fabric, a pleasant smell, a beautiful painting—these originate outside ourselves and then we "take them inside us" by processing and experiencing them through our sensory nerves and brain.

When we walk into a room, at first we might notice how it smells, whether wonderfully from an aromatherapy candle or horribly from mildew. Over time, usually very quickly, we become accustomed to the smell and cease to notice it. Perhaps at this point, after the smell has begun fading from our consciousness, someone new enters the rooms and reminds us ("What's that wonderful scent?" or "What smells so terrible in here?") until they, too, get used to it, and it fades into the background once again.

Scientists call this kind of sensory adjustment hedonic adaptation. It applies not just to direct sensory pleasures such as sights, sounds, or smells but also to virtually every kind of external circumstance, including major life changes. New relationships (or exiting an old one), new jobs, new locations, new cars—all create a surge of temporary happiness that quickly subsides as our nervous system acclimates to the new object or sensation in our lives. Quite literally, it doesn't take long before the thrill is gone.

A landmark study published in *Journal of Personality and Social Psychology*, titled "Lottery Winners and Accident Victims: Is Happiness Relative?," provides dramatic proof that hedonic adaptation works not only at the level of direct sensory input but also in much broader and deeper ways. The researchers looked at three groups of people: lottery winners, accident victims who tragically became paraplegic, and a control group who neither won the lottery nor suffered severe trauma. Predictably enough, the study found that in the first few months after winning the lottery, the recipients experienced a large upward spike in their level of happiness, while the happiness level for the recently paralyzed subjects fell dramatically.

That's not surprising, as anyone who has ever received shockingly good or bad news can attest. What's startling is what researchers discovered beginning at sixth months and becomes unmistakable at the twelve-month mark: within a year, the happiness level of those that had won the lottery had fallen all the way back to, and in some cases well below where it had been prior to their windfall. Conversely, after about a year, the paraplegic subjects had adjusted to their new life circumstances, and their happiness levels had recovered entirely. *In fact, they were generally much happier than the lottery winners!*

This is hedonic adaptation rendered in sharp relief. The "happiness" gained from becoming fabulously wealthy quickly drains away. We become used to our lives as wealthy people, and the thrill and security derived from our new material possessions fades. On the other hand, the accident victims were able to adjust to their radically changed lives—perhaps even gain strength and wisdom from it—and despite the horrific nature of their experience, they were able to relatively quickly regain and even surpass their previous levels of happiness.

Another study in the *Journal of Experimental Psychology* highlighted a different aspect of hedonic adaptation: our psychological inability to guess correctly our response to life-altering situations. The study looked at the happiness levels of patients on kidney hemodialysis—which is no fun, as some of you might know. Those on dialysis need to receive many hours of treatment several days a week just to stay alive, and, barring a kidney transplant, they must do this for the rest of their lives. They also must make extreme dietary changes and most have to alter radically their daily schedules and often those of loved ones and caretakers. Sounds awful, doesn't it?

Except that according to the study, those with end-stage kidney disease were no less happy than the healthy subjects. However, when members of the latter group were asked if they *thought* they would be unhappier if they had kidney failure, the majority were absolutely certain that their lives would be worse. Fortunately, they were wrong. Most of us will be just fine—and if we aren't fine, it's not really because of the illness itself but because of the kind of people we are regardless of what's ailing us physically.

The Spirit

Betty learned that happiness and bliss don't require a lot, at least not externally. We don't need a particular job, or spouse, or bank account, or social status, or to be the star of our own reality TV show—or anything. It's so very simple. Yet, if it's so simple, how come we miss it?

From an early age, we begin looking outside ourselves. One of our first impulses is to use our senses—sight, taste, smell, hearing, and touch—to explore our outer world. This is natural and expected. We need our senses to survive; to alert us to dangers, keep us safe, and seek out positive opportunities. The challenge is that we become so accustomed to using our senses—and our senses alone—that even as we grow older, we never surrender the incorrect belief that stimulating our senses is the *reason* for our existence. We confuse our survival instinct as the primary place to find lasting fulfillment. Our senses, designed and intended as merely a subordinate *tool* for use in certain situations, instead become the only way that we explore our world. We forget, or never discover, that we have other capacities, that there are other places to look. As the saying goes, to a carpenter with a hammer, all the world's problems look like nails. That's us: we think that sensory stimulation is the solution to everything.

As infants, we subconsciously learn that accumulating "stuff" might be the source of happiness. It starts with a blanket, pacifier, or stuffed animal. These objects give us a false sense of psychological security or amusement, but they can't offer genuine, lasting solutions. Think of what a pacifier really is: a fake substitute for our mother's breast, meant to trick us into thinking that we're being fed or to remind us of our parent's comforting security. In truth, it provides neither nourishment nor genuine security. Babies only *think* it does.

What begins as a well-meaning attempt by our parents to gain a little peace and quiet accidentally becomes a subconsciously stored blueprint for happiness. We falsely come to assume that collecting the right kinds of objects will make us happy. As the years progress, we slowly expand our desire for material comforts into clothes, cars, houses, vacations, and luxury goods.

It goes deeper. We look outside ourselves not only for stimulation but also to uncover the mysteries of existence. Yet the world outside of us is in constant flux, yielding little in the way of enduring meaning. The ancient Greek philosopher Heraclitus observed that the only constant is change; the very nature of our world is impermanence. Today we know this more than ever. Whether we are scientific rationalists or fundamentalist believers, we all agree that the world had a beginning (whether through a big bang or a God creating it in six days) and is certain to have an end (whether in the distant future through a Big Crunch or heat death, or sooner in Armageddon and Judgment Day). Long before the universe itself dissolves, we are facing our own personal dissolution in death.

Between birth and death come millions of smaller changes, both trivial and important. Our bodies change, our knowledge changes, our experiences change, the people around us change, and our fortunes change. The world outside us is in constant flux—and often the inner world of our body and mind as well.

We look for security in the world around us, in relationships, in a large bank account, in a special diet and good health. Yet these are all ephemeral. Even if we have "the best" relationship, eventually we or our partner will die. Even relationships that are working well at the moment might implode. We hear of a couple separating and say, "But they seemed so happy!" We know that could happen to us; our partner could be miserable, and we might not even know it. Money comes and goes. Our health can disappear in one trip to the doctor; even if we follow every guideline for good health, it can all vanish in a single car accident that wasn't our fault. There is no permanent security in the outer world of things or people.

We must embrace this, not hide from it. The world of things and sensory pleasures is fleeting. There can be no security and no lasting happiness in the temporal world of constant flux. We can't conquer all disease or prevent every war or ward off every environmental catastrophe. We can't control other people, especially not their emotions and needs. Anything and everything that is dependent on finding unchanging happiness in the external world must fail in the end. It is as certain as death itself.

When we look closer, we make the startling discovery that for every pleasure, there is a corresponding pain. For example, a fun night of drinking brings a hangover. We could even think of this as the philosophical extension of the scientific principle outlined in Newton's third law of motion: "For every action, there is an equal and opposite reaction."

Imagine receiving a massage, something that most of us find enjoyable and relaxing. The first sixty to ninety minutes of massage are often pleasurable, or at least pleasant. Imagine that massage continuing for two to three hours. We would likely grow bored, ceasing to notice it, as either we fell asleep or our mind drifted. Now imagine the same massage continuing not for hours but days. First, our skin would turn red, then peel and crack, and then become deeply painful as the masseuse eventually wore us down to the bone. If we were strapped down to the table and massaged continuously in the same place long enough—a day, a week, or a month—we would literally die from it as the skin broke down and blood started to flow. What began as a pleasure would become an excruciating pain. Literally, torture.

While this example is extreme, it captures what really happens to one degree or another with all our pleasures. Eventually they not only bore us but also hurt us. Of course, we usually stop before things become downright gruesome—but not always; witness the countless millions who have drunk or drugged themselves to death. In every case, getting drunk or high started as fun, though it usually doesn't end that way.

Most of us don't follow a particular pleasure all the way to its ghastly conclusion. Instead, sensing that a particular outward pursuit is growing tedious or painful, we tell ourselves that it must have been just that one specific object or activity that's failed us, immediately turning our attention to a new pursuit, as the cycle begins again. On and on we go, pursuing one desire after another, like hamsters on a treadmill.

We continue this way for years, perhaps lifetimes, before we realize that in the end, every attempt at pleasure—at manipulating the external world to our liking—has done nothing but put us on a collision course with suffering. We have put our faith into things that cannot and will never satisfy. This was the great insight of the Buddha—and countless numbers of saints and sages before and after him.

At a certain level, we know this. What happens after an exciting day? We crash, we need rest. Eat too much dessert, we feel full or get fat. Have too much sex, we end up feeling depleted, or with a disease, or in some kind of relationship mess. We go on a shopping spree, but then the bill comes due. Look at any child: filled with excited energy one moment, collapsed in heap, barely able to keep his eyes open the next.

Pleasure is not limitless, and the external world eventually loses its excitement and simply becomes exhausting. But we can go much too long before we figure this out. Why? Because of the endless variety inherent in the external world. There are literally billions of combinations and permutations of sensory pleasures, stacked and sequenced in unique ways. When one pleasure runs its course, we unhesitatingly look for a replacement. Usually we try to swap out the failed pleasure for something new as quickly as possible so that we needn't experience even one moment of sensory deprivation.

Perhaps now you can already begin to see why many of our most common strategies for achieving lasting happiness are doomed—why we are digging in the wrong place altogether. Given how widespread our most common happiness mistakes are, it's imperative that we take time to examine each of them in depth. Our desires can be so strong, so blinding, and so all consuming that it's difficult to convince ourselves that there isn't *some* satisfaction to be found in them. Until we are so convinced, they'll distract us from finding the hidden bliss within.

The Experiment:
The Fleeting Nature of Sense Pleasures

Note: If you are keeping a Bliss Journal, you can write down this exercise and your responses to it.

Think of a song that you really like. Find it on CD, your iPod, or whatever format you normally use to listen to it.

1. Listen to this song as many times as possible over the next day. You can do this two ways: either set aside at least an hour or two right now, or, if that's not possible, carry around a listening device with you over the next twenty-four hours.
2. Listen to the song from beginning to end in a loop for the next one to two hours without a break, or carry it with you for the next twenty-four hours and listen to it every spare moment possible—while traveling, on break, working out, before bed, and so on.
3. If you find yourself growing tired of the song, yet the allotted time has not yet expired, keep listening. Don't stop, no matter what.
4. After you've listened as much as possible, reflect on what you've just learned, noticed, and experienced. Did the enjoyment it originally brought you begin to fade? Did you start to grow bored or tune it out? Did you ever get to a point where you were not only bored but also outright sick of the song?

5. Recall that this was one of your *favorite* songs. What does it mean to you that you so quickly grew tired of something you loved?

6. How confident are you that stringing together an endless parade of sensory experiences is the key to lasting happiness?

Online

Additional videos and resources for this chapter are available at www.theblissexperiment.com.

CHAPTER 3

Money and Luxury

Many wealthy people are little more than janitors of their possessions.

—*Frank Lloyd Wright, American architect*
(1867–1959)

For the next three chapters, we'll take an in-depth look at our most common misconceptions and failed strategies for finding lasting happiness.

The belief that material wealth makes us happy or confers meaning to life is a widespread myth. Those of every age, gender, race, nationality, religious background, and era are prone to this error. Between my family, friends, private high school, Stanford, and then as a spiritual teacher, I have come across countless people determined to get rich, often by any means necessary. Even those who don't care to be obscenely wealthy often tell me that they desire to be at least a little bit wealthier than they currently are; if only they had another 10 percent to 20 percent more money, life would be better.

I've seen more people make major life and career decisions in pursuit of wealth than any other reason. I know attorneys, CEOs, and doctors who hate their lives but can't and won't find another calling because the money is too enticing to surrender. At one time or another, we all imagine our lives would be better if we were wealthy, or at least a little better off than we are now. Fortunately for us, it turns out that there is almost no truth to this most common delusion, though for reasons that may surprise you.

The Story

Lyle is the richest person I know. While I've *met* many very wealthy people over the years, Lyle is someone I *know*. We've had many personal discussions, spent countless hours together, and I've socialized with his family and friends. He has hundreds of millions of dollars, acquired through a wide number of businesses and investments. He's a generous philanthropist, sitting on the boards of numerous nonprofit organizations, as well as a dedicated family man with four children.

Lyle owns a megamansion in Connecticut, a ski house on Lake Tahoe, and an oceanfront villa on a Caribbean island. He flies on private jets, has a fleet of nannies, assistants, and personal chefs, stays in the penthouse of five-star hotels, eats at the world's finest restaurants, drives exotic luxury automobiles (when not being chauffeured in limousines), and counts innumerable politicians, actors, and rock stars as his friends.

He is the life of the party and the center of attention everywhere he goes. He holds forth like a king at court as his friends and well-wishers hang on to his every word. He expects to be fawned over. He tells funny stories, is witty, bright, well read, generous to his friends and family, and, to anyone observing from a distance, seems like one hell of a great guy.

For all his wealth, Lyle is profoundly unhappy. For one, he has a terrible secret: he is an alcoholic and, possibly, a drug addict. He has been drinking heavily and doing drugs for decades. I've watched him drink an entire bottle of vodka, get stoned, do some blow, then top it off with nitrous oxide, mushrooms, or ecstasy all in one night. There was at least a ten-year stretch where Lyle was drunk or high every time I saw him. A subsequent quiet stint in a rehabilitation facility didn't work entirely but at least slowed him down.

Occasionally, Lyle and I would talk heart to heart. Outwardly, his life was relatively stable. His family was wealthy (though he grew this wealth considerably through his own intellect and skills), his parents loved each other and never divorced, and he went to good schools, from elementary through graduate. He married his college sweetheart, who was a wonderful woman: smart, pretty, grounded, and kind. His children are also great— probably due mostly to their wonderful mother.

Lyle confided in me what drove him to drinking and drugs: despite having every material possession and every advantage, life felt meaningless. He didn't trust most of his "friends" because he couldn't be sure that they really liked him for himself and not for his wealth. He divorced his loving wife (and the second and third) because he felt so isolated and distant that he had lost the capacity to receive and give genuine love. He knew that although he had a staff of people who did his bidding and people kowtowed to him wherever he went, it was only because he paid their wages, bought them stuff, could bankroll their business, or was a high-spending customer.

Worse, he had grown tired of his life of luxury. After years of accumulating things, he knew that none of it made him the least bit happy. We both noticed that even as his net worth climbed, his patience and temper worsened. If a server in a restaurant ignored him for even two minutes, he flew into a rage. If something he bought wasn't absolutely perfect in every way, he sent it back. The more luxuries he experienced, the more each new thing had to be that much better, more perfect than the last. Great wealth not only failed to insulate him from life's challenges, it actually heightened them. Even the most minor imperfections or failures completely destroyed his equanimity. He could no longer enjoy the little things in life—or really much at all.

Lyle felt trapped. He had achieved the American Dream, yet it left him cold and empty. He had no one to talk to. Most of his "friends" were really just sycophants who couldn't understand and were in fact clamoring to be in his halo of wealth. No psychologist or fellow rehab patient had experienced his level of wealth. No one understood him at all, not even his ex-wives and family. He told me once, "I look around the room, and I feel like an asshole complaining about my life when everyone else seems to have such real and terrible problems. I just can't do it. I don't know what to do."

The Science

There's a tremendous amount of research proving that money and luxuries don't generate happiness. It comes from myriad angles: comparing the well-being of people from different economic backgrounds, surveying wealthy and poor individuals, and looking at long-term health and wellness outcomes for specific groups of people.

From a macro perspective:

What do Ghana, Mexico, Sweden, the United Kingdom, and the United States have in common? They all share similar life satisfaction scores despite per capita income varying tenfold between the richest and poorest countries. Which is to say: despite our incredible wealth, Americans are no happier than the west African Republic of Ghana!

Separately published research concludes that although American standards of living have sharply increased sharply since the early 1970s, our level of happiness hasn't risen at all.

If anything, it may have declined, given that antidepressants are now the most prescribed drugs in America. This is not unique to the United States, incidentally. From 1981 to 2007, during the time of the greatest economic boom in the history of China, its national happiness levels have plummeted.

At the individual level:

- A survey of 49 of the richest people in the world, selected from the *Forbes* magazine list of wealthiest Americans, showed that many of the superwealthy admitted to being unhappy. On average, the superwealthy reported only slightly higher levels of happiness than a randomly selected control group from the general population. Most important, *not a single one of these 49 wealthiest Americans believed that money was the major source of their happiness.* They ranked money as one of the *least important* aspects for attaining well-being.
- A study tracked 12,000 people from their freshman year in college through their late thirties. Researchers found that those in college who explicitly made "getting rich" a key life goal were on average *less happy* fifteen years later than those with more uplifting goals.
- In a study of 374 employees working at Cornell University, researchers concluded that "higher income was associated with *more* intense negative experienced emotions . . . but *not* greater experienced happiness."

Given that the pursuit of money and luxury is a universal human obsession, this raises the question, why are we so determined to get something that clearly doesn't deliver?

Nobel Prize–winning economist Daniel Kahneman has at least one answer. He designed a series of studies that demonstrates that humans are highly susceptible to forming "focusing illusions." A focusing illusion occurs when we mistakenly exaggerate the importance of any single factor for achieving a desired outcome. In a confusing world with a nearly infinite number of variables and choices, our minds are often confused, uncertain, and overwhelmed. There is so much that we simply don't know—whether statistical probabilities or real-world facts—that oftentimes life circumstances force us to make choices based on incomplete information or understanding. To help us whittle down the chaos and define a course of action, we tend to latch onto just one or two salient facts or experiences and blow them out of proportion, ascribing to them importance that they simply don't have in reality. Kahneman's research demonstrates conclusively that accumulating wealth is one of the most common focusing illusions.

I do want to point out one exception, the *only* one that researchers have ever found. Those who are so poor that they cannot afford even the most basic things to survive—food, clothing, and shelter—do report a relatively *mild* increase in their happiness levels when they are able to gain these minimal levels of "wealth." Beyond that, neither incremental nor large jumps in income make much difference.

The Spirit

It's no surprise that money and material objects are one of our primary focusing illusions. As discussed, we've been trained from an early age to look to the material world for comfort. Material objects also surround us. They're everywhere. They're easy to see, feel, hear, touch, and taste. Since we explore our world primarily through the senses and material objects are really nothing but a collection of sensory experiences, they are naturally attractive to us. Moreover, we are bombarded with them. Virtually everyone we know or see is constantly displaying or talking about their objects. Corporations spend trillions of dollars manufacturing and marketing their wares. There are so many types of objects and experiences available, it doesn't matter what kind of person we are, our interests or hobbies, as there is always some object out there designed precisely to fill any and every desire.

Ultimately, however, it's not just focusing illusions or brain chemistry that explains our fascination with wealth and luxury. The deepest reasons lie beyond the boundary of physical science in the very nature of reality, consciousness, and human existence.

Money and material objects are wholly external to us; even when we ingest foods or drugs, they retain a certain sense of "otherness." Objects can't penetrate to the core of our being, nor can they make lasting changes to our consciousness. Wealth doesn't make us feel peaceful, joyful, contented, or loving. It doesn't help us to understand or connect with others. Both Mother Teresa and a Mafia hit man could go on the same luxury cruise, and in neither case would we realistically expect that the trip would change either of them at a deep level.

How could it? Do we really believe that sleeping on 1,000-thread-count sheets will by itself bring us peace, wisdom, or love—or uplift our consciousness? When it's laid out clearly, we can see how absurd a notion this is. It doesn't, and it can't. At a certain level, we all know this.

It's everything *else* we do with our lives that defines us: our thoughts, deeds, aspirations, and consciousness. If mere *things* had any kind of consistent or normalizing influence on people, we would discover that folks exposed to the same things started to think, feel, and behave in the same way. This is obviously not the case.

The Downside of Wealth

Placing our happiness at the mercy of wealth and luxury tends to produce the opposite result: it makes us feel even more uncertain and insecure.

The world of things is fleeting and ephemeral. Our wealth can be wiped out either by a mistake we make or through something that has nothing to do with us, like a global economic downturn, a plunge in the stock market, financial fraud, or a run on the banks. Responsibility for wealth often comes with a fearful need to preserve and protect it.

Wealth also doesn't solve the mystery of our existence or insulate us from death. If we can't take it with us, and it can't keep us from dying, and it doesn't help us understand the meaning of life—well, that's a giant clue that it can't possibly be the ultimate answer to much of *anything*. At best, money and luxury are like administering painkillers to a dying patient. It makes the journey more comfortable, but it doesn't treat the underlying disease or prevent the inescapable.

Far from making life just a bit more tolerable, it actually makes it *worse*. Like my friend Lyle experienced, money can make us more irritable, more impatient, more difficult to please, and more isolated. We become dependent on money, objects, and situations being just right. If they're not, we're *un*happy; sometimes we can't even function. The wealthier we are, the more we worry that our friends and family like us more for our money than for ourselves. It's no wonder that the suicide rate for wealthy and successful people is actually higher than for the poor.

Placing Conditions on Our Happiness

To believe that we need external possessions is to place conditions on our happiness. It makes us prisoners to only a small set of possible outcomes. Not everyone can be wealthy. It's like playing a game of Russian roulette with your soul. What happens if you don't accumulate enough wealth? Or you do, briefly, but then it vanishes? Has your chance for happiness been destroyed?

To place our happiness at the whim of others, of complex economies and financial systems, most of which are out of our control, is like choosing to live in a psychological prison. Right now, as you're reading this, repeat to yourself, "I won't be happy until I have a million dollars, or a billion dollars, or a mansion, or am retired with a big bank account." Now ask yourself this: How do you feel as you repeat that? Not so good, I'll bet.

What We Really Want

Here's a startling truth: we don't *really* want money or things, we only think we do. What we actually want is the underlying benefit that these objects represent. A thing is nothing more than a *delivery vehicle* for a quality or experience we seek.

Recently, I found myself fantasizing about owning our own swimming pool. Brook and I live in an apartment building in an urban part of Los Angeles. The weather is nice year-round. After letting my mind fantasize about a nice, private pool for a while, I caught what I was doing and asked myself a simple question: Why do I *really* want a pool?

I wanted to sit in the warm sun and swim in the cool water. A private pool would give a sense of solitude and peacefulness. I imagined it would also be an aesthetically beautiful environment with the landscape and glistening water. It would be quick and convenient to access, since it would be right where we live.

Those are the *surface* reasons why I wanted the pool. When I thought about it more deeply, I realized that each of these reasons represents *qualities* that I wanted to access and experience. The sun represents energy, vitality, and healing. The cool water represents relaxation and calmness. The privacy of it represents solitude and peacefulness. The environment represents beauty. The convenient location represents the ability to slip into the experience at a moment's notice.

In other words, as I reflected on it, a private pool represented vitality, healing, calmness, solitude, peacefulness, and beauty—all of which I'd like to access without delay or difficulty. I didn't really want the pool per se, I wanted more of these qualities in my life. I fixated on the pool as a delivery vehicle to obtain those qualities.

Objects Are Neutral Vessels

Using external objects as intermediaries for attaining the qualities we really want is indirect, inefficient, and uncertain. What happens if I never get a private pool? Does that mean I'm forever barred from experiencing these qualities? Further, as the wealthy can attest, merely having the objects doesn't guarantee receiving the underlying qualities we seek. We have to actively develop the understanding and skills necessary to extract the benefits from the intermediary delivery vehicles. If we don't know how to do this, it can be like receiving delivery of a locked package that we don't know how to open. Technically, we possess it, but in reality, we can't really get at what's inside.

The cosmic joke is that the box is empty anyway. Pleasures and joys aren't truly inside the object, they're inside *us*. Think about this: a poor person might derive pleasure from cheap drug store candy. A rich person might be able to receive pleasure only from imported Belgian chocolate. In both cases, they actually receive the *same* amount of pleasure. It's not the object that contains intrinsic joy. It's our thoughts, feelings, and orientation; our inner consciousness dictating our response to that object.

Instead of yearning for objects, we can instead learn how to access those states of consciousness directly. We don't need millions of dollars so that we can buy these delivery vehicles. Instead we can have it right now. And then twenty-four hours per day, every day thereafter. It's not only more direct and efficient, it's more certain. In fact, it's guaranteed.

An Important Caveat

That said, money and luxury aren't inherently evil. It's not bad or wrong to have nice things or to be wealthy. A certain amount of money can be positive if approached with the right perspective. The challenge is to avoid heaping unrealistic expectations on wealth by blindly pursuing it while ignoring more important things.

As we'll explore later, there are even some circumstances where objects typically associated with wealth or luxury can be beneficial. We certainly don't have to give away our money or quit our high-paying jobs. We need only reevaluate our underlying understanding and motivations.

Whatever our bank balance, realizing that we needn't *prioritize* the accumulation of money and possessions (and often debt) removes a tremendous weight from our shoulders, leaving us lighter, happier, freer. The less we introduce intermediaries between happiness and us, the faster we can access bliss.

The Experiment (1): Gaining Perspective

1. Visualize or write down something nice that you bought in the last year; preferably something that you strongly desired. Choose something *not* of lifesaving importance, just something you *wanted*.
2. Remember how you felt when you acquired it or first experienced it. Recall any feeling of excitement, happiness, importance, or pleasure.
3. How long did that excitement last? A day? A week? A month? A year? Do you still feel it as vividly today as when you first purchased it? Did it ever disappear or lose intensity?
4. If so, what did you do when the positive feelings subsided? Did you begin thinking about acquiring something else? Have you already bought something else since then?
5. How many "exciting" possessions do you estimate you've bought in your lifetime? Things that you believed would make you just a little happier if you owned them?
6. Has any purchase, ever, given you permanent joy? Do you expect your next purchase(s) to do so? If so, is that likely to prove true?

The Experiment (2):
Uncovering the Illusion of Luxury

1. Visualize or write down an object or experience that you have *not yet* bought but want.
2. Why do you want it? Write a list of all the benefits you believe this item will confer.
3. Create a second list based on the first: what are the underlying *qualities* or *benefits* you hope to gain through this thing (for example, calmness, vitality, healing, beauty, love, and so on)?
4. Is there a way that you can experience these qualities and benefits directly, without needing the intermediary object? What actions can you take now to increase that quality/benefit inside yourself, regardless of whether you have that thing or not?

Note: It's okay if you don't yet have a clear sense of how you can directly experience these benefits. By the time you complete this book, you'll be able to return to this exercise with a variety of solutions.

Online

Additional videos and resources for this chapter are available at www.theblissexperiment.com.

CHAPTER 4

Sex and Romance

Sex builds no roads, writes no novels, and sex certainly gives no meaning to anything in life but itself.
—*Gore Vidal, American author and playwright (b. 1925)*

Sex and romance are the most commonly pursued human experiences, even more than money and luxury, for even those who have no hope for or interest in great wealth still get married, have children, have affairs, and spend a great deal of their time thinking about them. While there is a high bar of entry to the world of luxury hotels, mansions, yachts, and exotic cars, sex and romance are available to everyone, no matter his or her station in life.

Much of Western pop culture is dedicated to extolling their virtues, including almost every pop song ever written. Even male-driven action movies often make sure to include at least one female character and a romantic subplot. While there's some truth to the trope that men often focus on sex, while women yearn more for romance, the reality is that each gender pursues both.

It's probably not surprising that the ultimate value of sex for happiness and meaning is being called into question. Perhaps it is surprising that I bundle romantic "love" and relationships together with sex. The reason will soon be clear.

The Story

Max is a famous rock star. *Very.* Millions in the West—really, anywhere that Western rock has infiltrated—have heard of his band, even if they aren't fans of the music. I first met him years ago while I was at Stanford. I happened to have backstage passes to his concert in the Bay Area. One of my friends was close with Max, so he introduced us. Through this mutual friend, Max and I continued to run into each other over the years, often while he was on tour.

Though it wasn't outright acknowledged by those of us who saw him across the country, it was clear that Max had different "girlfriends" (more like repeat groupies) in almost every city. He would send roadies or members of his entourage into the crowd before and during the shows, handing out backstage passes to any woman who seemed his type. After the show, the women would come backstage, where there was always an after-party. Max would have a chance to meet them; the ones he liked were invited to attend the "after-after-party" that took place in a hotel suite where the band was staying.

I would see him in those hotel suites late at night, always with a young, beautiful woman—or two or three—on his arm. Sometimes I would watch as he and the others would divvy up huge piles of cocaine and take turns doing lines. As the party started to wind down, he and the women would eventually disappear into his private bedroom. The same scene would repeat itself in city after city, year after year. A never-ending parade of women, all treating rich, famous, and talented Max like a god.

Years later, I ran into Max when I was visiting my friend. Over dinner at an upscale Italian restaurant, we reminisced about the "good old days." Max admitted that those years were actually the loneliest of his life. He was usually drunk or stoned when he slept with his girlfriend-groupies. Not only was it meaningless for him, he eventually came to despise it. Decades of sleeping around with the world's most beautiful women left him confused, lonely, and eventually in rehab both for drugs and sex addiction. Sex *never* gave him even a fleeting moment of genuine happiness. Eventually, he said, it even ceased giving him pleasure. He had grown completely numb to it, an empty ritual that he continued partly for the sake of his image but mostly because he didn't know what else to do or how else to behave. It was an addictive habit, not a source of joy.

Max eventually broke free of this habit. He settled down, got married, and even had children. He seldom thought about other women, nor did he enjoy reminiscing about those wild years. Unfortunately, he now had a new set of challenges: he had never learned how to relate to a woman as an equal partner. His marriage, though better than the endless parade of faceless female fans, was volatile and continually strained. He and his wife repeatedly separated, then reconciled. Max's drinking had recently taken a radical upswing. He was disappointed and confused that his marriage and settled lifestyle hadn't been as transformative as he'd hoped. He'd been convinced that he'd picked the "right" woman. After years of sampling so many, he was certain that he knew genuine chemistry when he felt it. He had his pick of thousands, and this was the one that seemed best suited. There were no compromises with her, no sense of settling for something less. She had seemed perfect in every way. So why were they fighting all the time? Max didn't have any answers, and I didn't feel like I was in a position to offer suggestions.

As of the last time we spoke, they were together, but I got the distinct feeling that storm clouds were on the horizon.

The Science

Because sex, romance, and relationships are so important to us, there's no shortage of research on the topic. America has become much more sexually open and adventurous since the 1950s. Not only do we talk about and (sometimes graphically) depict sex much more honestly, the average person experiences it more often as well. It's not uncommon for people to have five to ten times the number of sex partners than our grandparents' generation did. Casual sex is now an accepted part of mainstream society. The number of extramarital affairs is also skyrocketing.

It's not just young people partaking in this sexual revolution, either. The combination of women now constituting half the workforce (thereby increasing the opportunities for both genders to meet potential sex partners) and high divorce rates has lead to a slew of older adults "back on the market." This creates more opportunities for casual sex encounters across all age ranges. Despite this, research shows that:

- Just as we've already seen with the spike in wealth and living standards, the radical increase in sexual activity has coincided with *declining* levels of overall life satisfaction and happiness.
- Women, in particular, despite a huge increase in their sexual partners and activity, have reported steadily *declining* levels of well-being since the 1970s.

Clearly, if sexual openness and access to more partners were salient factors in happiness, our reported levels of well-being would be on the rise. Sexual activity can't be as important or influential as we believe. This is supported by some compelling data:

- A recent study in the *Journal of Sex Research* found that women who engaged in the most casual sex reported the highest levels of depressive symptoms.
- A 2004 study published in the *Scandinavian Journal of Economics* reported that people with just one sex partner, engaging in regular but *not* frequent sex, are happier than people having frequent sex with many partners.
- Men who cheat on their wives or use prostitutes are less happy than those who don't.

While many people are willing to concede that sex by itself isn't a solution for enduring happiness, they are more resistant to the claim that romantic love isn't much better. Unfortunately, studies overwhelmingly demonstrate there is truth to this observation.

Since 1999, the National Marriage Project (NMP), a research initiative now at the University of Virginia, has published an annual report on the health of marriage in the United States, titled *The State of Our Unions*. According to the 2010 edition, people who marry because they believe they've found their romantic soul mate generally have far more unstable, volatile, and shorter unions than those who marry for more mundane reasons.

Likewise, a multitude of researchers and psychologists around the world has discovered that the "passionate/romantic" phase of a relationship generally lasts for no more than eighteen to thirty-six months. A recent British poll of ten thousand people sponsored by the *Daily Mail* found that the average passionate romance faded after about two and a half years.

And a study conducted in Germany followed nearly twenty-five thousand men and women for fifteen years. Seventeen hundred of them got married during that time. All twenty-five thousand subjects were reinterviewed each year. Researchers concluded that those who fell in love, conducted a courtship, and then married showed *no long-term increase in their happiness compared to those who didn't marry.*

The Spirit

As with wealth, the fundamental reason that sex and romance don't generate happiness is that they are external. To believe that we *need* sex or romance is to become dependent on others for our fulfillment. It is to tell ourselves that we are intrinsically incomplete. This pulls our focus outside ourselves and into the world of sensory pleasures, reinforcing the notion that happiness is "out there" in another person. Not only does that make our happiness contingent upon circumstances outside our control but also, as with chasing any externality, it's an inherently uncertain, anxiety-provoking way to live.

To believe that sex or romance is necessary is once again to take an indirect approach to lasting happiness. The ecstasy of sex is really our yearning for bliss; the desire for romance is our attempt to experience unconditional love. Ultimately though, both sex and romance are circuitous, inefficient, and temporary strategies. There are faster, more direct, and more satisfying ways of finding bliss.

Sex

Sex is a topic fraught with conflicting emotions. In my classes, usually at least one attendee is concerned that I might be prudish, conservative, traumatized, or dogmatically antisex. I assure you that none of this is true. Like many of us, years ago, I tried screwing my way to happiness. If it had worked, I would gladly tell you. The thing is, it just doesn't.

Recently, a student asked me sincerely, "Isn't an orgasm a form of bliss? If we could find a way to orgasm frequently, wouldn't that be good?"

That's not a ridiculous question. Those moments of orgasm are frequently described in blissful sounding words such as *ecstasy, thrilling,* and *mind-blowing.* Unfortunately, there's a world of difference between orgasm and bliss. An orgasm, like all pleasures, is counterfeit bliss.

Sex is a sensory pleasure. As we've discovered, *all* sensory pleasures fall victim to hedonic adaptation. The more we engage in sex, the more quickly we'll become numb or immune to it. This is one reason why sex addicts—who have more sex than most—report that they don't enjoy it very much. It becomes a compulsion, not a pleasure. What began as fun became dark and joyless.

As intensely pleasurable as a good sexual experience can be, it's always fleeting and incomplete. If an orgasm were complete by itself, there wouldn't be a need to experience it with a partner. We should all be perfectly content to engage *solely* in self-pleasure. Sure, lots of people *augment* their partnered sexual activity this way, but I've yet to meet anyone who wished that masturbation was his or her primary experience. This tells us that the act alone must not be as intrinsically enjoyable as we claim.

Like all desires, sex is susceptible to the spiritual equivalent of Newton's third law of motion: for every action, there is an equal and opposite reaction. As pleasurable as an orgasm can be, ultimately there is not only something missing and hollow about it, but it usually generates some sort of negativity that offsets any pleasure gained. At a physical level, sex is always depleting to some degree (for the man, at least). Or it results in unpleasant diseases or an unwanted pregnancy. Psychically, it can trigger feelings of humiliation and inadequacy, or lead to emotionally messy situations of one sort or another. Even if a particular interaction (or two) turns out "perfectly," without negative consequences, the more we engage in it, the more certain it is that unpleasantness will eventually emerge. We can't look at a single experience (or two) in isolation. Over time, if we employed sex as a primary happiness strategy, any initially positive experiences would fade, while adverse situations and emotions would gain ascendancy.

Fulfilling our desires *never* leads to their cessation. Instead they intensify. Thus, once we clamor for sex—and get it—we generate a stronger and stronger desire for more and more. We never achieve fulfillment or satiation. At that stage, like all addictions, the pleasure is diminished or completely lost. We are consumed by continuous, self-inflicted pain.

In contrast, bliss has no dark side or negative qualities; it is pure, unadulterated light. It never gets boring or turns against us. It is energizing and invigorating. It is the source of all energy, the creator of it, not something that consumes or depletes it. Bliss is not only internally generated but also complete and satisfying in and of itself. It is not addicting but liberating.

Of course, sex has positive qualities. For example, it can be a way of forging a deeper connection with a loved one. Not to mention that it's necessary for having children and continuing the species. In no way am I implying that celibacy is a prerequisite for bliss—so long as we understand that neither is sex its source.

Romance

People are often surprised—even upset—when I include romantic relationships on the list of failed places to search for bliss. I'm often asked, "Don't you believe in love?"

Of course I do. True love. Unconditional love. Divine love. As we will see later, developing the ability to love unconditionally is *essential* to lasting happiness. Romantic relationships often have little to do with genuine love. Yes, it's possible that they *might*. The problem is: they also might *not*. Romance and unconditional love are *not* synonymous. It is possible to feel passionate toward someone without feeling, expressing, or even understanding unconditional love. Inversely, it's possible to feel and express unconditional love without being involved in a romantic relationship.

What most of us mean by "romance" is a combination of passionate desire and fuzzy emotion that transports us to perfect bliss. Never mind that most of our objective evidence tells us that this approach is severely wanting. Despite the mania for romance and soul mates, not only are divorce and infidelity rampant—most divorcing and cheating couples at one time claimed undying, passionate love for each other—but there's a good deal of evidence supporting the futility of this approach.

For starters, as has been pointed out by numerous anthropologists and historians, romantic love is not found in all cultures and time periods. It appears to be a relatively recent concept and mostly confined to some of the Western cultures and those places that Western culture has permeated. This lack of universality alone should make us suspicious.

The larger difficulty with the "romantic model" is that it not only concedes that we are incomplete beings but *revels* in it. It doesn't matter whether we subscribe to the ideal of a soul mate—that one perfect person who makes life (and us) complete—or a more adaptable version that holds there are a limited number of "right," "compatible," or "perfect" people for us. Either way, the message is that we are lacking something that can be filled *only* by someone else. Not only is this fallacious, it actively *undermines* our pursuit of bliss by blinding us to the genuine path of inward discovery.

Seeking love externally reduces our "beloved" to just another object to be acquired—little different from a nice house or a fancy car—which will, in turn, deliver to us something that we cannot experience ourselves. The delusion rests on the notion that we *procure* love rather than *uncover* or *develop* our capacity for it. If you think about it, this is a materialistic and mercenary understanding of love, and not nearly as "romantic" as it seems.

Romantic love concentrates as much or more on what we're *receiving* instead of on what we're *giving*. Of course, all romantics have some sense of giving, perhaps even sacrificing, but always there is equal or greater emphasis on obtaining something in return. Romantics must stay hypervigilant about receiving their just due, since the very premise of the romantic model is that we're incomplete in and of ourselves. Reducing love to this kind of quid pro quo equation guarantees that a litany of negativity will eventually surface. If love is a transaction, then it must stay balanced and equal. If one partner (or both) starts to feel that he's not getting enough in return for the love he's giving, out pops the usual array of harmful emotions: jealousy, resentment, rage, disappointment, depression, or anxiety (or all of the above).

Real love is not something we acquire outside ourselves but a quality and capacity we harbor within. It's an *internal* process of expanding our ability to feel and express love regardless of outward circumstances.

Genuine love—unconditional love—requires no reciprocity. It is entirely selfless. I open my heart to another regardless of how she feels in return. This is a limitless form of love, not held hostage by environment or someone else's perception. It's an internal feeling that doesn't require the recipient to consent to it or return it. One can feel unconditional love toward someone indifferent to us, or even downright hostile. We can even cultivate and feel it in the face of pure evil. In a way, this is the great test of unconditional love: can we continue to feel it even when its object offers nothing in return, perhaps even wishes us ill?

Bliss is a state of mystical union with God, the Universe, the Divine, Pure Consciousness—however we want to phrase it. Romantic love undermines this kind of mystical union. Ironically, it creates separation. While we might feel like "my partner and me" are joined together, united in our "us-ness," this actually cuts us off from the rest of the universe. If my soul mate and I are one, then everyone and everything else instantly becomes "other." We've opened a chasm between the world and us. The separateness intrinsic to this mind-set precludes the ability to attain a true mystical union.

As with wealth and sex, I'm not against relationships (I'm in one myself), marriage, or love. But I am in favor of the *best* possible versions of them. There is a great deal that we can learn from relationships of all kinds, including those with intimate partners. At their best, committed relationships are outstanding vehicles through which we can learn selflessness, compassion, and genuine unconditional love.

This improved understanding of genuine love actually *improves* our intimate relationships by removing their mercenary qualities, as well as much of the unnecessary pressure and burden of expectations. We no longer expect or require the other person to complete or fix us; we accept that responsibility for ourselves. This allows our relationships to become vehicles for personal transformation.

The Experiment:
Expansion of Love Visualization

Note: You can do this exercise anytime you want to remember that love is a choice within you, not something to be found externally. Or as a reminder whenever you encounter someone with whom you're having difficulty. See if it helps you change how you view yourself and them, too.

1. Close your eyes and visualize love as a light that shines inside you, centered in your heart. Take a moment to see it clearly living there, pulsing, vibrating. Visualize its shape, size, and color.

2. Once you have a clear image in your mind, now visualize that light expanding from your heart to encompass your entire body. Imagine it filling the entire space you're in: your home, work environment, or outdoors. Imagine this light gradually expanding to include all your friends, family, and loved ones, as if they were standing in front of you. Continue visualizing that light expanding until it covers your city, state, country, and the entire globe, including all human strangers, those of every race and nation, and all creatures of this earth, great and small. Feel that light of love healing and bringing joy to all who are sheltered within its protective rays.

3. Now visualize someone inside your bubble of loving light who you may not like or who may not like you. Feel that person equally surrounded, healed, filled with happiness and joy—all emanating from that light that radiates from your own heart center. Feel that choice to love unconditionally come from deep inside of you. Feel it connecting and binding you to all of creation. Feel that love transforming the world, healing, and bringing peace and joy to all those within its protective sphere. See all of creation dancing, smiling, and laughing within the radiant waves of love emanating from within you.

Online

Additional videos and resources for this chapter are available at www.theblissexperiment.com.

CHAPTER 5

Fame, Beauty, and Power

Fame has also this great drawback, that if we pursue it, we must direct our lives so as to please the fancy of men.

—*Baruch Spinoza, Dutch philosopher (1632–77)*

It is amazing how complete is the delusion that beauty is goodness.

—*Leo Tolstoy, Russian author (1828–1910)*

Ultimately, the only power to which man should aspire is that which he exercises over himself.

—*Elie Wiesel, Romanian-born writer and Holocaust survivor (b. 1928)*

Fame, beauty, and power are the final three specific urges we'll examine. We're grouping them together because they are similar to one another but distinctly different from luxury, sex, or romance. They aren't susceptible to hedonic adaptation in the same way because they aren't experienced directly through our senses. They are more abstract, akin to observations of and *reactions* to the external world, residing less inside us than in others. We are watching and responding to how others respond to us and feel thrilled and stimulated by their response.

By *fame*, I mean not only the urge for celebrity or international renown. Even when outright fame is impossible or not sought, we often find ourselves jockeying for social distinction among whatever smaller circle we inhabit. This applies to power as well. It needn't mean "world domination." It might mean power within the family, at the workplace, in a religious organization, or over any comparatively small number of people. By *beauty*, I mean the desire for physical beauty among human beings, not beautiful paintings, sunsets, and objects.

Here we are concerned mostly with the conscious pursuit of fame, beauty, and power for their own sake. If they are merely the *unintended* or indirect by-products of our main interest, negative consequences may not accrue. However, in all three cases, we'll find that the conscious, direct pursuit of fame, beauty, and power might be the most disastrous kind of happiness mistake we can possibly make.

The Story

Chiara was a beauty queen. In her late teens and early twenties, she won several local and regional beauty pageants in her home state of Texas before moving to Los Angeles. She had classic American looks: blonde hair, blue eyes, and a curvaceous figure. She dropped out of college to come to LA to parlay her beauty into a modeling or acting career. Though Chiara did get some low-level modeling gigs, she never quite made the big time. By thirty, it was clear that her career wasn't happening.

She decided that before she got too old or her looks faded, she needed to attract a wealthy husband. Chiara had no difficulty doing so and soon married a multimillionaire. They had three children. Unfortunately, he developed a drug addiction that made his behavior increasingly erratic. After an incident of domestic violence during a drug-fueled rage, she filed for divorce.

In her early forties, Chiara found herself a single mother. She discovered it was difficult to attract men her age. She didn't have a career; although she'd done some volunteer work for nonprofit organizations, she had focused primarily on raising her children and shopping, dining with girlfriends, going to spas, country clubbing, and traveling.

Her primary postdivorce plan was to stay in great physical shape and use her social connections to find a new husband. Chiara ratcheted up her diet to new extremes—she had been on a constant diet for close to thirty years—in her quest for physical perfection. She felt that her looks and body were her only assets. It was her job (really, her life's work) to maintain them as much as possible. After a series of disappointing dates and brief relationships, she was introduced to a *very* wealthy widower who was unabashedly interested. The problem: he was in his early seventies. Chiara felt it was her best opportunity. With few marketable skills (and little desire to work) plus two children, she accepted his proposal.

Chiara and Harley had the marriage we might have predicted. Her financial needs were taken care of, but it was a distant, unloving relationship. Not only was she young enough to be his daughter—he actually had four children of his own, one of whom *was* older than Chiara—they had little in common. She acted more as his de facto nurse and social companion than mutual partner. They had sex only when he felt like it; it never occurred to her to initiate, partly because she had no interest and partly because the dynamic was that she served him, seldom the other way around. They spent little time together except at social events or when traveling. Chiara spent her days working out and shopping. Her husband was constantly critical, sometimes vicious. Though he never denied her materially, he constantly reminded her that she and her children were dependent on him for everything. She felt demeaned, although she also knew it was true.

She began an affair with her married personal trainer—a slightly younger man with whom she spent more time than she did with her husband. When that affair disintegrated, Chiara fell into a deep depression. She stopped working out or tending to her looks, seldom leaving bed. Her fights with Harley escalated.

Through the intervention of her oldest son, she saw a psychiatrist and started taking antidepressants and other medications. That gave her just enough of an energy boost that she began exploring her spiritual self, which is how we met. She took one of my classes.

These days Chiara feels better about herself. Her marriage is still distant, often hostile, but she has started doing yoga, meditating daily, reading inspirational books, and pursuing her own spiritual growth as much as possible. The last time I saw her, she said to me, "I felt worthless. All I had to offer was my face. But now I'm older, and men don't notice me. I spent thirty years of life obsessed over something that made me miserable every day."

The Science

The impact of fame and power on those who already possess it is difficult to study because there is a small pool of subjects from which to draw, most of whom are unlikely to agree to participate in a psychological study, especially one that may embarrass them. Fame, especially, must be studied less directly, primarily by measuring the impact of its pursuit upon those that haven't yet achieved it but identify it as a primary goal.

A recent study did just that: researchers asked students their life goals and then tracked their self-reported levels of happiness postgraduation as they set out to fulfill those goals. The study explicitly measured extrinsic versus intrinsic types of goals; extrinsic meaning "external things outside of ourselves" and intrinsic meaning "interior, inward directed." They discovered that:

- Students who chose good looks, material wealth, or fame as key pursuits—extrinsic goals—reported significantly *less* overall happiness than those who had inward and loftier ambitions.
- Not only were those who pursued beauty or celebrity comparatively less happy, the extrinsic goals were identified as the *source* of their ill-being.
- It took only *one year* of pursuing beauty and fame for their happiness to deteriorate substantially.
- A separate study of four hundred schoolchildren between the ages of nine and twelve found that those who believed that fame and beauty were key to self-fulfillment were much more likely to develop depression than those who didn't.

Sociologist Orville Brim, PhD, director of the MacArthur Foundation, conducted a series of studies in which he concluded that the lifelong pursuit of fame was one of the most deleterious goals we can have. Not only do most never achieve it but also even those who do seldom feel rewarded or satisfied. It becomes an insatiable, bottomless pit of dissatisfaction. It tends to destroy relationships, generate negative self-image, and often produces other harmful negative emotions such as blaming, anger, and resentment.

Beauty is easier to study. Psychologist Nancy Etcoff is a faculty member at Harvard Medical School. In her research, Etcoff identified a number of benefits that beautiful people receive, especially preferential treatment. Despite every advantage, *beautiful people reported that it had absolutely no impact on their happiness*—it might even have decreased it.

This is supported by a fascinating study on runway fashion models, considered the pinnacle of the modeling profession. These jobs are reserved for the most beautiful and magnetic women in the world. Researchers compared the well-being of these elite beauties against a group of average-looking nonmodels. They discovered that the models reported far less happiness and life satisfaction than the average-looking people and, furthermore, exhibited a significantly higher incidence of negative personality disorders.

As noted, the effect of power on well-being is a difficult area to study, as powerful people are unlikely to participate. This is especially true of the most powerful world and political leaders. We can, however, look at business leaders and those who hold power in less public and all-encompassing ways.

Researchers have consistently found that too much power in the setting of corporations engenders severe negative consequences for the power holders. A 2008 study at Ohio State University found that powerful people tend to ignore other people's opinions, even when others are right and listening would have benefited them. Holding power makes people cocky, egotistical, and falsely self-assured. They begin to believe that by virtue of their position alone they must be smarter and better than everyone around them. This often leads to serious mistakes and negative performance outcomes. At a personal level, powerful people begin to isolate themselves, have fewer friends, and often disrespect—even disdain—their fellow human beings. Over time, this has disastrous effects on their well-being.

Worse, Dache Keltner, a professor at the University of California at Berkeley and director of the Berkeley Social Interaction Laboratory has found that power, once acquired, *tends to make even good people act like sociopaths*. The effects of power can be so severe that Keltner likens their behavior to those who have suffered brain damage to their frontal lobes! Some of the terrible consequences of power include:

- behaving overly impulsively and insensitively toward others;
- being more likely to interrupt, speak out of turn, and fail to look at those speaking;
- a tendency to tease people in a hostile, humiliating fashion;
- a wide range of rude, even antisocial behaviors: shouting, profanities, blunt critiques, throwing things, and so on; and
- an inability to feel empathy and compassion for others.

Similar studies led by Adam Galinsky at the Northwestern University Kellogg School of Management have found that holding power makes people self-centered, myopic, and careless toward the feelings and experiences of others. In turn, this makes subordinates dislike the power holder, further contributing to declines in happiness among the powerful.

The Spirit

Pop quiz: Who are Edwin Booth, Edmund Kean, and William Charles Macready? Answer: the most famous actors of the nineteenth century. Haven't heard of any of them? They were the Brad Pitt, Tom Hanks, and Tom Cruise of their day—perhaps more so. Now try these names: Paul Muni, Charles Laughton, and Luise Rainer. Haven't heard of them either? That might be particularly troubling to the fame seeker because each of them won at least one Academy Award *in the twentieth century*. Rainer not only won Best Actress *twice* in a row but also, as of 2011, was *still alive!*

I recently read an article about Zsa Zsa Gabor, who'd just been admitted to the hospital. Crowned Miss Hungary in 1936, she moved to America, became an actress and socialite, and was known for her glamor and beauty. What struck me were the two photos appended to the article. The first, taken in 1954, showed a radiantly beautiful woman, similar to actress Grace Kelly, the future princess of Monaco. The next, taken in 2011 at the age of ninety-four, showed a plain, frail woman who looked like anyone's great-grandmother. There's nothing *wrong* with this; it's how it *should* be. But it's a stark reminder of how beauty fades for everyone, even the most beautiful women.

Here's another pop quiz: Who are Gratian, Joannes, Justin, Galba,

Otho, Geta, and Balbinus? Answer: each was a Roman emperor. Now, being a Roman emperor was the pinnacle of authority; not only did he have more power than virtually any being in history, he was considered divinely ordained, even divine himself—a god on earth. And yet those powerful men are now forgotten. At least fifty of the eighty-five or so Roman emperors were assassinated, forced to commit suicide, or killed during battlefield coups against them. If you had the "good fortune" to become emperor of Rome, there was a nearly 60 percent chance that you'd be murdered for your throne. This figure doesn't include those who went mad or were deposed but allowed to live out their remaining years in exile. Few held power until their natural deaths.

There are many reasons that we gravitate toward fame, beauty, and power. In addition to the increased opportunities for wealth, sex, and romance, we believe that they will provide us with some combination of:

- social acceptance, friends, and access;
- love;
- self-esteem;
- respect and recognition;
- influence over others or even human history; and
- existential comfort (the ability to cheat death, generating a kind of immortality in the sense that we won't be forgotten even after we've died).

Why They Fail

The problem here is that fame, beauty, and power don't genuinely provide a single one of these things. Not one.

To begin with, as the examples of Zsa Zsa Gabor, Gratian, Joannes, and the rest suggest, we all know that fame, power, and beauty are fleeting. They don't last. Beauty is *guaranteed* to fade; power and fame are highly likely to. It's exceedingly rare—in the neighborhood of one hundred million to one—for someone to sustain the same level of fame and power over a lifetime (unless the person dies young or achieves it late in life). By nature, then, these things can't possibly provide a lasting solution. At best, they're temporary bandages that mask and distract us from our deeper problems. Worse, the longer we delay serious attempts to know ourselves, the deeper the hole we descend into and the less time we'll have later to enact the necessary repairs.

Even if we somehow beat the odds and held fame, power, or beauty for a lifetime, we still wouldn't be happy. By placing our faith in other people to grant us our happiness (by being recognized as famous, beautiful, or powerful), we thereby undermine any real authority such people could ever have for us. The problem is this: we know that we're empty inside. We wouldn't feel so driven for the recognition of others if we weren't. When others turn around and grant us adulation or approval, we immediately understand that it must be for superficial reasons. They don't and can't really know who we *are*. They haven't even properly detected and responded to the emptiness inside us. Yet they're heaping attention on us anyway. Which means that whatever they're giving us must be equally shallow and unreal. Thus, their endorsement rings hollow and unsatisfying. We don't really respect them. How can the endorsement of someone who doesn't truly know me—my mind, my heart, and my spirit—possibly have any lasting meaning or import? The entire exchange of attention is a giant Ponzi scheme in which any self-reflective player knows that everyone, himself included, is an empty sucker, but where everyone is depending on the appeal of the fraud to generate an endless supply of new fools.

The upshot of this basic reality is that is that most of what we hope to gain—social acceptance, friends, love, self-esteem, and respect—is immediately disqualified. We can't accept these shallow people as our friends or value their love. We know that they are behaving foolishly, so it doesn't enhance our self-esteem. (Later we'll examine if self-esteem is a positive goal anyway.) Self-respect can't be generated by people we disrespect. The ability for fame, beauty, or power to boost our self-esteem and self-respect is especially laughable. By definition, self-esteem and self-respect are just that: "self," not "other." What we receive is "other-esteem/respect" not "self-esteem/respect." There is no connection between the two.

Worst of all, fame, beauty, and power don't merely fail to grant happiness, they actively *destroy it*.

Relying on others for validation and approval heightens our insecurity. We've made ourselves dependent on something external, over which we have at best partial—and often no—control. This not only makes us inse-cure, it often generates fear, helplessness, and anxiety.

Relying on masses of people for happiness also makes us more self-conscious and self-absorbed. Being the center of attention and discussion creates a hyperawareness of—and often an extreme vigilance over—our image and actions. Dwelling on the self constantly is the surest possible way to make ourselves neurotic and self-obsessed, often triggering bouts of crippling rumination and self-judgment as we continually measure our-selves against ideals and rules set by those whose attention we are so des-perate to attract. We start living wholly outside of ourselves, neglecting our innermost self, because our first responsibility is to influence the bestowers of our fame, beauty, or power. One misstep, and it can all go away.

This generates a terrible psychic burden, often leading to resentment toward the world and heightening, not lessening, our sense of isolation. We don't merely devalue those who "love," "respect," or even fear us, we develop active hostility and antipathy toward them. We know that they are false, phony, weak, and superficial. Negative emotions roil inside us, leading to either bitterness or depression.

Fame, beauty, and power are by nature zero-sum games. This means that in order for us to have them, someone else can't have them. Each only makes sense if it is relatively rare and limited. If everyone is famous, beauti-ful, and powerful, that's the same as saying that no one is famous, beautiful, or powerful. Since there are always more people wanting these things than there are "open slots," this makes them intrinsically competitive. The vast majority of people who play this game are guaranteed to lose. It's a low-percentage strategy.

Further, as with any competition, even a successful pursuit creates stress, uncertainty, hypervigilance (always looking for threats), fear (of los-ing, of someone harming us to get what we have or prevent us from getting it in the first place), and above all, a huge number of "losers." Competition requires that most people don't win—at least not for long—and that they become acutely aware of their failure, complete with all of the attendant negative emotions that failure entails. Most likely, too, competition also breeds cheating and ruthless behavior. We end up spending a great deal of time with and inside the sphere of influence of some very negative and nasty people. We also become suspicious, even paranoid, sometimes right-fully so. Much of the world is clamoring for our position at the top.

As if all of this weren't bad enough, competition "winners" are also *guaranteed* a certain amount of criticism and resentment, not only from opponents and "losers" but also from the general public, the media, and/ or critics—none of which will reinforce feelings of self-esteem, respect, friendship, love, or admiration.

In the cases of fame and power, there is also the loss of privacy, espe-cially if it escalates to the highest levels, which can make us feel captive prisoners. To be known and dependent on the public encourages a feeling of always "being on," never being able to relax or let down our guard. It also forces us to have interactions that we don't want or enjoy, as people jockey for our attention.

Lastly, as implied in our opening examples and throughout this section, none of these truly generates immortality. Not only do we still die but also, in almost every case, history *does* forget us—very quickly. In rare cases in which our name or contribution endures for generations, it's more likely due to infamy (Caesar, Napoléon, Hitler) than goodness. At best, only a small fraction of the population remembers us, usually only the specialists in whatever field we gained our notoriety. Really, though, even if we are remembered by millions (for good reasons), what does it matter to us? It doesn't change who we are at a deep level. Nor did it keep us from dying. Moreover, the real truth is that no one really cares—people are too busy with their own lives to care about your name "going down in history."

The Special Case of Power

As deleterious as chasing fame and beauty are, power is worse. It has an especially negative effect on the holder. Fame and beauty allow us to *in-fluence* others; power allows us to *command* them. The greater our ability to order, force, or coerce another person into doing our will, the more we imperil our soul. It's no wonder that scientific research reveals that power mimics brain damage and almost inexorably leads to sociopathic behavior.

Sometimes holding power is our legitimate responsibility. Certainly the world needs leadership at all levels of society. The mistake is to believe that the exercise of power is anything but a burden, responsibility, and challenge. As the nineteenth-century British historian Lord Acton wrote, "Absolute power corrupts absolutely." Once we begin to believe that holding and exercising power will make us happy or really has *anything* intrinsically positive about it, we're in deep trouble.

One of the fantasies often animating our desire for power is the dream of changing and molding the external world in ways more to our liking. Whether on a global, corporate, or familial level, we believe that power will help us remake our world—however big or small—for the better. Any attempt for one person to lastingly influence the external world is bound to fail. The outside world is simply too resistant. No emperor, dictator, president, or CEO can change enough things grandly and permanently enough to generate any kind of inner satisfaction.

Despite our grandiose fantasies, at some point every form of power will hit its natural limit—usually in the form of other people and their competing agendas, including their own strong desire to curtail, undo, or take away our power. Which isn't to say that people don't try to convince themselves and others differently. Of course they do. But the more grandiose our claims, the further detached from reality we become, leading to self-centeredness, dishonesty, inauthenticity, and disconnectedness. With that come emotional pain, deep fear, and crippling insecurity.

The Experiment: Asking Why

1. If you are or have been interested in fame, beauty, or power, make a list of what you hoped to gain through it. Be honest with yourself.
2. Rank each of these reasons in order of importance.
3. Review your ranking and ask yourself, "Is fame, beauty, or power *the best, most effective, and most realistic way* of achieving each of these goals? Are there better ways of fulfilling them?"
4. If there remains something on your list that you've concluded is *best* accomplished through beauty, fame, or power, feel free to continue to pursue it for that reason(s) and that reason(s) only.

5. For the remainder, create a list of priorities and action items. Set the intention and vow that you will find the best, most enduring solution. The *Bliss Experiment* will assist you in doing this.

Online

Additional videos and resources for this chapter are available at www.theblissexperiment.com.

CHAPTER 6

The Amazing Power of Habit

Men's natures are alike; it is their habits that separate them.
—*Confucius, Chinese philosopher (551–479* BC*)*

We've explored where *not* to look for happiness, meaning, and truth. Shortly we'll turn our attention to examining more fruitful places to search. But first we must examine a key tool in our search for bliss, one that when used improperly, leads us subconsciously in negative directions. When harnessed properly, however, it becomes a key ally in our success.

Digging for bliss—stripping away all the layers of useless dirt and rock that cover it—requires understanding how habits are formed and changed. That might seem strange. What does such a mundane thing have to do with happiness or bliss?

Simply put, habits are the supervisors of the actions we take and the actions we avoid. They help govern what we do and how effectively we do it. Bad habits can guide us off course and keep us from unearthing our deepest layers.

Habits are thoughts, emotions, or actions that we've repeated frequently enough that they've become reflexive behaviors, performed without conscious thought. They can be good, bad, or neutral. They are the efficient bureaucrats of our body, mind, and spirit: they don't *enact* the internal laws that govern us, they *administer* our choices as effectively as possible. Habits eliminate the need to consciously think about and direct energy toward critical tasks. Good habits make our lives easier. Bad habits hold our minds and behaviors in a vice grip of negativity, acting as obstacles to our happiness.

For our Bliss Experiment to be effective, we must take some time to understand how habits work and how we can change unhelpful ones. Otherwise we'll struggle to implement the key ideas and practices necessary for bliss.

The Story

Alban, in his early thirties, is from a Mexican immigrant Catholic family now living in Southern California. His father is a truck driver; his mother, a housekeeper. He has three sisters. Alban's mother raised them with a combination of Catholicism and superstitious folk wisdom. For example, from childhood, they were taught to cross their fingers when they sneezed, so that they didn't accidentally exhale their souls.

Alban was a compulsive worrier. He thought it was due to his family's potent blend of Catholic guilt and folkloric beliefs—or perhaps he was just born that way. He was constantly worried about something. If he didn't hear from his parents or sisters for two days, he became concerned they were sick or dead. He worked for a small advertising and marketing company as a graphic designer. He was constantly in fear of losing his job despite the fact that his role was critical and his performance reviews top-notch. Even as he worried needlessly about being fired, Alban also fretted that he wasn't earning enough money. He had a nice girlfriend and a good relationship, but he didn't think that they could afford to get married and start a family—despite the fact that between them, they were at least middle class, with prospects of higher earning in their future.

Alban hated to fly; he was sure that the plane would crash or be hijacked by terrorists. He was afraid that our government would mistake his Latino complexion for that of an Arab and send him to Guantánamo Bay, where no one would ever hear from him again. He feared the government might revoke his citizenship, even though he was born here and is as much a US citizen as anyone. (Alban's parents aren't US citizens, but they do have green cards.) He was also afraid that Southern California was going to be devastated by an earthquake and that everyone he knew would die.

He worried about less far-fetched things as well. During a massage, Alban's practitioner noticed a lump on his back. His doctor told him it was a harmless mass of fatty tissue called a lipoma; it didn't even need removal. But Alban couldn't help but constantly run his fingers over it. He was sure that the doctor was wrong, and it was cancerous. Despite the fact that he never felt sick, he obsessed so much about it that he finally had a surgeon remove it—only to discover definitively that the lump was indeed harmless. He hated driving on the highway because he worried constantly that big trucks might hit him. He was an even worse passenger: always flinching when his girlfriend made a left turn into oncoming traffic or drove through a yellow light.

In short, Alban worried constantly about *everything*. As soon as one worry evaporated, new ones popped up in its place. He was driving himself crazy but couldn't stop. His mind continually generated new fears no matter how often they were disproven. He tried rationalizing to himself, deep breathing, and even psychotherapy. None worked. Though spiritual practices like meditation greatly help with worries, Alban's were so severe that he couldn't even bring himself to try. At first his habitual worrying was stronger than the meditation technique he learned.

Together we realized that we needed to work first on changing his mental habits in a direct way. As I explained to him, he had built up such powerful habits of worry that until he learned to change them consciously, he would have great difficulty feeling peace and joy. We designed a dedicated process and program to help him control his worries by tackling them as habits of the mind. A month later, he reported a noticeable decline, leaving him feeling happier and more peaceful. Alban was also able to do some of the other practices with more success. He wasn't "cured," but he felt more in control than ever and that it was finally going in the right direction.

The Science

Habits are learned behaviors. They aren't inherited genetically. By watching people inside MRI scanners, scientists can actually see new habits being formed in the brain. They've observed that while we are first learning a new behavior, the prefrontal cortex area of the brain lights up. This is the most advanced part of our brain, where processes such as reasoning, decision making, setting goals, and other cognitive functions are carried out. As we become familiar with the task through repetition, activity in the prefrontal cortex declines, but it increases in another part of the brain, the basal ganglia. This is where our motor skills and other processes that don't require conscious thought reside.

Studies vary in their findings, but virtually all agree that bad habits can be reversed relatively quickly. The most optimistic report I've seen pegged it at twenty-one days. The worst-case scenario is eight months, but only for the most difficult habits in the worst situations. A study of astronauts by NASA found that it took about thirty days. Other quality studies have put the number at about sixty-six days.

Since habits are repeated behaviors, a better way to measure the formation of new habits might be via the number of repetitions. A study in the journal *Neuroscience* suggested that new habits develop in as few as fifty repetitions. This may explain the time disparity in the above studies. The faster we get to fifty repetitions, the faster the new habit is created.

The above research implies that habits should be relatively easy to create or change. Yet why does it *feel* so difficult? Why are we so prone to relapsing?

The main reason that relapses occur is that a new habit is not given an opportunity to "set" properly, either by giving it enough time or repetitions.

A secondary difficulty concerns how our brains respond to pleasure. Dopamine is a neurotransmitter that helps control our brain's reward and pleasure centers. It enables us to identify rewards and take action to attain them. Intensely pleasurable experiences—alcohol, drugs, sex, certain foods, even shopping—trigger its release, subsequently creating a reward circuit in the brain. This circuit registers intense experiences as "important" and creates lasting memories of it as pleasurable. That, in turn, subtly prompts us to do it again. The more we do, the stronger the urge becomes.

Higher-order attainments aren't included in the dopamine reward circuit. Dopamine is primarily the domain of sensory pleasures and short-term gains. For example, positive outcomes that require longer-term commitments to emerge, like eating broccoli, don't trigger the same kind of dopamine response.

A third reason is what's called restraint bias. A 2010 study published in

Scientific American revealed that we often have an inflated sense of impulse control. When we prematurely declare ourselves "cured" of a bad habit, we don't properly guard against putting ourselves in a situation where that bad habit can reassert itself.

Another study demonstrated that the brain "remembers" conquered bad habits, at least for a while. In certain situations, the original "brain groove" that bad habit created hasn't yet been fully erased. It's there, lying dormant. If we expose ourselves to situations that trigger that habit too soon after conquering it, it can reactivate.

Setting a strong intention at the outset of forming a new habit improves our success. A 2002 study of people beginning a physical fitness routine for weight loss found that those who made a formal vow to complete the program stuck with it longer and to greater effect than those who didn't:

• Those who made their vow public—by speaking it out loud to a group of peers, announcing it on Facebook, or declaring it to God—had the highest success rate.

• Members of a second group made a quiet vow to themselves without telling anyone or offering it to a "higher power." They had more success than the third group, which did nothing, but less than the strongest vow group.

• Those who made no vow, whether publicly or privately, were least likely to finish the exercise program.

• Similarly, a separate study of tobacco users in a smoking cessation program found that those who made an intensive commitment to quit had higher success rates than those who didn't.

The Spirit

My spiritual teacher, Paramhansa Yogananda wrote, "The health, success, and wisdom outlook of your life entirely depends upon the issue of the battle between your good and your bad habits." He explained that this is because "we usually do not do what we wish to do, but only what we are accustomed to do." Without understanding how habits work and how we can change them, it's very difficult to make quick progress on our journey to bliss.

Many of our shortcomings and failures are due primarily to bad habits rather than to ill intent. Recall the story of Max, the rock star. He had long ago lost interest in sleeping with so many women; the sex wasn't even pleasurable anymore. That was just his routine after each concert; he was on autopilot. Addiction is a deeply ingrained habit. At a certain point, although bad habits cease bringing us pleasure and even make us feel worse, we still feel powerless to stop.

Many of our harmful emotions are the product of bad mental habits, not carefully considered or appropriate responses to difficult situations. Alban couldn't stop worrying about even the most ridiculous things.

Habits are not who we truly are at a deep level. They are neither genetically determined nor reflective of our Highest Self. Too often we meekly cave in to our bad habits by telling ourselves, "That's just who I am," "I have no choice," or "It's genetic." Even if we notice family members engaging in similar behaviors, that means only that we *learned* it from them. They are not inevitable or unbreakable.

Spiritual practices, especially done over sustained periods of time, create an inward environment in which bad habits can't take root. Calming activities such as meditation, yoga, and exercise quiet our mind. These practices alter the brain's biochemistry, in essence making dopamine rewards feel less pleasurable and thereby lessening their destructiveness.

From a more spiritual perspective, these practices give us mastery over all aspects of our being. A spiritually enlightened being has no negative habits of any kind. Even his or her positive habits result from conscious decisions. Spiritual masters have so much control over their minds that they can prevent negative habits from ever taking root. If one somehow did sneak into her brain, as soon as she became aware of it, she'd be able to eliminate it immediately.

Qualities Necessary for Changing Our Habits

Gaining control over our habits requires developing four spiritual qualities: awareness, concentration, willpower, and energy.

We can't root out negative habits or choose positive ones unless we have awareness. We must learn to identify our bad habits and imagine their positive replacements. Introspection is essential. We must be willing to look at ourselves as clearly and objectively as possible. Journaling, praying, and meditating are all ways of doing this. We can also ask people we trust for their observations. No matter how we gain awareness, the important thing is that we make the conscious decision to face ourselves.

That's only part of what awareness means. The second aspect is that once we identify a habit we'd like to change, we have to reflect on it and understand it. Why did it start? What was our original intention or goal? Usually habits begin because we thought that activity would help us attain a particular desire. Understanding what we hoped to gain from that bad habit helps us generate positive substitutes. For example, if we began smoking because we found the nicotine calming, we can use that insight to generate the idea for a positive replacement. We'd look for a more constructive alternative that would do a better job of creating that calm feeling, such as meditation or progressive muscle relaxation.

The second quality is concentration. Recall how the brain operates when forming habits. Initially our prefrontal cortex—the center for reasoning, making choices, setting goals, and other cognitive processes—is very active. It takes mental effort to create new habits. When we want to learn something new, we must study and apply ourselves. Often we remove all distractions, go over it again and again, and spend time consciously thinking about it. We put our sole focus on it as much as possible. We can't just wave a magic wand or wish it into existence, and then ignore it, forget about it, or treat it as secondary. We must prioritize it.

Next we must learn to harness and build our energy. It takes great energy to change a habit. Habits are like ruts or grooves cut into our minds through repetition. Once a groove is created, we flow along with it; we even feel stuck inside it. In order break out of a groove or change a direction, we have to exert enough extra force to push it from that groove.

Additional Tips

There are some supplementary tips to bolster our odds of success. Not all of these are appropriate for every habit or situation. We must use our own judgment as to which of these tips work best in a given circumstance:

1. Start small. If we don't have a lot of practice at consciously working with habits, it *may* help to start with achievable, realistic goals and build from there. We can also take a large goal but break it into smaller increments or phases.

2. Replace bad habits with good ones. As Spinoza said, "Nature abhors a vacuum." If we only remove something negative without simultaneously adding something positive, it's much harder.

3. Beware of triggers. We usually overestimate our self-control. In doing so, we recklessly put ourselves into situations that are likely to trigger a relapse. Paramhansa Yogananda put it this way: "Environment is stronger than will power."

4. Link two activities. Linking is when a first activity acts as a cue for the second. This works best when the first activity is already familiar and regular. For example, when I first started meditating, I began my morning meditation practice immediately after brushing my teeth. After a while, the very act of brushing my teeth primed me to meditate.

5. Interrupt bad habits. A recent study found that people who habitually eat popcorn at movie theaters are so accustomed to it that even when researchers intentionally gave them stale popcorn, they didn't even notice and ate just as much as they normally did! However, if the subjects were instructed to eat the stale popcorn with the opposite hand than they usually employed, they ate much less. Changing hands made them more aware of its low quality. Small disruptions to our routines can jolt us out of unconscious habits.

6. Find a partner or small group. Practicing a good behavior with someone else helps keep us motivated and accountable—a positive form of peer pressure. Two people can even agree to work on different things together. For example, a couple might make a pact: one partner might work on not panicking in stressful situations; the other, on not reacting angrily.

7. Create a substitute reward system. As we learned, certain types of intense pleasures trigger a dopamine response that's often powerful enough to overrule our rational faculties. We can create an alternative reward system. For example, if we stop smoking for "*x* length of time," we allow ourselves to do something else that we've been wanting. Diets

often use "cheat days." If we follow it perfectly for six days, we reward ourselves with a day on which we can eat anything. This can dramatically increase our success. Pleasures usually generate an *immediate* dopamine rush. A substitute reward system can't have too much delay. If we can't collect a reward for a year, during those moments of temptation, it will feel too far away. We'll be more likely to cave in to the near-term reward.

Never Quit

Most important, don't quit, even if we slip. Yogananda said, "A saint is a sinner who never gave up." The process of creating habits requires repetition. Sometimes we must repeat the very attempt itself again and again. Each time we try, we build strength. Our early efforts, even the failures, are never lost. They slowly build our awareness, concentration, willpower, and energy. Eventually we'll succeed.

The Experiment: Rooting Out Bad Habits

1. Think about, identify, and write down all habits you can think of that are *preventing* you from achieving happiness or bliss.
2. Identify those habits that are *helping* you.
3. Choose *one* habit that you are ready and able to change right now.
4. Reflect on the positive reason(s) you initially began the habit or anything good you originally hoped to gain through it.
5. Think about new, positive ways to achieve this goal. Think of every positive activity that can replace the negative habit.
6. Identify specific thoughts, feelings, circumstances, or events that trigger your negative habit. List as many cues as you can, including environments, people, or emotions. Perhaps it's something you avoid. Or a time of day, or a visual, auditory, or olfactory cue. Which of these can you change or avoid?
7. Make a list or plan including everything that you feel is necessary for implementing the positive habit.

8. Make a formal pact with yourself that you will do this. Choose a specific moment you will start. It can be today, tomorrow, or an exact date by which you will have everything in place to begin. Swear a vow to yourself, to God, your Higher Self, or whatever feels comfortable for you that you *will* do this.

Tip: Later we'll explore the use of affirmations. You may also wish to find or create an affirmation for this new habit and practice it regularly.

Online

Additional videos and resources for this chapter are available at www.theblissexperiment.com.

PART 2

Looking in the Right Place

We now have a clearer understanding that looking for happiness in our external world is a mistake. As we begin the process of turning within, we're confronted immediately with some challenging questions. What does it mean to look inward? Who am I inside? Are there better and worse ways of doing this?

Merely to turn "inward" isn't quite precise enough. We all have a lot going on in our mind and our innermost selves. Not all of it is likely to be useful.

In a certain sense, each of us has several "selves." There is our Higher Self, which can be thought of us our soul, highest potential, or deepest essence. We have our lowest self: that egoic, sometimes uncivilized part of ourselves that pulsates with our selfish needs and desires, forever wanting immediate pleasure or gratification, no matter the consequences. We have our past self: who we were, what we experienced, and what we recall from our personal history. We have our future self: who we want to become, our hopes, dreams, and goals. And we have our present self, the being that is with us right here and now in this present moment. Which of these is truly *us*? Where is bliss to be found among all these selves?

Among all of our selves, there is only one true self. This self is where we look for bliss. But in order to find our True Self, first we must release any false selves that may be harming or distracting us from our quest.

Bliss happens only in the eternal present: the Now. This is the one and only domicile of our True Self. Living in the past or future blocks our inward journey to bliss. It's impossible to feel traumatized, victimized, wounded, preoccupied, distracted, or goal obsessed and be in bliss. These are mutually exclusive states of consciousness.

Dwelling in the past or the future entails living outside of reality. Only this moment is real. While we remember aspects of our past or have a vague sense of what might happen in the future, ultimately both are illusions. Everything we experience happens *only* in the present. Every memory or daydream—and all the sensations and emotions they conjure—actually occurs right now, in this moment—neither "back then" nor "by and by."

When we truly discover this and feel it in all of its pure intensity, we have finally found the right place to begin looking for the hidden bliss within.

CHAPTER 7

Releasing the Past

> If you believe that feeling bad or worrying long enough will change a past or future event, then you are residing on another planet with a different reality system.
>
> —*William James, American psychologist and philosopher (1842–1910)*

We now understand that looking outside ourselves for happiness, meaning, and truth is a mistake. As we begin looking inward, we must first examine a particular kind of inner experience that is equally unfruitful: our past.

We unwittingly withhold happiness from ourselves by allowing past events and feelings to intrude upon our present. Traumatic memories or negative emotions prevent us from feeling genuine happiness *now*. We needn't have experienced a large-scale trauma. The day-to-day minitraumas that we inflict upon one another through family, friends, relationships, peers, business associates, and the like generate plenty of grist for the mill.

On the flip side, sometimes when we dwell on the past, we see ourselves as the perpetrator, not the victim. Consequently, we feel the need to punish ourselves as atonement for past sins, as if we don't *deserve* happiness. Shame, guilt, anger, fear, and a host of negative emotions prevent us from discovering the bliss within. Our past becomes our own worst enemy.

The Story

In this chapter and the next, we'll hear the story of Shanice and DeShawn, an extraordinary couple. They are bright, energetic, socially engaged, artistic, and in love. Together they seem destined for greatness. Shanice is a talented painter, though for now she earns most of her income working as a freelance art director and graphic designer. DeShawn is an attorney, working for a nonprofit organization that focuses on social justice. He offers legal advice to lower income people, predominantly African-American, facing legal challenges from California state government agencies, the federal government, or corporations. Much of his time in recent years has been spent helping low-income families avoid foreclosure.

One of the many things they share is how they were raised. Both grew up in South Central Los Angeles, where crime rates are high and graduation rates low, but both had highly motivated parents who helped them avoid the worst of it. Sadly, in these neighborhoods, that required avoiding the public schools. Shanice was sent to a private Catholic girls' school (though her family isn't Catholic) on a scholarship, and DeShawn was admitted into the Los Angeles Unified School District's gifted and talented program.

There was only so much their families could do to insulate them from their neighborhoods. The two of them knew many kids who joined gangs, wrestled with drug addictions, dropped out of school, suffered teen pregnancies, and even went to prison. Some were from their own extended families.

In the next chapter, we'll hear more about Shanice. Now we'll delve more deeply into DeShawn's story. He was filled with anger over many of the things he saw during his own childhood. So much so that it began greatly affecting his work, at one point bringing him to the brink of being fired and losing his reputation and career.

He felt that the school system and government were corrupt and mostly didn't care. Nor did the police or social service agencies. His anger wasn't confined to the government. DeShawn's most blistering attacks were aimed at the parents who allowed their kids to deal drugs, become gangbangers, work as prostitutes, or in one way or another sabotage their own communities.

DeShawn struggled to come to terms with his childhood experiences, despite long since having escaped. One of his close friends in middle school later joined a gang and became a street-level drug dealer. DeShawn knew that his friend was a good kid with a good heart. But he didn't get the educational opportunities that DeShawn did. He attended the regular public school and became yet another casualty of a broken-down, dysfunctional system notorious for failing to educate its students. DeShawn admitted to feeling both anger and guilt. He escaped, while his friend didn't. It seemed arbitrary. In his mind, their divergent fates boiled down to two key moments.

First was the test they took in eighth grade. That one event forever altered their destinies. DeShawn was placed in the gifted and talented program at a functioning school. Although his friend had skills, capabilities, and dreams, he was written off forever. The second was when they were both shoplifting at a local pharmacy. It was DeShawn's idea, yet only his friend got caught. His friend never turned him in. DeShawn's record stayed clean, and he continued in the gifted and talented program. His friend, however, got his first juvenile arrest. DeShawn felt guilty that he didn't step in and either share or take all of the blame.

He was also overwhelmed by an abundance of stories of a never-ending parade of good people hitting dead ends or shattering their lives with just a few impulsive decisions. He felt that he couldn't let go of his anger until no one else had to go through these things. His anger and guilt fueled his crusade for change.

While that is admirable in some ways, the difficulty was that DeShawn couldn't be objective or think clearly. Sometimes he saw injustice when there wasn't any: in his first job as an attorney, he exploded in anger and physically threatened the assistant district attorney, accusing him of racism when the ADA—who was Latino—offered an African-American accused of assault a plea deal that DeShawn thought ungenerous. What DeShawn didn't realize was that the accused already had a prior conviction for the same crime. The ADA was being lenient. DeShawn almost lost his job, but after apologizing profusely, he instead received an official reprimand.

After accruing several other warnings for inappropriate anger and emotion, DeShawn was told that the next outburst would cost him his job. This was a major wake-up call. He saw how his past experiences often clouded his present judgment. He began to see that as much as his childhood memories motivated him, they also hurt him. He wondered if there was a more effective way he could advocate for change.

The Science

Memory doesn't work like a photocopy machine, perfectly storing exactly what happened in unbiased detail. It's more impressionistic: we file away fragments, feelings, snippets of conversations, and the like, reconstituting them as needed in the present. These recollections are almost always flawed. More importantly, our recall errors are not random; they are consistently biased toward remembering the negative.

For instance, when researchers showed volunteers in a study a series of images—positive, negative, and neutral—then tested their recall, the subjects *overwhelmingly remembered the negative images best*. They showed substandard abilities to remember the positive and neutral imagery, despite being shown an equal number of images in each category for the same amount of time. Likewise, another study demonstrated that people give greater emphasis to negative events, objects, and personal traits when re-telling their life stories. Not only do we remember negative events better than positive ones, we remember negative *traits* about other people more than positive ones.

Critically, according to a landmark study published in *Psychonomic Bulletin & Review*, memories can also intrude upon and contaminate our present, leading to skewed perceptions of the world around us. For example, it's been found that if we ruminate on the past while driving, these memories negatively alter our understanding of what we're seeing on the road right in front of us. (To ruminate is to think about something over and over again, while continuously reliving the cascade of original, nega-tive emotions each and every time.) We literally start "seeing" things that aren't there or claim they are behaving differently than they really are.

Partly because of negative-memory bias, dwelling on our past is a recipe for emotional disaster. According to researchers at Stanford University, people who ruminated on their pasts had much higher rates of depression than those who didn't. This held true even in the rare cases when the ruminating thoughts were largely correct. Obsessing about our past cre-ates emotional and functional deficiencies. *Even accurate ruminations* don't bring about positive benefits. Similar studies showed that ruminating on the past increases our feelings of shame or guilt, which, in turn, can lead to higher incidences of depression, anxiety, mood disorders, and suicide, as well as serious health consequences caused by suppressing the immune system.

The flip side of these studies is that *ceasing* to dwell on the past leads to remarkable improvements in our happiness. Results from studies conducted in England showed significant reductions in depression, anxiety, self-criticism, shame, inferiority, and submissive behavior. There was also a considerable increase in the participants' ability to calm themselves.

And the best news? *The benefits are the greatest for men and women suffering from chronic difficulties, especially the most severe emotional traumas.*

When properly understood, framed, and treated, past traumas and negative memories can be a positive catalyst for personal and spiritual growth. A 2008 study of 1,739 adults suffering from posttraumatic stress disorder (PTSD) found that those who recovered from traumatic events emerged from their ordeals with markedly increased strength of character.

One of the most successful ways to overcome acute trauma is to face it head-on, not fight it or run away from it. In an Australian study of volunteers who suffered from severe PTSD brought on by assault or war, those who had therapists guide them—using a variety of techniques including visualization and cognitive retraining—step-by-step through the trauma until they no longer reacted emotionally had far better outcomes than those who received traditional talk therapy or no treatment at all. By reliving the trauma in as much detail as possible, the victims were able to keep it from consuming them. They trained themselves to reframe what happened to them from a neutral or positive perspective, allowing them to release it forever. Those who either repressed or relentlessly relived the trauma without objectively trying to release it stayed traumatized, their symptoms often worsening as time progressed.

The Spirit

Bliss happens in the Now, when we inhabit this moment so perfectly that it saturates and uplifts our consciousness. It is *impossible* to simultaneously ruminate about the past and feel bliss. For this reason, every Bliss Experiment requires the ability to throw off the yoke of our past.

This isn't as radical as it may sound. It's axiomatic that healing our past is essential. This scarcely needs proving: nearly every branch of psychology—Freudian, Jungian, cognitive, gestalt, transpersonalist, and so on—proclaims the need to overcome past wounds. One of our initial responses to major traumatic events—a plane crash, school shooting, terrorist attack, natural disaster—is to dispatch trauma counselors for survivors and witnesses. This is in recognition that past hurts impact our current and future lives, and that without intervention, the odds of a negative outcome increase greatly.

Psychology and Spirituality

There is, however, a critical difference between psychology and spirituality. Many of the traditional psychological approaches emphasize the efficacy of plumbing our past, sometimes again and again. In a sense, they believe that the deeper we can look backward—at the early conflicts from infancy, our formative relationships with our parents and families, and those key milestones of childhood development—the happier (or at least less neurotic) we'll be.

The spiritual perspective largely disagrees. Bliss requires that we look backward only in a limited way. The goal is to release our past, to *cease* dwelling on it—in effect, to make it disappear from our consciousness. We must learn our lessons dispassionately, extract the wisdom we gained from those experiences, and then let them go. Ultimately it is a fruitless place to dig or dwell; there is no happiness, meaning, truth—let alone bliss—to be found there.

Admittedly, working with our wounds and traumas is difficult, delicate work. Some of us have experienced genuine horrors that cannot and should not be glossed over or insulted by platitudinous drivel. Sometimes we may benefit by working directly with a qualified professional. There are some contemporary therapeutic approaches that work harmoniously with bliss practices. Therapy or psychiatry can be helpful temporarily ("temporary" can be years), especially to aid us through a trauma or a particularly difficult period. Ultimately, though, we also must understand that the therapeutic and pharmaceutical models stop far short of blissful self-realization. Bliss practices begin where therapeutic exercises end.

The Nonexistent Past

In some ways, ruminating about the past is even more delusional than seeking wealth, sex, romance, fame, beauty, or power. At least those have a concrete, material reality. The past is like a ghost; it's truly a figment of our imagination.

Not only does an unreleased past intrude on our present, our propensity to overinflate the significance of negative memories means that those emotions are certainly slanted, perhaps totally erroneous. This is why dwelling on our past generates depression and anxiety. The more we look backward, the less accurately we see what's really happening in the Now.

Ruminating on the past means constantly rerunning old tapes, grasping onto old expectations, seeing the world through outdated lenses. Like a mirage that isn't there, we find ourselves drinking the sand or, like Don Quixote, tilting at innocuous windmills that we mistake for enemies. We don't hear what others are really saying in the present. We don't accurately process what's really happening now. We're too busy only half-paying attention while we instinctually react to situations that don't exist, emotions that aren't felt, and words not spoken.

In doing so, we make a new round of mistakes that generate additional hurt feelings, negative reactions, and a further repository of memories to skew and misinterpret in the future. Unless we consciously shed these ghosts, we'll find ourselves locked in a vicious, self-reinforcing, never-ending cycle.

The impetus to change comes when we realize that no matter however difficult it can be to release our past, it is even more painful to cling to it. Our negative memories and emotions are powerless to create a better now for us. We *must* make some conscious effort to shed these in order to live fully in the moment.

Integrating Our Past and Present

There are more and less effective ways to release our past. One of the most common and least effective ways of doing so is by using alcohol and drugs to help us forget. This *never* works, as alcohol and drugs only temporarily suppress past memories, leaving them to resurface later, often at the most stressful times. Or they create so much collateral damage in our mind and body that the "cure" becomes worse than the initial trauma.

There are two healthy, effective ways to release our past: integration and forgiveness. For the remainder of this chapter, we'll discuss integration. Forgiveness will be discussed in the next chapter, after we hear the story of DeShawn's partner, Shanice.

Painful memories intrude on our present because we haven't properly processed and integrated them into our experience of the Now. We become captives of our fears, afraid to examine past traumas because they are scary and confusing. We are emotionally overwhelmed. Often our first impulse is to fight against them, push them away, and wish them to disappear. We try to manipulate our external world to ward off these experiences. The problem is that avoidance or pushing away only makes them worse.

Failing to integrate and release our past hurts, traumas, and memories—both bad *and good*—creates a kind of temporal schizophrenia, opening a gap or duality between our past and present selves. When we are not spiritually integrated in the present, our past ghosts act like multiple selves trailing behind us, anchoring us down, continually forcing us to look behind us and fear the bottomless chasm.

Acceptance, Dispassion, Reimagination

The three steps to integrating our past with our present are acceptance, dispassion, and reimagination.

Acceptance comes from admitting, even embracing, what has happened to us and allowing it to become part of our present self. Instead of fighting against what happened, wishing it hadn't, refusing to look at it, believe it, or admit its impact, we stop resisting and allow it to *be*. We accept that whatever happened is now part of who we are. We learn to face it without any kind of emotional reaction; working at it earnestly until the memory provokes zero emotional response.

We accomplish this by turning *into* the trauma, not away from it. Resistance only adds fuel to the fire. We must learn to see our past experiences and ourselves objectively, like a neutral observer would. Just as we aren't devastated by the trauma of someone we don't know on the other side of the world, so too must we learn to feel that way about our own. We consciously practice seeing the event and ourselves as dispassionately as possible. Dispassion creates positive distance: a kind of psychic space and mental breathing room that give us greater clarity. That space allows us to consciously change our reactions to the event. We can see what kind of different choices we might have made to prevent it or reduce its impact, how we can learn from it.

Finally, we can reimagine our past by retelling our story, emphasizing the good that has come from our experiences—or the good that *could* come from it, if only we allowed it. Neither our minor issues nor major traumas need define us, let alone destroy us. We can use them as catalysts to making ourselves better, happier, and stronger people. From my own experience, I know that the worst things that have ever happened to me have helped me become the person I am today. I am happier, wiser, and more blissful for having gone through all that I have. The more we dwell on any positives, even the smallest and slightest, the easier it is to integrate that negative memory into our present experience.

Once fully integrated, our bad memories cease to have power over us. It's not that we've *forgotten*, it's that we stop *reacting* to them. They simply *are*. When we truly accept something, we stop turning it over and over again in our mind, automatically breaking the cycle of rumination and negative emotions. The state of no reaction is a sign that we have brought our past into the present. They have merged into one. No longer is something terrible lurking "out there," stalking us, holding power over us. In that moment of acceptance and integration, our past ceases being other; it's happily part of our Now.

The Experiment: Retelling Our Story

1. Choose a negative event, interaction, or memory. Recall it in as much detail as possible, including what happened later.
2. Make a list of everything good that came from it. These can be internal realizations or outward benefits: people you met, opportunities that arose, or relationships that deepened.

3. Practice acceptance. Grant yourself permission to accept what has happened to you. Stop fighting it; invite your past into your present life story. Repeat to yourself, "What has happened is in the past cannot be changed. I am grateful for every opportunity." Visualize your mind and body relaxing around this fact, feeling soft, calm, and peaceful. Notice if you carry any physical or mental tension around admitting this to yourself. If you notice tension in your body, make an effort to relax those tense body parts.

4. Examine the event or memory with as much dispassion as possible. See yourself as a neutral observer might. Pretend that you are an outside scientist, therapist, or clergyman studying yourself from a distance. How would you describe what happened? What were all the involved parties thinking and feeling? What motivated them? What could we have done differently to change the outcome, either prevent or minimize it, if anything? What lessons would you draw?

5. Retell the event or memory positively, as if you were the happiest, kindest, most understanding person on earth. If you have difficulty doing this, visualize someone else—a therapist, minister, wise guru, or compassionate friend—doing it for you. What would that person say? What good came from it? You can also include possible future positives that might still happen because of this event.

6. Feel gratitude for what's happened to you. If not the event itself, be thankful for the person it's helped you to become, the changes in your life you've made because of it, the people you've met—all that has come from it. See the upcoming chapter on practicing gratitude for more about this.

7. Visualize the past merging into the present. Feel it losing negative power over you. Repeat this exercise as many times as necessary to release the trauma or memory.

Online

Additional videos and resources for this chapter are available at www.theblissexperiment.com.

CHAPTER 8

Turning the Page

Forgiveness is the key to action and freedom.
—*Hannah Arendt, German political philosopher (1906–75)*

Releasing the past often requires forgiveness. This is especially true when we find ourselves victimized by others or when we feel shame, guilt, or remorse for bad acts that we've perpetrated against others. In one case, we must forgive someone else; in the other, ourselves.

There is a great deal of misunderstanding around forgiveness. This is not surprising. It's a fraught topic—by definition certain to contain a great deal of negative, even conflicting, emotions. Forgiveness is best understood as an internal act; it is something we do for ourselves, not for others.

In chapter 7, we began the story of DeShawn and Shanice. We concentrated mostly on DeShawn's experiences. Shanice has a very powerful story of her own.

The Story

Though she never shared the details with me, during her teens Shanice was the victim of an attack. The perpetrator was a neighborhood boy she knew in passing. Shanice has gone through therapy; in college, she briefly joined a support group. Although she is a functional, productive, and motivated person, she had issues with intimacy and trust. Not atypically, she also felt shame for what happened to her, although she knew it wasn't her fault. Part of her shame stemmed from her desire to please her parents, whom she loved and respected. They had tried so hard to protect her from the dangers of her neighborhood. Her distress was compounded by feelings that she had let her mother and father down—although I never got the impression that her parents felt this way themselves.

Shanice frequently thought about her attack, sometimes vividly reliving it. She had terrible flashbacks and immobilizing panic attacks. She felt rage at her attacker, not only for what he did to her but also for hurting her entire family; he had disrupted their hopes and dreams of a better life for Shanice. At first she found her rage useful, as it fueled her painting and creativity. As time went on, however, the downside of the rage manifested more obviously. She struggled in her relationship with DeShawn, though he was loving, supportive, and understanding. She admitted that it affected her ability to feel genuine intimacy and trust. They also had a tendency to spiral downward in rage-fueled fights, since both were capable of great anger. Small fights over trivial things could quickly escalate into screaming matches from which it took days to recover.

This left her feeling discouraged and also wary of feeling too much. When she allowed herself to feel, often it would unlock a stream of negative and uncontrolled emotions that scared and depressed her. It was easier not to feel anything. Only when Shanice painted did she allow unrestrained feelings to come through. It was probably no accident that she liked the solitary nature of painting. She didn't have to worry about her rage, fear, anxiety, and depression affecting anyone else, most especially DeShawn.

Eventually she realized change was needed. It was severely impacting her relationships: with DeShawn, with her family, with her friends, even her work colleagues. Shanice found a therapist specializing in sexual abuse. Remarkably, she told me that it didn't take long for her to feel better. Wisely, this counselor focused immediately on helping Shanice forgive: first herself and then, later, her perpetrator. Forgiving didn't mean reconciling with her perpetrator. In fact, she hasn't seen him since the attack. She doesn't know where he lives, if he's in jail, or even if he's alive.

Since learning forgiveness, Shanice feels that a great weight has been lifted from her consciousness. She's much happier, and less angry, anxious, and depressed. Her relationship with DeShawn is closer and better than ever. She was even surprised that her painting didn't suffer, something that she was afraid might happen. Her painting did change, however: it's no longer as violent, swirling, and dark. But she finds great joy in her new style; there are even early signs that it will sell better, since she recently landed her first solo exhibition.

Shanice says that the most exciting part of learning to forgive was how quickly it unfolded. It took her and her therapist a few months of working together before Shanice made the decision. Once she firmly and clearly made up her mind to do so, her attitude and emotions changed very quickly. The hardest part was making the initial decision. The forgiveness itself was effective immediately. She described it to me as like dropping a weight: "One minute it's on me, weighing me down, straining me, and the next, it's just *gone*."

The Science

The scientific evidence in favor of forgiveness is as irrefutable as any scientific conclusion can be. There are a multitude of university-affiliated and nonprofit research organizations dedicated to studying forgiveness and applying those results to individuals and society. Of particular note is the pioneering research being conducted by the Stanford Forgiveness Project, organized by Dr. Frederic Luskin of Stanford University.

Virtually every subtopic within the field of forgiveness has been studied: for the individual, the family, the state, and the world, including large-scale applications of forgiveness for those who have suffered from the violence in Northern Ireland, South Africa, Sierra Leone, and the attacks on 9/11. This work has also been successfully applied and researched in a variety of corporate, medical, legal, and religious settings. One study, particularly applicable to Shanice's story, was conducted at the Cincinnati Children's Hospital Medical Center. It examined the impact of forgiveness on victims of childhood sexual abuse:

- Victims who were able to forgive their abuser had much less chance of suffering PTSD and reported higher levels of self-esteem than those who didn't.
- Forgivers had much lower rates of postattack depression, anxiety, and stress.

- Practicing forgiveness also lowers blood pressure, boosts all-around physical health, reduces physical pain, and helps prevent people in recovery from substance abuse from relapsing.
- Forgiveness transforms *all* relationships, including marriages and friendships, and helps us feel more connected to the world around us, which is reflected in increased volunteerism, charitable donations, and other altruistic acts. Conversely, those who never forgive experience marked declines in their relationships and feelings of connection to the world. They feel more alone and isolated.

The amazing power of forgiveness goes far beyond the individual. Studies prove that it decreases the overall crime rate by breaking the cycle of retribution and violence; shortens and prevents wars; and is universally effective across all cultures, countries, races, economic status, and religions.

The Spirit

The power to forgive is a spiritually transformative act. It's no accident that one of the most important moments in human history is when Jesus looked down from the cross and said, "Forgive them, Father, for they know not what they do." Forgiveness is inherently divine, for by releasing our claim on hatred, fear, anxiety, depression, revenge, and negativity, we create space inside ourselves for compassion, wholeness, peace, wisdom, and love. Those are the building blocks of bliss.

That it took a spiritual master like Jesus to forgive tells us just how difficult it can be. As Mahatma Gandhi said, "The weak can never forgive. Forgiveness is the attribute of the strong." It's a heroic act, requiring extraordinary courage. It might seem impossible to imagine. We remember what's happened to us, which can summon so much rage, fear, anxiety, and desire for retribution that it might feel almost insulting that anyone would ask it of us. Bringing ourselves to the point of *wanting* to forgive another is the hardest step. Once we make the decision, the rest unfolds easily and naturally.

Much of our difficulty stems from where we focus our attention. We often dwell on the perpetrator, who usually deserves rage, even retribution.

It's even more maddening if the person's transgressions have gone undetected or unpunished. We may be the only ones who know what he or she has done; perhaps worse, even if others know, we might be the only ones who seem to *care*. That only fuels our anger.

When we shift our focus away from our perpetrator and onto ourselves, forgiveness makes more sense. We've already seen the myriad deleterious impacts that holding on to past hurts has on us: it makes us miserable, harms our health, undermines our current relationships, and generally interferes with our life. Most important, it blocks our ability to feel happiness and bliss. Refusing to forgive keeps us in a perpetual state of victimhood; the first time at the hands of our perpetrator, and forever after at the hands of ourselves.

Sometimes when I am especially struggling with my willingness to forgive, I remind myself that living well is the best "revenge." Dwelling on my past hurts gives those who hurt me power over me. I am allowing them to impact my life. The last thing I want is to give them the satisfaction. Put more positively, disallowing them the ongoing ability to impact my life reclaims that power for me. I become the master of my destiny, not them. Only by choosing positivity, beauty, kindness, and love do I get the life I truly want.

It's helpful to remember how we felt when others have forgiven *us*—the relief, the release, the lightness—or our misery when they wouldn't. None of us is perfect. A vengeful outlook will inevitably rebound on us, since we too, as imperfect beings, will commit transgressions that require forgiveness.

As Hanna Arendt implied in the quotation that opens this chapter, forgiveness is the only way to a present and future free of bondage. Judgment, hatred, revenge, and its attendant negative emotions trap us in the past. Harboring these attitudes is to claim that change and transformation are impossible, that life is static, fixed, and irrevocably broken. If we relentlessly look backward, we lose not only the ability to see this present moment but abandon all hope of changing the course of our future.

Every small, individual act of forgiveness is a step toward a better world. Look at South Africa after apartheid. Unlike so many African countries that disintegrated after independence, South Africa—largely because of the wisdom, compassion, and vision of Nelson Mandela and Archbishop Desmond Tutu—not only didn't collapse but set a shining example for the world. The nationwide forgiveness project chaired by Archbishop Tutu, called the Truth and Reconciliation Commission, was essential to this success.

Forgiving Ourselves

Forgiveness is not always aimed at others. Often we must forgive ourselves: for our failings, mistakes, high crimes, and petty misdemeanors. Even when we have done something genuinely awful, our only hope for redemption is to uplift our consciousness. If we wallow in misery, self-pity, or self-hatred, we become continual channels for that negativity. And negativity never stays confined inside us; it *always* leaks onto others, in small and large ways. Healing ourselves not only helps us but also lessens the prospect that we'll hurt others in the future.

"Sin" is atoned for through love, not hatred. If we want to remove evil from this world, we must root it out of ourselves, for evil is uncontrollable. Self-forgiveness is the only lasting way to stop the cycle of violence, against others and ourselves.

Though self-compassion can be the most difficult of all, we must remember the words of the Yogananda's own spiritual teacher, Swami Sri Yukteswar: "Forget the past. The vanished lives of all men are dark with many shames." We all make mistakes, some merely embarrassing, others deeply disturbing. It is the inevitable result of our human imperfections.

Forgiving God, the Universe, or Humanity

When there is no individual to blame, as in a natural disaster, or the scale of the offense is unimaginably colossal—the Holocaust or a ruinous economic collapse—instead of blaming an individual or group, we sometimes look for a much larger scapegoat: God, the universe, or humanity in general. A common argument for atheism is that the universe is so cold-hearted, even vicious, that God either can't exist or is so mean-spirited as to be unworthy of our attention, let alone worship. Some feel genuine rage at this terrible, accidental, chaotic, mistake of a world; others see it as an unfunny cosmic joke.

I'm sympathetic to this viewpoint, as I once held it myself. There's a profound theological discussion we could have, but this isn't the place for it. For now, I will say only this: forgiveness in this context means a willful shift of our focus from the external to the internal. What happens outside of us is ultimately neutral. It's how we choose to understand it and react to it that makes the difference.

The belief that someone or something "out there"—whether a personal God or the impersonal "laws of nature"—is hurting us is an interpretive *choice*. It has the tinge of blaming and victimhood; it's a belief, not a fact. A disempowering one at that. Blame, anger, and hurt—including at God or the universe—hinder our abilities to experience the bliss within.

Common Misunderstandings

There are a number of common misconceptions about forgiveness; we often use these misunderstandings as reasons to avoid it.

Forgiveness and reconciliation are *not* the same. Reconciliation is external; forgiveness, internal. Reconciliation requires reestablishing positive contact with those who have harmed us. It's a direct exchange between the parties, perhaps even a resumption of the relationship. In some cases, reconciliation makes sense; in others, it doesn't. As should be clear by now, bliss is about the internal, not the external. As such, bliss does *not* require outward reconciliation. What matters is our internal state of consciousness.

Forgiving is not the same as forgetting. Sometimes allowing a bad memory to vanish from our minds *can* be helpful—whether accidentally or purposefully—but in my experience, we are usually best served by *not* forgetting, only forgiving. Wisdom is acquired by learning from our past experiences, good and bad. When we can remember them dispassionately, without being captured by swirling negative emotions, there is much to gain. Remembering our past can propel us to new heights, both personally and societally. Ignorance is not bliss, and there is no bliss in ignorance.

In cases in which laws have been broken, forgiveness doesn't mean surrendering our right to legal redress. If a remedy is possible—say, locking up a child molester or launching a civil suit against a fraudulent company—it probably *should* be pursued. As always with bliss, we're concerned primarily with our internal attitudes. Do whatever is appropriate, but with as much calmness, equanimity, and clear-mindedness as possible.

At the macro level, as much as we should try to forgive brutal dictators, terrorists, or genocidal maniacs, this doesn't mean that we shouldn't do our best to stop them—even if it means war. As much as possible, we mustn't succumb to harmful negative emotions while performing our righteous duties. If it's the right thing to do, that alone is motivation enough; we needn't saddle ourselves with crippling harmful emotions as well.

The Experiment: The Process of Forgiveness

1. Make an unbreakable commitment to do this *for yourself*—not for the perpetrator or anyone else. You alone have the power to choose forgiveness. Decide that your own happiness and bliss are the priorities.
2. Pick an event, relationship, or interaction. It may be something that happened to you or something that you did to another. Recall what happened and your feelings about it. Try to stay objective, listing as much or as little detail as you feel necessary. More detail can help when you are unsure what it was exactly about a situation that left you feeling so hurt. In cases of obvious trauma, you may not need to list a lot of detail. Sometimes discussing it with a trusted person—family, friends, a therapist, spiritual counselor—helps clarify your own thoughts and feelings. Or you can write in a journal or find some other way to express it privately.
3. Gain perspective on what you're feeling. See what you're feeling as not something truly in this now-moment but as a reaction to something that happened in the past. List the ways in which this present moment—right now—is *different* from the past, and how the past is "leaking" into your present and distorting it.
4. If possible, summon empathy for your victimizer—or yourself, if this is an exercise in self-forgiveness. Empathy does *not* mean agreeing with or condoning. It's the process of understanding what the person (or you) was trying to achieve by committing that act. Try to feel what he (or she) might have been thinking, needing, and feeling. You may even feel badly

for him in the sense that the perpetrator got it so wrong and made such a terrible mistake. Picture the person's fear, confusion, and ignorance— even stupidity. Imagine the pain he must be in and the problems, even personal hell, his confusion creates for himself.

5. Rewrite the story of your trauma, grievance, or mistake so that it has a positive outcome. Look for the ways in which you can use this to gain wisdom, become a better person, achieve your life goals, or find new opportunities. Whenever necessary, remind yourself of this positive narrative.

6. Release any expectations of punishment. If there is a way that the perpetrator can or should be punished, it is perfectly fine, even positive, to pursue that remedy. Practice feeling dispassionately about that, as if you are just the vehicle through which impersonal justice must be administered. If there is nothing you can do—or the offense doesn't rise to that level—instead release your desire to be the personal vehicle for their punishment. Have faith that the universe will take care of punishing him. Let another be the vehicle for judgment and punishment, or even to decide whether that is necessary at all. Release all expectations that the person will even be punished in an outward, detectable sense. See the ways in which he is already living as punishment. There is no greater hell than to be trapped in a negative consciousness. Whether the world recognizes it or not, he is probably in hell right now.

7. Concentrate on this visualization: mentally picture negative thoughts, emotions, or desire to harm another as a heavy ball or weight. Imagine releasing it over the edge of a cliff and watching it fall away from you, leaving you feeling light and free. Or see yourself as an eagle, struggling to gain altitude and soar on life's winds until you drop the dead weight you've been carrying in your talons. As you let go of your past hurts, see yourself soaring free through the sky.

8. Hold on to or reinforce your forgiveness by repeating the above process, in whole or part, as often as necessary.

Online

Scan the Microsoft Tag above to view a brief video, "Forgiveness," or go to youtube.com/seanmeshorer.

CHAPTER 9

Forgetting the Future

I have known a great many troubles, but most of them never happened.

—*Mark Twain, American writer (1835–1910)*

We've explored how living in the past displaces our attention from the fullness of this moment, often with disastrous consequences. There is a second, equally mistaken temporal place we look to for happiness and bliss: the future. While the primary mind-set of looking backward is rumination; for looking forward, it's worry. Together they form a one-two punch guaranteed to deny us bliss.

We are terrible at predicting the future both externally and internally. The world is simply too complex, with too many variables and too many people making decisions we know too little about, for us to be any good at it.

We all know and joke about how bad meteorologists are at predicting tomorrow's weather—let alone the forecast for next week or next month. In reality, predicting the weather is infinitely simpler than predicting the trajectory of a human life, family, or civilization. We all know to pay minimal attention to weather predictions—especially for anything beyond the next few days—yet we'll spend countless hours, days, weeks, and even months of our lives endlessly trying to extrapolate much more complex future events, including where we'll be in five years, and how our careers, relationships, children, health, and finances will turn out, not to mention the courses of companies, technologies, and even countries.

The Story

From a young age, Ari had a clear picture in his mind of how his life would unfold. He visualized a moment in time in which he had achieved his goal of becoming a wealthy, respected doctor with a beautiful wife, two children, and felt complete satisfaction. He organized his entire life around this vision.

Ari grew up in a moderately wealthy Long Island family. He attended a prestigious private school, was high school valedictorian, and got accepted into Harvard—the college of his dreams. His application was perfect: Ari had made sure that he had the grades, the extracurricular activities, and the overall life story lined up exactly how the Harvard admissions committee would like. At Harvard, Ari continued dating his high school sweetheart, who was not only beautiful but also shared his life goals in every way.

He was intent on again finishing first in his class so that he could continue his education at Harvard Medical School. Ari also pined for, and eventually gained entry into, one of the prestigious final clubs—the Harvard equivalent of fraternities—to bolster his resume and give him a spate of contacts among the rich and powerful. Once in Harvard Medical School, he poured himself into his studies. His new goal was to land a prestigious fellowship given only to a few medical school graduates in the entire country. He was desperate to become a world-famous brain surgeon.

After becoming a doctor, Ari married his high school sweetheart. Soon after, she became pregnant with their first child. They moved to Florida, where the tax situation was advantageous, and he was offered a highly lucrative position. They bought a minimansion and became pillars of the community.

Approaching his fortieth birthday, Ari took stock of his life. He had achieved everything he had visualized: the career, money, status, wife, children. It was precisely at that moment that Ari realized he was miserable and sank into a debilitating depression. He could barely get out of bed to go to the office. He mostly ignored his children. His marriage was strained almost to the breaking point. Even his fellow doctors noticed. What went wrong?

As Ari reviewed his life, he recognized a lifelong disconnect between who he truly was as a person and the future vision that he had created for himself. The truth is that he never really wanted to be a brain surgeon, perhaps not a doctor at all. At a minimum, he would have preferred pediatrics or family practice. He overrode his feelings because the money and status with those disciplines—or some other profession entirely—weren't as high as with brain surgery. He never really cared about joining a final club; he didn't even like most of the members. Yet Ari had spent countless hours with them just in case the connections might eventually prove advantageous. He realized, too, that although he loved his wife, they didn't have much in common on a deeper level. She represented what he *thought* a good wife should be, but genuine understanding was missing. He had children because that was the conventional expectation rather than any deep-seated drive to be a father. Even living in Florida was about tax breaks and real estate prices, not because that's where he truly wanted to live.

Almost every major life choice that Ari had made was geared toward receiving a future payoff or fulfilling a vague fantasy, even though every decision made him anxious and unhappy. He spent a lifetime brushing aside what he was feeling and experiencing in the moment, always telling himself that it would get better when he "got there," as if there were some future moment that he would cross a finish line, and all would be perfect from that point forward.

As he crept closer to forty, Ari realized there was no finish line to cross; no moment that all of his sacrifices would pay off. He was consumed with anxiety and agitation. He put himself on antidepressants and antianxiety medication, but these had little effect because he made no attempt at any other kind of change, in either his life circumstances or mental outlook. His downward spiral continued until those around him worried that he might be suicidal.

I tried to help Ari see his options as much as possible, largely by guiding him to calm his endless future dwelling and help him get in touch with what he was feeling and experiencing in the here and now. He found that exceedingly difficult. His mind kept drifting toward the future, relentlessly trying to calculate what *might* happen down the road.

Though he made progress, eventually Ari and I lost contact. He admitted that he wasn't ready to implement lasting change. The last I heard, he had pulled back from the brink of suicide but was still struggling. I'm not sure if he was ever able to come more fully into this present moment. For his sake, I hope so.

The Science

Humans adjust to situations and events in surprising ways. Even if "bad things" happen to us, they may not be nearly as devastating as we fear. They might even turn out to be the best thing for us. One recent study found that although we base many of our decisions on "affective forecasts"—predictions about what our emotional reactions will be to future events—in reality, we're consistently mistaken.

We seldom visualize the future situation in all its complexity. Our future worrying is too broad; we fail to factor in key details that end up changing *everything* about how we really end up feeling. A study published in *Psychological Science* shed light on this. Subjects tried to predict in advance how they would feel if a certain event happened. After that event took place, the same people were asked how they now felt. Contrary to their original predictions, the event made little or no difference to people's internal well-being. If they were happy before the event, they stayed happy after, regardless of whether they interpreted the event itself as good or bad. Conversely, if they were unhappy before, even if they predicted that the event would make them happy, it had no effect.

The researchers found that we fail to accurately predict the emotional impact of future events because we're too focused on the event itself and not enough on our own inner faculties, resources, and capabilities. External events have little to do with our internal happiness and well-being, *even when we believe that they will matter a great deal*. Who we *are* internally is much more important than what happens to or around us.

Another type of predictive mistake we make is to assume that our future tastes will resemble our current tastes. Economists from Harvard and the Massachusetts Institute of Technology discovered that we process fears and make decisions based largely on what we currently like, need, or want. We assume those will *always* hold true. In turn, we put great effort into securing a future that has even more and better of what we value now—only to discover that when the future arrives, our needs, wants, interests, and desires have completely changed.

Worrying about the future has severely negative physical and mental consequences. A study published by the American Heart Association demonstrated that chronic worriers have a higher incidence of coronary heart disease than nonworriers, while according to another study, people who worry excessively about the future have higher rates of anxiety and depression and lower rates of happiness and well-being. Perhaps worst of all, incessant worrying actually *increased* their sensitivity to current and future traumas. That is, if something bad came to pass, the worriers experienced it with heightened distress compared to how non-worriers experienced the same event.

The Spirit

The future is an illusion. It doesn't exist and can *never* exist. To constantly project, worry, and daydream about the future is to live in unreality. In some ways, it is more destructive than living in the past, because at least obsessions about the past have *some* basis of reality to them. We can experience only the Now. Life is a series now-moments. As soon as the future arrives, it's a moment in the present.

When we can see the fundamental unreality of the future, we open ourselves to a major shift in awareness. Now is the only reality. The rest is a fantasy, illusion, dream, or nightmare. Living in the now is waking up.

Three Ways of Living in the Future

There are three primary ways we live in the future. Most of us do all three to varying degrees and in different combinations. The most common and destructive form of future dwelling is what-if thinking. When I was twenty and working through my anxiety and depression, I spent a lot of time talking with a transpersonal therapist. One day, after I'd expressed anxiety about something or another, Michael said to me, "You know, Sean, 'What if?' are the most neurotic words in the English language."

I never forgot that simple, powerful observation. His "What if?" didn't mean the creative, exploratory impulse or our boundless capacity for innovation. Instead Michael was referring to those personal, emotional, fear-based scenarios that we constantly generate: What if I get sick? What if I fail? What if something terrible happens? What if she doesn't love me? What if I lose my job? What if I can't do [fill in the blank]?

Fear can take place in the present: for instance, if someone put a gun to my head, I might feel pure fear in the Now. Worry is different. It's a *future-projected fear* that generates anxiety. The overwhelming majority of what-if scenarios never happen. If we could count our what-if thoughts, then tallied how many actually manifested, it would be an infinitesimal percentage; at least 99 percent wasted mental energy. Even when a worry comes true, we've probably incorrectly imagined our actual response or failed to factor in critical details that alter the outcome, rendering all that time spent worrying unproductive and not helping us cope any better.

As you may recall, a focusing illusion is the tendency to isolate one or two variables and overestimate their impact to the exclusion of everything else. This helps explain the continual mistakes we make in projecting our future: we fear losing our job but overlook that an equal or superior opportunity might result; we fear a failed relationship but never consider that it might clear the way for something healthier. Even if something "bad" happens, we fail to credit our own internal resources and adaptability.

The second way we live in the future concerns excessive goal orientation. Our society rewards results, not processes. This has its benefits but also a downside, because doing anything for the sake of a future reward pulls us out of the present moment. Goal-seeking behavior sacrifices the present for the future. We do something not for the present satisfaction, wisdom, or joy it provides but in exchange for a future reward—one that might never come or pay off in the ways that we'd hoped.

One thing is for sure: no one hands out rewards for just *being*. Nor do the rewards usually take into account *how* we got the result. Our parents didn't ask us if we cheated to get that grade, no one looks too closely at whether the CEO or bond trader broke any laws. Society continually rewards us not for the journey itself but for completing it—never mind how.

Just as concerning: often these goals aren't personally meaningful. They are other people's goals that we've internalized; from our parents, our friends, our teachers, our leaders, our religion, our society. We can spend our entire lives chasing goals and rewards that others tell us we *should* want rather than what we truly *do* want.

What do we feel when we complete our goal? Perhaps we tell ourselves that completing this or that gave us a sense of satisfaction, even happiness. If we examine it more closely, we discover that more often we're experiencing *relief*, not genuine happiness. We're thankful that, finally, a burden has lifted. Peace of mind briefly returns—until we eagerly take on the next goal.

We also tend to visualize just a moment or two of our future payoff. If it's winning a prize, for example, we fantasize about the moment we receive the reward: the walk across the stage, the congratulatory handshake, and the standing ovation from the crowd. What we forget is that life goes on afterward—and that we will quickly adjust, the thrill will fade away. Much too soon, we return to "normal." Then we must set out once again to find the next goal to achieve.

This doesn't mean that people who work hard or long hours are automatically unhappy. Nor does it mean that setting goals is bad. *If you really love what you're doing, then you've found a way to blend the promise of future rewards with the immediate experience of joy in the present.* This is increasingly rare. Too often our goals turn against us, becoming a cruel taskmaster, robbing us of the present moment. We become like Ari, motivated more by a future reward than the immersive and expansive bliss of living in the now-moment.

The third way we live in the future is through fantasy and daydreaming: about getting rich, meeting the perfect lover, winning the Nobel Prize. Some daydreaming can be useful. It can put us into a nonlinear, nonrational, intuitive state in which creative solutions manifest. Spending too much time in fantasyland disconnects us from the eternal Now. If we spend an hour elaborately fantasizing about living in a gold palace surrounded by the finest luxuries, what will be the psychic impact when the daydream ends and we look around our dumpy apartment? Probably our anxiety and depression will increase, and we'll be less capable than ever to appreciate and enjoy what we're experiencing right now.

Many of our future fantasies don't help us move forward. They are elaborate ways to escape from and *avoid* our present reality. They're *designed* to take us out of the moment. We want this because we haven't yet learned how to fully inhabit the present in a positive way. The dilemma is that only the Now is real. Too much time in fantasyland means that we're surrendering our ability to actually engender and implement that better future of which we're dreaming. We can't learn, change, or make spiritual progress if we're not present.

Planning Without Worrying

This doesn't mean that we can't and shouldn't plan for the future. Planning is not the same thing as worrying, fantasizing, or being excessively goal oriented. We can't just show up at a doctor's office without scheduling an appointment—that requires planning and future projection. So too does making dinner, buying concert tickets, or setting up a date for next Friday. For that matter, if we genuinely feel guided to *be* a doctor, we have to think about how to achieve that. We need to take certain courses (in fact, we have to figure out what kind of school we should attend, since they might not all have medical programs), we have to take the right standardized tests, apply, study, and choose a specialty. Every business and organization must do a great deal of advance planning. Products don't magically manufacture, market, and distribute themselves.

The key is to plan without worrying. We must strive to let go of fears, personal attachments, and desires for too-specific outcomes. We must divest ourselves of the mistaken belief that we need the world "out there" to unfold in a certain way for us to be happy. Even when we do set broad goals for ourselves, we must remember to continually feel and evaluate them in the present moment, always checking them against our authentic selves to ensure that we haven't slipped into worry, negativity, or fantasy.

The Future Is Now

The future is a vague and always-shifting target. Our present, and our way of being in the present, continually affects what will occur. The future is seeded in the Now. We cannot see, control, or understand the future. All we have, all we are, and all we can command is our present being. When the future "arrives," it is really just another present moment.

When we stay immersed in the present, worry and anxiety melt away. By releasing the past and shedding our thoughts of the future, the deck is clear so that we can finally see ourselves with clarity. This is the only way we can properly evaluate if what we're doing, feeling, thinking, and being is right for us—or if we've fallen into the trap of making ourselves miserable for the sake of some future goal or daydream. Most important, this opens up the possibility of bliss by allowing us to connect fully to the present.

The Experiment: Back to the Present

Whenever we feel ourselves unnecessarily worrying, planning, or daydreaming about the future, we can train ourselves to notice this and come back into the moment. By interrupting and creating distance from our thoughts, we manifest calmness and clarity.

1. Notice what your mind is doing right now: its thoughts, feelings, and inner activities. Now tell yourself, "That's my mind doing its thing." Practice labeling your mind activities. For example, if your mind is excessively concerned about whether you'll have enough money in the future, say to yourself, "Worrying." Or if it's dreaming about winning the lottery or one day owning a Ferrari, say, "Fantasizing." Or inventing new goals, "Planning." If it is dwelling on the past, say to yourself, "Ruminating" or "Obsessing." You can invent as many labels as occur to you. Try to label each and every one of your thoughts for the next minute or two.

2. Get into a comfortable sitting posture, in a chair, on the floor, or whatever works for you. Pay attention to your breathing. Breathe through your nose. Notice your belly and lungs rhythmically moving in and out. Feel the cool air in your nostrils as you inhale, the warm air as you exhale.

3. Begin counting your breaths. Count each breath, with a full rising and falling (in and out) as one repetition. Count ten breaths. Say the number silently in your mind. When you arrive at ten, count backward back to one then repeat the cycle again: "one, two, three, four, five, six, seven,

eight, nine, ten . . . one, two, three, four, five, six . . ." If you get distracted, gently bring your mind back to counting and keep going. Practice this for three to five minutes. You can do it with your eyes open or closed.

4. Now take as much time as you need to look around your immediate environment. Notice the landscape, interiors, any specific objects, and the colors in your line of sight. Listen for sounds, pay attention to smells or sensations. Try to keep your mind calm and nonjudgmental. Just notice, without criticizing, worrying, or feeling one way or another about your experience.

5. Throughout your day, whenever you notice that your mind is thinking too much about the future, repeat this exercise. Practice labeling your thoughts first, then interrupting them by counting your breaths. You can do it for several minutes or just a repetition or two. Always be sure to conclude with noticing your environment as much as possible.

Online

Additional videos and resources for this chapter are available at www.theblissexperiment.com.

CHAPTER 10

Awareness Pure and Simple

I have realized that the past and future are real illusions, that
they exist in the present, which is what there is and all there is.
—Alan Watts, British-American philosopher and writer (1915–73)

To this point, we've focused largely on places *not* to look for bliss, whether
in the external world or in the inner realms of our imaginary past or future.
After we've turned away from the external, released our past, and forgotten
our future, we are finally left with this present moment, the infinite here
and now. Finally, we discover the one true place to find bliss.

The irony is that the present moment is easy to overlook. It can seem
like this small, fleeting, even trivial thing—yet in truth, it's our *only* reality.
It's all that will *ever* exist. We often feel alienated from it, as if it's a distant
tableau meant only to serve as the background to our endless traumas, fantasies, and dialogues in the foreground of our minds. We talk with others
while silently entertaining completely separate thoughts and conversations
in our mind; we get wrapped up in emotions created by our past memories
or future dreams; we walk or drive through our daily life in a half-aware
reverie, barely even noticing what's actually happening around us—all the
while failing to connect to or even be aware of this moment right here and
now.

The Story

Jonathan grew up in Highland Park, a suburb of Chicago. He was raised
in a reform Jewish family and attended a prestigious private day school.

Though his family was not particularly religious, Jonathan went to weekend Hebrew school and was bar mitzvahed at thirteen. As part of his Jewish education, his temple classmates joined together with kids from several other Chicago-area congregations for a yearly field trip.

For seventh and eighth grades, Jonathan's parents allowed him to skip the trips. For ninth grade, however, they insisted that he participate. The boy dreaded it: he didn't know most of the other kids, including his randomly assigned roommate, nor was he much interested in his religion or heritage. The field trip was to a Jewish yeshiva: an educational institution dedicated to the study of the Jewish laws and Scriptures. Also attached was a rabbinical college where young men and women trained to become rabbis.

Like most teens, Jonathan's main interest in the trip was to meet girls and have fun away from his parents. This was the dominant view; many of his fellow weekenders came stocked with alcohol, drugs, and a party vibe. Since all the kids stayed in a dorm together—boys and girls on separate floors—everyone came ready for a little after-hours fun, especially once the adult chaperones went to sleep. On Friday night, after the Shabbat dinner and orientation program, people snuck into one another's rooms for a series of hushed parties. Jonathan's roommate, whom he had met earlier that day, was friends with a kid who brought some weed. Jonathan got stoned for the first time.

Since he didn't know most of these kids—none attended his high school—Jonathan felt free to act differently than usual. He wasn't popular at his high school. No one here knew that. No one had preconceived notions about him, how he should behave, or his social status. Nor did he have to worry about identifying the popular kids, either to avoid them or suck up to them. It was a liberating environment; they could all be themselves, at least for the weekend.

On Saturday the kids ate together, attended a temple service in the morning, and then did group exercises in the afternoon. Few, if any, paid much attention to the religious aspects, especially since they were all from Reform synagogues and secular environments. They were far more interested in cracking jokes, having fun, and making plans for the Saturday late-night parties and hookups.

After dinner, something interesting happened. The evening program took place inside the main temple sanctuary. It was led by two young rabbis-in-training—a man and a woman—who were only ten to twelve years older than Jonathan. The rabbis-to-be brought all the kids onto the stage, near the ark, where the Torahs were kept. (The Torah is the first five books of the Old Testament. For Jews, it is the holiest and most important Scripture.). The rabbis turned off the lights. Only candles lit the room. Everyone sat in a loose semicircle, facing the leaders. In calm, soothing tones, they began telling stories explaining the meaning of that morning's Torah reading. The man brought out a guitar and led some folk singing.

Jonathan began to feel peaceful and light, which was surprising and unexpected. He looked around and noticed that everyone responded similarly. The kids were quiet and focused, some leaning on each other in a supportive, bonding way. He looked at the flickering candles, the holy ark of the Torah in front of him, the calm, smiling faces, and suddenly, for the first time in his life, he felt fully present. A sensation of pure awareness rose inside him. He wasn't worried about any trivial problems or histories with anyone in the room. He knew he wasn't going to see most of these kids again, or at least not anytime soon. His school, studies, the major project due for biology on Wednesday, everything—his entire life in Highland Park—seemed remote, like it had all fallen away. His mind grew quieter and calmer than he could ever remember; he felt profoundly connected to those around him: the rabbis-to-be, the other kids, the wider Jewish community that he usually ignored, even the synagogue and the Torah itself—which suddenly seemed to be radiating a peaceful, centering power into the room. He wasn't worried about anything, he wasn't even thinking about anything, he was just feeling pure awareness and acceptance. In that moment, everything seemed perfect.

Later that night, the kids again snuck into one another's rooms. But not to party; just to quietly talk, share, and be together. No one drank or did drugs. They simply enjoyed one another's company. Jonathan had never experienced anything like it. It wasn't an out-of-body experience, he didn't see a bright white light, God didn't appear and speak to him; it was a profound, quiet knowingness and a pure, unfiltered experience of the Now.

His life quickly returned to normal on Monday, but Jonathan never forgot that night. Years later, when we met and he recounted it to me, his only questions were: What was that and how can I feel that again?

The Science

The research presented in the last three chapters makes it clear that living in the past or future is a mistake. Simple deduction, then, tells us that happiness and bliss must be the domain of the present. Still, it's worth examining a recent, intriguing study reinforcing this.

One of the benefits of modern technology is that it allows scientists to find creative tools of exploration that were previously impossible. In 2010 the journal *Science* published a study conducted by Matthew Killingsworth and Daniel Gilbert at Harvard University. Ingeniously, the two of them devised an iPhone application that allowed nearly 2,500 participants to track their thoughts, moods, activities, and awareness as they went about their daily lives. At random intervals, their phones asked them how they were feeling, what they were doing, if they were thinking about something other than what they were doing, and whether whatever they were contemplating was pleasant, unpleasant, or neutral.

The app made it easy for participants to accurately log what they were doing, and the information was electronically sent back to the researchers for analysis. The results might best be summed up by the article's title: "A Wandering Mind Is an Unhappy Mind." Their research showed that when our minds drift from whatever activity we are doing in the present moment—especially by thinking about past events or planning for future ones—our self-reported levels of happiness *plummet*.

Killingsworth himself explained it well: "Human beings seem to have this unique capacity to focus on the nonpresent. They have the ability to reflect on the past, plan for the future, and imagine things that might never occur. But at the same time, human beings are clumsy users of this capacity, and it tends to decrease, rather than increase, happiness."

A different study found that those who live more fully in the present are *less* likely to delude themselves or have incorrect illusions about reality. Those living in the present are not only happier but perceive the truth of their circumstances with greater accuracy.

The Spirit

To live in the present moment is to be fully aware and immersed in what we're doing *right now*. It's a state of relaxed concentration, *relaxed* being a key word. We often understand concentration as energetically taxing, even mentally or emotionally draining. We visualize scrunched up foreheads, tensed shoulders, or a taut hypervigilance. This isn't at all what being present in the moment means or requires. It isn't draining, it's invigorating; it's not tension producing, but tension releasing.

Living in the present, the Now, requires intentionally choosing our state of consciousness instead of drifting mindlessly. It means paying full attention to what we're doing and experiencing; being open to and aware of the environment and ourselves. While it's true that certain practices such as meditation sometimes make it seem like it's a special or especially difficult state to cultivate, in reality, living in the present is simple and natural. It's a choice that becomes a positive habit.

We can be awake and aware during any and every moment: talking, working, eating, running errands, or making love. It's not a practice, it's a state of consciousness, a way of being—one that dramatically increases our happiness and opens the doorway to bliss.

The Fullness of the Present

Immersion in the Now is a state of fullness. Drifting into the past or future creates an unsettling emptiness—a kind of temporal duality in which there's a gap between what's happening now and what happened in the past or what we dream of for the future. This effectively splits us into our past self, our present self, and our future self. Between these pieces lies a disconnected chasm that gives space for rumination or worry to do their damage, as fear, anger, anxiety, and the gamut of negative emotions seep into our consciousness.

Being fully present stitches together that duality, unifying us, making us whole. It is a state of oneness. In oneness is completeness—they are synonymous—which is why being fully present emanates fullness and satisfaction.

There is something mystical about this kind of fullness. When we are fully present, everything feels alive and transformed. Everything is heightened: our senses, our mental acuity, our feeling of connection. We see everything, hear everything, and feel everything. But not in a negative or overwhelmed way. We are completely calm, centered, and in control. Really, we're completely *out* of control, but not in the usual sense. I mean in the positive sense that our ego, with its normal fears, desires, negativity, and needs, recedes quietly into the background. We stop feeling like there is a separate *I* apart from the Now, all distance and duality is resolved. There is no *I* who can feel in control or out of control, or have a negative experience of any kind. Our entire being is utilized, all of our faculties focused and maximized. There is no waste, no leakage, and no loss. There is only wholeness.

Living in the Now changes our experience of the world and ourselves. It fundamentally shifts how we understand and relate to our inner and outer worlds. When Jonathan found himself fully immersed in the moment, he was able to see the people around him, even the rabbis and trappings of the Jewish faith, altogether differently. Just the night before, his peers were people to party with, curry favor with, try to impress. His own Jewish religion was an uninteresting, even boring, puzzle filled with strange people doing strange things that had little personal meaning for him. Yet for just that weekend, his life was transformed. He felt a peacefulness, knowingness, and connectness that was new, vital, and exciting. Externally, nothing had changed: he was with the same people, practicing the same religion, doing the same activities that he always had done. And yet now everything was different. Not just different, *better*.

Benefits of the Present

To live in the present moment is to be aware of everything: our thoughts, feelings, reactions, environment, and activities—whatever is happening *right now*. When we do this, interesting things occur. First, we get to know ourselves much better. We start to notice our habits and personality. The more we see and understand ourselves, the easier it is to make positive change—and the more effective those changes are, since we know that they are in accord with our deepest self.

Living in the present is also intrinsically much less stressful. If we're living in the past—especially our traumas—or worrying about the future, we're not going to be in a very good mental space most of the time.

We experience more fully and learn more from those experiences. Too often, when we are only drifting through the present, we miss the wonder of what is happening right now, whether that is beautiful scenery, an inspiring event, or a simple satisfaction. Each moment becomes infinitely richer and more rewarding. Being present doesn't just allow us to fully experience all of life's extraordinary moments, it makes every moment feel extraordinary.

Living in the Now allows us to see and understand truth more clearly. It's the only way to differentiate between what's real and what's a projection. Instead of allowing our past traumas, emotions, and experiences to bleed into and distort the present, we see and feel things as they truly are. Our responses become appropriate to the moment, not to something that happened yesterday or last year. We stop reacting to imaginary ghosts.

Finally, living in the present helps us to be more open, less judgmental, and more accepting, both of others and ourselves. It creates a kind of buffer space, a quiet peacefulness that calms the flow of judgments, criticisms, and negative emotions that continually bombards us. We see the ways in which we're deluding ourselves and our impact on others. If we're aware and centered, we have much more bandwidth available to observe and record what's really going on: how the things we do or say (or don't do or don't say) positively or negatively affect those around us.

Being in the moment and practicing mindful awareness manifests the doorway to bliss. It's like an enchanted, magical map. When we center ourselves fully and completely in the moment, the location of the treasure appears magically. For the first time, we see very clearly where to look for lasting happiness and enduring truth.

The Experiment: Savoring the Moment

1. Find or buy a piece of fruit: an apple, orange, grape, berry—whatever you like.
2. Find a quiet, private place to sit. Set the food in front of you and close your eyes, taking a breath or two to relax.

3. Think about the history of this food. Sometime in the past, someone planted the fruit. Visualize the entire scene: perhaps a tree being planted, then growing to maturity, then finally sprouting fruit. See the entire farm, with all the trees and roots going down into soil, sun shining, and water glistening. Imagine the fruit growing, slowly ripening until it was ready to be picked. Visualize the person picking it, either by hand or with equipment. Imagine where it was inspected, packaged, loaded on trucks, and driven to the market where you purchased it.

4. Imagine, too, all the people that were involved in this process. Whoever planted the fruit, tended to it, picked it, packed it, drove it, displayed it at the market, and so on. All those different faces and places, people with their own backgrounds, stories, hopes, challenges, dreams. They were born, raised, clothed, fed, educated in some way or to some degree, and, of course, ate countless amounts of food themselves. Think about all those people, the equipment, and the stores. Who built the market? Where did all that food and equipment come from?

5. Now notice what is going on inside yourself as you reflect on this miraculous piece of fruit. How do you feel? There is no right or wrong answer. You may feel gratitude, amazement, or nothing at all. Or you may even be annoyed at all the resources needed to produce this single piece of fruit. Maybe it makes you feel connected to the great chain of life, or maybe you are just bored, tired, or are starting to think that this whole exercise is stupid. It's all okay. Just notice what's going on inside you right at this moment.

6. Now pick up the piece of fruit. Look at it as though you have never seen this kind of fruit before. Feel its texture and shape in the palm of your hand. Notice the color, the variations in shading, perhaps even green or brown spots. Now smell it.

7. Now open it. Slice it with a knife or peel it with your hands. Listen for any sounds this makes. Watch closely and see what it's like as the flesh peels away.

8. Is there anything about this fruit that you've never noticed before?

9. Now bring it up to your mouth. Do you have a desire to eat it? Perhaps a feeling welling up inside encouraging you to take a bite. Just notice that.

10. Now close your eyes, open your mouth, and eat a piece. Feel it in your mouth, chewing slowly. Focus all of your attention and awareness into

this. The taste, the texture, the sound of chewing. Notice the saliva, your tongue, and your teeth all effortlessly going about their business.

11. Pay attention to any thoughts you might be having. Is your mind wandering? Are you comparing it to another fruit you once had or another food altogether? Are you enjoying it or thinking it tastes bad? Are you finding this exercise interesting or idiotic? Do you want to take another bite?

12. Keep going, eating the fruit and noticing whatever you're thinking, feeling, sensing, for as long as you wish.

13. When you are done, look around the room you are in and try to feel a connection with your environment. Listen and observe.

14. Reflect on how you felt while doing this exercise. Were you able to immerse yourself in it, or did thoughts of the past or future continually intrude? If you were able to stay (mostly) present, what did you notice or feel while you did this? Was this different from your usual experience of eating fruit?

15. Take time every day to savor something that you normally hurry through or don't give your full attention. Practice noticing and being absorbed in whatever you're doing. Realize that you can live every moment with this level of awareness.

Online

Additional videos and resources for this chapter are available at www.theblissexperiment.com.

PART 3

Digging Deeper

Finding the hidden bliss within requires being present, in the Now. Once we've located the right place to look—in this present moment—our deepest work begins.

We've seen how the past and future are fantasies concocted in our mind. Once we're fully present and aware, we have the opportunity to observe ourselves, what our mind is doing, saying, feeling, and thinking—all its myriad quirks and behaviors.

Being in a state of centered awareness allows us to understand better that which we call our mind. As we do, we frequently notice that not everything happening in the Now is always so pleasant. Even a mind free from ruminating about the past or worrying about the future often gets itself into all kinds of trouble.

Learning to understand, redirect, and take control of our mind is an essential step on our journey. We are not our minds. The mind is a tool that we are meant to use for the realization of our highest potential. For most of us, however, that tool has completely taken over, like an inmate running the asylum. Once we regain mastery over our mind, we also gain the ability to peer behind it, finally making direct contact with bliss.

CHAPTER 11

The Never-Ending Stream

We are shaped by our thoughts; we become what we think.
When the mind is pure, joy follows like a shadow that never
leaves.

—*the Buddha*

As we turn our awareness inward, we can see that we all have a seemingly
endless procession of thoughts, commentary, conversations, and images
running through our mind. Our internal dialogue is filled with negative,
judgmental, or self-defeating thoughts, resulting in a roller coaster of harmful emotions.

This frequent, sometimes relentless negativity represents the next layer
that we must examine and see if we can peel away. Doing so clears one of
the most intense obstacles that we face on our journey toward bliss.

The Story

Willow is a bodywork practitioner and spiritual healer living near Atlanta.
Originally, she specialized in Hellerwork Structural Integration, a straightforward, relatively non-"woo-woo" type of body therapy that combines
deep tissue massage with a chiropractor's approach to proper body alignment and positioning.

One day a client mentioned that he was prone to kidney stones and was
experiencing early symptoms that always resulted in a full-blown attack.
Spontaneously, Willow stopped the bodywork and moved her hands over
his kidneys. She kept her hands there and silently prayed for and visualized

a painless dissipation of the problem. After a few minutes, she resumed the regular session. The next week, the man returned with a remarkable claim: the kidney stones had disappeared painlessly! He was convinced that Willow was responsible, since previously, once those symptoms came on, they always led to a painful passing. He had received no other treatment.

Willow began incorporating spiritual healing into her bodywork. She read books on it, including techniques used by other practitioners. As word spread of her "healing talents," people called requesting only spiritual healing, without any interest in Hellerwork. Person after person told her that she'd helped them. One woman claimed that Willow had cured her of cancer. Eventually those with just about every disease and problem claimed the same: from back pain to shingles to heart disease, people felt that Willow had healed them. The owner of a small publishing house in Virginia heard about her and asked her to write a book. It seemed like she was on her way to a satisfying and successful life.

About ten years later, I met Willow when she attended one of my classes. Willow was almost broke and thinking about filing for bankruptcy. She had been divorced after just two years of marriage. She was childless and now past childbearing age, which deeply saddened her. Though she still saw clients—when she could get them—the buzz around her had long since cooled. The woman in front of me was bitter, pessimistic, filled with blame toward others, and felt that life was manifestly unfair. I wouldn't have guessed that she was a spiritual healer; she seemed deeply in need of healing herself.

Willow told me that things began to unravel when she started quarreling with her publisher-to-be. She was sure that he was trying to take advantage of her in some way, despite the fact that he was always kind, fair minded, reasonable, and flexible. Still, her "intuition" kept telling her that some danger was lurking beneath the surface. She made a series of unreasonable demands, including a royalty rate that no author, not even Stephen King, receives. She had also concocted a litany of disaster scenarios in her mind about what would happen if she didn't carefully police her publisher and protect herself: he would cheat her, he would stick her with a bad book cover, he would change her writing in unacceptable ways, and so on. She missed her deadlines but always placed the blame on someone else.

Eventually the publisher cancelled the book before publication. He told her it wasn't worth the hassle.

She then got into a terrible fight with one of her wealthiest and most influential clients, whom Willow had healed of fibromyalgia. In turn, this woman had recommended her to several friends and wrote a testimonial letter that Willow could use for marketing herself. She had asked the client for a large loan to open a healing center, but the woman turned her down because Willow had no business experience and no partner to help. Willow felt like this woman "owed" her, since she was rich and Willow had healed her even when conventional doctors couldn't. She was so upset that she refused to continue treating this woman and even ripped up her testimonial.

She also felt that her husband had destroyed her life by divorcing her (because she was so negative and difficult to be around) and leaving her childless and alone.

Not only did she blame her publisher, patron, and husband for her unhappiness, but Willow also characterized them in the extreme: they were evil people who wanted to control her, and then, when they couldn't, they enjoyed destroying her life. If only those people hadn't screwed her over, life would be great. She would be a well-known, financially secure spiritual healer with a wonderful family.

She was even mad at God because she had all this healing ability, but God wasn't giving her the right opportunities to use it! She knew of other healers with big book deals who become well known even though Willow thought they were frauds. It was all so unfair.

The Science

"Negative thoughts" can be defined as any of the myriad types of unconstructive thoughts or unpleasant emotional states such as anger, anxiety, depression, futility, pessimism, and so forth that routinely pass through our minds.

According to the National Science Foundation, human beings have on average fifty thousand thoughts per day, although some estimates put it as low as twelve thousand and others as high as sixty-five thousand. Most of us have no memory or experience of even a single moment in our conscious lives that we weren't thinking something.

Researchers have now begun to quantify the relationship between positive and negative thoughts and the ratio between them that likely triggers unhappiness, anxiety, and depression:

- A study of children between fourth and eighth grades showed that kids who have a high rate of "cognitive errors"—that is, holding negative thoughts that are incorrect, illogical, or plainly false—have dramatically lower self-esteem and higher levels of depression and anxiety.
- A similar study of elderly Americans demonstrated that those who have more positive thoughts are happier, while those with an abundance of negative thoughts are more depressed.
- A fascinating study in the journal *Cognitive Therapy and Research* tried to nail down the exact ratio between positive and negative thoughts that led to good or bad mental outcomes. Adults described as "functional" *but not necessarily happy* have at least 1.7 positive thoughts for every negative one. Mild dysfunctionality set in when the ratio of positive to negative thoughts hit 1:1. That is, for every positive thought, participants had an offsetting negative one. Extreme mental dysfunctionality, then, comes when we have more negative thoughts than positive thoughts, whereas happier people will have at least two positive thoughts for each negative one.

Our thoughts have a tremendous impact on our physical health and overall life effectiveness. Drs. Christopher Peterson, Martin Seligman, and George Vaillant, of the Universities of Michigan, Pennsylvania, and Harvard, respectively, conducted a groundbreaking study that has followed roughly five hundred subjects since 1937. Their findings showed conclusively that those with a pessimistic or negative explanatory style had significantly more health problems later in life than those who were positive.

Another study found that chronic pessimism was so destructive that it even had the ability to reduce the effectiveness of proven, powerful, and time-tested prescription medications.

As you can see below, the damming effects of negativity impact every aspect of our lives:

- A study examining key factors in successful long-term romantic relationships found that individuals who maintained largely positive thoughts about their partners (even to the point of idealizing them) have higher-quality and longer-lasting relationships.
- When researchers looked at groups of people with the same measurable skill and talent levels, they found that those salespeople who have a positive assessment of their abilities sell more and perform better than those who don't. The gap wasn't minor, either: optimists outsold pessimists by *double*.
- Positive thinkers keep their jobs longer and advance further in their careers than pessimists.
- Two different studies indicated that positive-thinking leaders create more effective organizations and obtain better results from their employees than negative-thinking leaders.
- Between two groups of swimmers with equal levels of talent, those with more negative thoughts performed worse than the optimists.

The Spirit

We are all quite insane—almost every one of us, me included. At least, that would be the conclusion that someone might draw if he could hear the continuous stream of thoughts, feelings, and images running through our minds. Even if we don't show it outwardly, we all have a tendency toward never-ending judgments, dialogues, reactions, and emotions that—especially if taken out of context—could make any one of us look stark raving mad.

A *mildly* dysfunctional person has over thirty thousand negative thoughts per day, and a severely depressed or pessimistic person, as many as fifty-five thousand! Even a functional, moderately happy person has as many as twenty thousand negative thoughts per day. I want to emphasize that we are talking about *unnecessarily* negative thoughts, ones that are *not* definitively true or factually proven. *Insane* might be putting it mildly . . .

The good news is that the research also proves that we needn't eliminate all or even most of our negative thoughts to radically boost our happiness. This is one reason why it's possible to make substantial progress toward bliss in just twenty-eight days. Even a relatively happy person can still have at least one of every three thoughts be negative yet still cross the threshold into everyday happiness. Perfection is not required.

The Mind River

In classes and workshops, I frequently use the metaphor of the mind as a river. Visualize a constant stream of thoughts, feelings, and images rushing through your head.

When we stand on a riverbank, we understand that we're seeing only part of the river; most rivers are far too large to see their source, middle, and mouth all at once. We also know that the part of the river we see in front of us is filled with millions of individual molecules of water that combine to seem like an unbroken whole. We also know that as the water rushes by us, it will be immediately replaced by more water arriving from upstream. We don't expect to see a spurt of water, then a dry gap, then another rush. Most rivers flow indefinitely and without cessation.

Similarly, we experience our mind rivers as an unbroken torrent. The constant rush of thoughts, images, and feelings cascading through our conscious mind seems unending. As we finish with one thought, we expect it to be immediately replaced by another. We're so accustomed to this process that it seldom occurs to us that it could be otherwise. Given that we have as many as sixty thousand thoughts per day, this isn't surprising. This deluge is so pervasive that many of us imagine this river is who we *are*. Since this river is all that most of us have ever experienced as "me," what else *could* we be?

A key step on our journey toward bliss is to discover that there is more to us than the mind river and to learn how to change it. There are three types of changes we can make. The first is that we can change the content of the river. For most of us, our mind rivers have a lot of mud, silt, and garbage floating through them. If we can filter those out, our mind river begins to sparkle. We can also change the direction of the river; perhaps ours meanders unnecessarily or leads us somewhere unpleasant. Third, we can learn to reduce the volume of water. Instead of a torrent, we can slow it to a trickle. We might even be able to stop the flow of thoughts altogether.

For the remainder of this chapter, we'll look at ways to purify our mind river. Later chapters will explore how we can redirect and reduce the volume of our thoughts.

Cleaning Our Mind River

In relation to the Happiness Scale, removing the mud—relentless negativity—from our mental river is critical for everyday happiness.

Continuing to develop our awareness is essential to this process. This is why it's so important to be centered in this now-moment. Awareness allows us to watch our minds, thoughts, and feelings. Just the simple act of doing so gives us separation, distance, and clarity. We have to practice watching our thoughts. When in a bad mood or about to take a negative action, it can help to pause just long enough to observe what's going on in our mind. I consciously try to visualize my mind river flow on by, as if my Higher Self were just an objective spectator. When something particularly ridiculous floats past, I tell myself, "There I go again." Or "That's just my mind doing its thing," or "What interesting thoughts I'm having!"

While it may seem like we have a nearly infinite variety of negative perceptions floating through our minds, in reality, most are just variations on ten common types. Knowing to look out for these makes it that much easier to cultivate awareness. The chart below provides a complete rundown. Let's look at two examples:

Overgeneralization is probably the most common type of negative thinking. Here we extrapolate a general conclusion from a small set of data. Whenever we find ourselves saying things like "He *always* does such and such," or "My boss *never* makes the right decision," or we convince ourselves that something will happen again and again just because it happened *once*, we're overgeneralizing.

Willow was a master at the second most common type of negative thought: blame. We've all found ourselves placing full responsibility for a negative outcome on someone else, as if we had nothing to do with it. Most of the time, that's not true or accurate; we've played at least *some* role in what's happened, even if we won't admit it. In those rare times that we *are* truly blameless, it still doesn't help us spiritually to dwell upon it incessantly. As we discovered in chapter 7, "Releasing the Past," doing so results in us revictimizing ourselves.

Awareness alone isn't enough. It's critical that we also learn to actively *dispute* our negative thoughts. Whenever we find ourselves feeling negative, it's helpful to analyze how it began and why it may not be entirely accurate. Usually some event, conversation, or action triggered the cascade. We must ask ourselves if what we're thinking genuinely tracks with *all* the known facts. Are there any facts or experiences that I'm forgetting? If so, does remembering them change anything? Have I engaged in any of the most common types of distorted thinking? Is there anything I can do to change my thoughts, change my decisions, and create a different outcome? If yes, what?

Most of our negative thoughts don't have any particular truth to them; they aren't grounded in reality or based on proven facts. They are demonstrably false or potentially false. What do I mean by "potentially" false? The act of thinking and believing them turns them into self-fulfilling prophecies. *Because* we believe them, we then take actions that maneuver reality into turning out that way. If we hadn't indulged those thoughts, then chosen to believe and act upon them, things could have turned out differently. Just like the lovers, salesmen, and swimmers examined in the studies cited a few pages ago, our ungrounded negative beliefs alter our lives for the worse. If we change our inner dialogue, our outer reality changes too.

We're not trying to suppress negative thoughts or paint them over with pretty colors, while they continually lurk below. That would be counterproductive. The goal of happiness and bliss is never to deny or run from reality, it's to fully understand it, embrace it, and experience it.

Achieving distance from and mastery over our mind is essential for bliss. If we don't realize that we can control our mind river, the less capable we are of peeling away this layer so that we can discover what lies beneath. Put another way: a needlessly negative and agitated mind can't possibly be a repository of abiding happiness and abundant joy.

Ten Types of Distorted Thinking

- **Polarized thinking:** things or people, including us, are only black or white, good or bad. There is no middle ground.
- **Overgeneralization:** we leap to general conclusions based on a single incident or piece of evidence. If something bad happens once, we expect it to happen over and over again. Look for statements that include words like *never, nothing, everything,* or *always.*
- **Mind reading:** without other people communicating to us, we "know" what they are feeling, thinking, and what their motivations are. If we feel it, it must be true. Our feelings about others or ourselves are always intuitively correct or valid just because we feel them deeply.
- **Catastrophizing:** expecting disaster. What-if thinking. The worst is always the only or most likely outcome—and the primary thing we dwell upon. It is concentrating on or magnifying the negative, while filtering out the positive.
- **Self-centeredness:** believing that everything people do or say is a reaction to us. Constantly comparing ourselves to others and thinking that they are doing the same. Falsely imagining that others are thinking about us at all!
- **Unfairness:** we feel resentful because we're sure we know what's fair, but other people or the universe doesn't agree with us.
- **Blaming:** holding others responsible for our pain or problems, or, inversely, blaming ourselves for every problem or difficulty. The feeling that other people or circumstances control us, that we are helpless victims of fate. Or there is something fixed inside us—genetics, addictions, or permanent illnesses—that are responsible for how we feel, what we do, how we relate to others, and what we can become.
- **Shoulds:** we have a list of inviolable rules about how we and other people should act, think, and believe. We use them to judge others or ourselves. Breaking the rules makes us angry or if we break them, we feel shame or guilt.
- **Need to be right:** we are continually trying to prove our opinions and actions are correct. Being wrong is unthinkable. We will go to any length to demonstrate our rightness.
- **Scorekeeping/prizewinning:** we expect specific people or organizations to notice and acknowledge our sacrifices and self-denial. We feel bitter when

the reward doesn't come exactly as we thought it should or in the way we wanted. A general belief that life's rewards are, or should be, externally noticeable.

The Experiment

The practice for this chapter is a three-step process. You can do all three exercises together or separately. They can be used on a daily basis or whenever you feel negative, moody, or overwhelmed by your thoughts.

Step 1: Watching the River Flow

In the last chapter, our practice focused on being aware of the present moment, especially of an external act (eating the fruit). Now let's do an inward variation of that exercise.

1. Find a comfortable place to sit. Close your eyes.
2. Visualize that your Higher Self is sitting on a riverbank, watching the river flow. The river isn't water; instead it's the constant stream of thoughts, feelings, images, judgments, dialogues, and such that is pouring through your mind *right now*.
3. Take two to five minutes just to watch this river. Try not to judge, label, or feel attached. Be a dispassionate observer, as if you are watching someone else's mind. You can even say to yourself, "There I go again." Or "That's just my mind doing its thing." Or "What interesting thoughts I'm having!"

Step 2: Distorted Thinking Review

In step 1, we watched our thoughts, remaining as neutral as possible about what we were observing, without judgment or labeling. For this next exercise, our goal is to label our thoughts with one of the ten types of distorted thinking described earlier.

1. Pick something relatively minor that's happened to you recently or that's bothering you now.
2. Make a list of everything that bothers you about this incident.

3. Now review your list. Do you recognize any of the ten types of distorted thinking in those thoughts? Write down any of the types of distorted thinking that might apply.

Step 3: Disputing Negative Thoughts

1. Taking your list from above, can you think of ways to dispute any negative thoughts you discovered?
2. For any form of distorted thinking that you've noticed, think of at least one way to dispute its accuracy.
3. Even if you don't really believe your disputation, play devil's advocate with yourself. Or visualize a third party you respect (or even an impartial judge) asking you questions. How would a neutral person see it? Would she agree with every point you are making? Even if she did, do you feel better or happier for holding on to this? Are there any ways in which these thoughts or feelings are harming you, even if you are sure they are justified?

Online

Scan the Microsoft Tag above to view a brief video, "The Mind River," or go to youtube.com/seanmeshorer.

CHAPTER 12

You Are Luckier Than You Think

A pessimist is one who makes difficulties of his opportunities,
and an optimist is one who makes opportunities of his difficulties.
—Harry Truman, *thirty-third president*
of the United States, (1884–1972)

The process of purifying our mental river requires infusing our mind with fresh, clean, and positive thoughts to replace any lingering negativity. In our exploration of habits, we discussed how nature abhors a vacuum; it is more effective to replace negative habits with positive ones rather than emptiness. It's the same with negative thoughts: it's easier to banish them when we actively replace them with positivity.

More importantly, it turns out that positive thoughts are almost always more accurate and truthful than negative ones. This can't be emphasized enough. We often believe, erroneously, just the opposite: that negativity is closer to reality than positivity. We might even believe that optimistic people are foolish, even embarrassingly saccharine. As the research proves, this is entirely inaccurate. Optimism is not only a practical and effective life strategy but also more authentic.

Above all else, an optimistic mind, under our volition and control, prepares the ground for the abiding experience of bliss.

The Story

Judith is a professional personal development author and speaker I've known for nearly twenty years. She has authored nearly thirty books, plus produced numerous audio recordings, videos, and complementary products. Yet chances are that you've never heard of her. Not a single one of her books has ever hit the best-seller lists. She has never been on a major national television program. She doesn't get hundreds, let alone thousands, of people at her talks. She's not wealthy, though I believe she makes a decent living. Still, Judith keeps writing, lecturing, and creating.

What's fascinating is that every time she is about to publish a new book, she tells me, "Sean, I think this could sell hundreds of thousands of copies." Which is remarkably optimistic, since it hasn't happened yet. I used to think that Judith was being a bit foolish. One time, after she'd talked excitedly about how successful her next book could be, I gently mentioned that her previous predictions had yet to prove true; perhaps it wasn't helpful to keep telling herself these fantasies. She replied calmly but with strength, "Sean, I can't afford to think that way. If I did, I'd never accomplish anything." Then she went on to share some amazing facts with me.

Judith said that even though no book of hers had ever sold enough in one week to become a best seller, over time, her nearly thirty books had outsold the vast majority of more famous authors. Worldwide, her total sales were now over a million units. Many big-time authors hit the best-seller lists by selling as few as fifty to one hundred thousand copies. And they achieve that only once, maybe twice in their lives. Likewise, Judith had spoken to tens of thousands of people—twenty to fifty at a time. More importantly to her, she was sure that she was genuinely *helping* people, not just selling them stuff. They had told her in person, in letters, and in emails. She was doing what she loved.

I had been thinking she was sort of a failure. Anyone looking at her from the outside might have thought so too. But Judith knows different. She's a success. A much bigger success than those who are more famous. If in the beginning, or after the first couple of books, she had thought the way I had—allowing herself to wallow in pity, blaming others, or giving in to negativity—she would have quit long ago. She's living her dream life, happier than most, and helping millions. All because she refused to see herself as a failure. The last time Judith and I spoke, she was just about to publish her next book. You know what she told me? "Sean, this one is going to help millions of people. I can feel it!"

Judith, I know it will.

The Science

Hundreds of studies by scientists across the world conclusively prove the benefits of optimism.

As we explored in the last chapter, pessimists are more likely to suffer from anxiety and depression. They also have significantly worse physical health and less overall success in life. Let's explore further why this is so.

It may be surprising to learn that *positive people have a more accurate perception of reality* and cope with stress better than negative people do. This was the finding of a study published in the *Journal of Personality and Social Psychology*. While pessimists dwell on their negative feelings, optimists look for the good side of a situation—or at least believe they will eventually find some kind of positive solution. What's more, optimists are more likely to seize upon solutions faster than pessimists, thus spending considerably less time immersed in stressful, negative situations.

Similarly, researchers at the University of Maryland discovered that optimists are more vigilant about their health and pay greater attention to information informing them about health risks. Negative people, on the other hand, tend to ignore this information or outright deny it. Not surprisingly, then, optimists live longer and are also less likely to develop dementia in their later years.

An amazing series of studies with far-reaching implications, published in the journal *Psychological Science*, demonstrated that people who were encouraged to feel positive about their visual acuity (that is, their eyesight; specifically the ability to see at a distance) scored better on eye exams than those who had negative beliefs about their ability. Think about that: both the pessimists and the optimists had the *same* physical capabilities and eye functionality, but those who *believed* they could see well really did see more. Optimism and pessimism literally changed the subjects' perception of reality. Put another way, their beliefs *changed* their physical reality. Seeing is not believing; believing is seeing.

We've all heard the statement "sadder but wiser." It is a common defense offered by negative people for their pessimism: "It may be more depressing, but I'd rather be depressed as long as I know it's true." In reality, it's the *opposite*. Sadder, more "realistic" people aren't wiser. A study conducted at Cornell University demonstrated that negative people are *less* accurate in predicting future actions and events than positive people.

Additional proven benefits of optimism:

- Optimists are more successful in their careers and interpersonal relationships. They see opportunities and are less likely to quit. Optimists are more persistent in striving for their goals and more likely to attain mastery at important life skills.
- Optimists have more friends, in part because others prefer to be around positive people and in part because optimistic people take better advantage of their opportunities for friendship.
- In a time of trouble, positive people who have the same number of friends as negative people make better use of the social support available to them, which, in turn, helps them get over the difficulty more quickly.
- Positive people are more engaged and immersed in life. Negative people tend to be withdrawn, disconnected, and in denial.

The Spirit

I have to admit: few people relate to negative thinking as well as I do. If Stanford offered a PhD in skepticism or cynicism, I would have graduated summa cum laude. Twenty years ago, I was convinced that pessimism was synonymous with truth and reality. Compared to your average spiritual teacher, I still maintain a noticeable streak of skepticism.

I've thought long and hard about why I naturally gravitate toward that perspective. For sure, I genuinely believe that a questioning attitude—not just believing whatever someone tells me—is not only useful but also necessary for spiritual advancement. If we allow ourselves to believe anything and everything, especially out of the false belief that people never lie, make mistakes, or misunderstand, we'll end up dazed and confused. There are many conflicting outlooks, theories, and perspectives. They can't *all* be correct. Gullibility and stupidity are not spiritual qualities. That's one reason I try to pair spiritual observations with scientific research. Genuine truth, spiritual or otherwise, should never offend our intelligence.

I also used to believe that assuming the worst was an effective coping mechanism. Many of us can't help but wonder if it might not be more devastating to think optimistically and then have one's beliefs dashed, that it's somehow emotionally "safer" never to get our hopes up in the first place. I've come to understand that this isn't at all what positive or optimistic thinking means. As such, I think it's helpful to discuss first what optimism is *not*.

Busting Optimism Myths

To be an optimist does not require a Pollyannaish or Panglossian outlook: the belief that the world is perfect, that whatever happens is perfect, and that we live in the best of all possible worlds. Self-deception is not required. Evil, ignorance, stupidity, and sheer human error definitely exist. Our world is a mixture of good and evil, kindness and meanness, beauty and ugliness, exhilaration and tragedy. Just because someone makes a claim about something doesn't at all require us to believe it. In fact, it's probably safe to say that a high percentage of what we believe or are told will prove wrong.

Nor does optimism require holding fantasies about the future. Life doesn't always work out in the end, at least not *externally*. In fact, as we've already discussed, bliss requires letting go of the future as much as possible, regardless of whether those fantasies are happy daydreams or anxiety-inducing fears.

Above all, genuine optimism has nothing to do with holding illusory beliefs about our capabilities or ourselves. The bliss process requires stripping away all that is false, including our egoic, I-centered selfishness. Neither self-serving interpretations nor inflating our skills, understanding, or intelligence has anything to do with real optimism.

What Optimism *Really* Is

Put as succinctly as possible: optimistic thinking is true thinking. They're synonymous. It's pessimistic thinking that denies reality—as the studies prove. Positive thinking means trying to see the full range of possibilities and making the conscious decision to pursue the best possible choices available to us. It's really that simple.

I realize that this runs counter to much of the prevailing folk wisdom of our times. Our culture seems to believe that negativity is more "realistic" than positivity. As we've seen, this is totally untrue. It's pessimists who have a difficult time perceiving reality accurately. Here's an example from my own life:

When my chronic pain was at its nadir—wildly out of control—I gave up my career running a publishing company and spent most of my days lying in bed, writhing in pain and riddled with medication side effects. My mind drifted to some *very* dark places. I started telling myself that my life was over, the pain would never get better (I didn't yet have a correct diagnosis), Brook would leave me, I would never accomplish anything again, and I was destined to die alone, broke, and miserable. Had I capitulated to that perspective, I could have pointed to any number of "facts" to "prove" it was all "true." I hadn't experienced a single pain-free moment in years, Brook was distressed by my illness, I wasn't working, I didn't have a clear diagnosis, and a large number of doctors and treatments had failed. I could have convinced many people, myself included, that this bleak outlook was simply a "fact," and that believing differently was sheer fantasy.

Yet it was entirely untrue. Here I am, living in Los Angeles, traveling the world speaking and teaching, writing books (and getting paid to do it), while Brook is happily reading by my side as I write this, and our relationship has never been better. Even though my body is in *pain,* I'm no longer mentally *suffering.* I could hardly be happier. The real truth is that this was *always* a possible outcome for me, though in those dark moments, I might have denied it.

At its heart, optimism is the knowledge that we are not helpless. If we scrape away the surface justifications, pessimists are really saying that they believe themselves to be largely weak and helpless, unable to shape, let alone control, their destinies. Neither strength, courage, nor energy is required, since the world is just a bunch of random stuff (most of it bad) happening *to* us. An optimist, on the other hand, understands that some form of change or improvement is *always* possible, even if only internally—the most important kind.

What I had to do, and what we all have to do, is admit to ourselves that we have choices. Even if we have few or none outwardly, at the minimum, we always have them inwardly. Real positive thinking isn't at all about believing that any kind of external reality is or isn't happening, or will or won't happen. Genuine optimism is about our *internal* mind-set, understanding, and decisions.

Positivity means surveying our options and orienting ourselves toward the highest and best, not the lowest and worst. *Willfully choosing something lesser when it's unnecessary is the most self-destructive form of negativity imaginable.* It also makes us complicit in whatever evil, ignorance, stupidity, or unpleasantness is happening around us. By dwelling on them, we are refusing to lend our energies to balance them out or improve our world or ourselves. To be pessimistic is to condemn us—and the world—to the worst possible outcome.

If we don't believe something is possible, we don't pursue it, or at least not with fortitude and conviction. We're more likely to abandon a course of action sooner. Who has a better chance of success: the girl who believes she can be an astronaut or the boy who's *sure* it's an impossible dream? That's the worst danger of negative thinking: it convinces us not to even try, to purposely choose destructive, unhelpful ways of being.

How to Be an Optimist

There are four specific practices that turn negativity into positivity:

1. We must *allow* ourselves to think optimistically. For me, this was the hardest step. Letting go of my fears that being positive would make me a fool or set me up for disappointment required internal convincing.
2. Make a conscious effort to change how we think and phrase our thoughts. In the last chapter, we talked about challenging our negativity.

It's time to take that one step further. After we've disputed our pessimism, we must actively rephrase it more positively. Whenever we catch ourselves being unfairly or inaccurately negative, we consciously reframe the thought in a more positive way. Here are some examples, based upon my own experience with chronic pain:

a. Instead of saying, "*All* doctors are clueless idiots," I started saying, "It's a fact that there are better and worse doctors in this world. Someone out there can probably help me; I just haven't found that person yet."

b. Notice, too, what optimism is *not*. I didn't say to myself, "All doctors are geniuses. Medicine will definitely cure me." Optimism doesn't require extremes; minor shifts often make all the difference.

c. Instead of saying, "I will *always* be incapacitated by crippling pain," I learned to say, "*Right now*, I'm in pain. It's cyclical; I have bad days and better days. I may or may not ever be 'cured,' but I can find ways to improve my functionality." Words such as *always* and *never* indicate helplessness and undermine our motivation for improvement.

3. At certain moments, we all feel singled out, as if the universe is plotting against us. We say things like "Why me?" or "God must hate me" or "I am a useless failure." Or perhaps worst of all: "I deserve this." The truth is that there is no reason to make it so *personal*. Just because I am in chronic pain, it doesn't mean that God hates me. That's an emotional reaction. I'm also not a failure because I had to quit my job—that was just the impersonal nature of the situation at that time. Seldom are these extreme forms of personalization proven, objective facts, they are *reactions*. Usually the reality is far more impersonal.

4. Look for the full range of possibilities and choose the best. I have never encountered a situation in which there were *no* choices. We may not have *every* possible good outcome available, but just because some things are "off the table" doesn't mean that *everything* is. If we're alive, we have at least some choices to make—and some of those are bound to be more positive and better for us. Choose those.

Optimism and Bliss

Learning to retrain our mind to think optimistically is an essential step on our journey to bliss.

Bliss requires energy and fortitude. Bliss doesn't always happen overnight. Pessimists are less likely to immerse themselves in these experiments, spend the time and effort necessary to master these skills and practices, and generally more likely to quit too soon.

Perhaps worst of all, as the research regarding optimism and visual acuity showed, the familiar trope "I'll believe it when I see it" might be exactly backward. It's more accurate to say, "I'll see it when I believe it." When it comes to uncovering bliss, this is even more the case. The ability to control our minds, as evidenced by the conscious ability to choose and infuse them with positive thoughts, is essential for bliss. As we'll see in later chapters, personal mind control is perhaps *the* central tool for uncovering bliss. Optimism is actually only a basic, introductory practice. If we decline to make progress here, we won't have the foundation necessary for later Bliss Experiments.

The Experiment: Reframing the Negative

Think of something affecting your life right now that is causing you to have lots of negative thoughts.

Part A

1. Try to understand as specifically as possible why you feel so negatively about this person, situation, or event. Pay careful attention to the reasons you've given for thinking or feeling the way you do.

2. Try to think about this person, situation, or event as objectively as possible. For example, do you really believe that it is a *permanent* problem that can never, ever change? Is it *universal*, across the board, without exception? Is it *personal* to you or not really specific to you at all? If some of your negative observations seem clearly accurate, true, and unchangeable, can you think of anything at all positive? List any and every silver lining or positive opportunity.

3. Practice reframing your original thoughts to remove any traces of distorted thinking. Without denying current reality, can you find a way to restate the problem so that you have stated it accurately but *without* exaggeration or negative bias?

Part B

Approach this like a brainstorming exercise. Give yourself permission to explore every possibility, including the most positive ones, even if you don't believe they're likely. There are no dumb ideas right now and nothing to be embarrassed about. Doing this exercise doesn't commit you to a particular action.

1. Using the original person, situation, or event from part A, tally the *full range of choices, solutions, options, or directions* you can imagine this unfolding or you doing—including all of the most optimistic and best-case scenarios, even if they don't seem likely. Be sure to include your negative, depressing, or "most realistic" options as well.
2. Reviewing this list, now identify *the best possible choice or outcome*, or at least the best possible one that you can allow yourself to believe has *any chance* of happening.
3. How can you reorient your choices, decisions, or life toward increasing the odds that the positive outcome happens? List out every action, strategy, or mental approach you can think of that could help make this positive possibility a reality.
4. Vow that you will invest as much of your intention, will, energy, and intelligence into making this best possible choice come to fruition. You will *not* abandon pursuing it—unless it becomes a proven, objective fact that it isn't possible.

Online

Additional videos and resources for this chapter are available at www.theblissexperiment.com.

CHAPTER 13

Thanks for Everything

Gratefulness is the key to a happy life . . . for if we are not grateful, then no matter how much we have we will not be happy—because we will always want to have something else or something more.

—*Brother David Steindl-Rast, Benedictine monk (b. 1926)*

One of the fastest ways to turn around a negative mind-set is to practice gratitude. I continually surprise myself with how simple and effective this is. Gratitude is easy to learn, requires no skill, and can be put into effect by anyone, regardless of background or beliefs.

In some ways, gratitude represents the culmination of mindful awareness, optimism, and living in the now-moment. It helps us see the full spectrum of reality while opening a clear pathway to higher states of bliss consciousness.

The Story

Jihan stumbled into one of my "Happiness" class series in Los Angeles without realizing its full scope. A second-generation Chinese-American, her parents immigrated to the United States from Hong Kong while her mom was pregnant with her. She heard about the class through Facebook, but for some reason didn't understand that it included a significant spiritual component. That discovery was a bit distressing for Jihan, as she was entirely secular. Both of her parents were atheists. Her father is an electrical engineer; her mother stayed at home full-time to raise Jihan and her younger sister, Limei.

After sitting through the first class stone-faced and silent, Jihan approached and informed me that she'd made a mistake and would like a refund. She had no interest in any of the spiritual content or practices, nor was she interested in bliss. She was looking to boost her everyday happiness and leave it at that. After talking a little bit and explaining the full range of what we would cover over the next month, Jihan decided reluctantly to stick it out. She had already cleared the time in her schedule, and it seemed like there would be just enough "nonspiritual" content for her to get at least something from it.

During the second week's class, Jihan told us that although she was only twenty-five, she'd already been married for two years but was having a great deal of trouble with her husband. He wasn't a bad person but had lots of little habits that annoyed her. She was starting to feel like she might have rushed into their marriage. She was also in graduate school, studying for her PhD in molecular biology. Her studies, while cutting edge, were grueling and much less exciting than Jihan had envisioned. She also found the entire department entrenched in power struggles and rife with tension. Professors battled one another for control, and there were intense rivalries between the various subspecialties. Recent university-wide budget shortfalls only exacerbated the situation, creating an atmosphere of competition for resources and respect.

Between her rocky marriage and tedious studies (which required several more years for her degree), Jihan was feeling boxed in, uncertain, and not at all sure that she could endure either much longer. On the other hand, she still loved her husband and did not truly want a divorce—which would be heavily frowned upon by her parents. She also maintained hope that once she got her degree, she'd have much more latitude to explore her own specific research interests.

It was abundantly clear from our conversations that Jihan was not interested in many of the suggestions for happiness and bliss presented during the course. Some struck her as too spiritually oriented; others she didn't have time for, or they simply didn't resonate with her. After pondering it for a week, I recommended that, for starters, she focus solely on the simple practice of gratitude. I also emailed her a variety of scientific studies proving its effectiveness, knowing that this was important to her. I asked her to do the practice at the end of this chapter for ten minutes every day for a week—focusing especially on expressing gratitude for her husband and the PhD program—then report back to me.

During the next week's class, Jihan was much more engaged than usual. She nodded her head in agreement at several points, participated in the conversation, and generally seemed more cheerful than during the first two weeks. Afterward, she told me, "I did the gratitude practice exactly like you said, and it was amazing! For the first time in months, I remembered why I married him. I remembered why I wanted to study molecular biology, too. A few days ago, we had this guest lecturer who talked about a new way of sequencing proteins. It was superclever and creative. That's exactly what I want to do. It gave me this idea for an experiment that I'm going to run by one of my professors.

"I ended up practicing gratitude much more than ten minutes a day, without even meaning to," Jihan continued. "I did it every time I got annoyed, and it turned around my mood. After not long, it became like a shorthand: I just reminded myself of a single positive thing about my husband or school, and then I knew that I had a whole list of other good things behind that one, so I didn't even have to take the time to run through them all, since I knew they were there, and I just let it go. Did I mention how amazing this is?"

The Science

Practicing gratitude is another area in which the scientific research is plentiful and consistent. Two of the leaders in the field are psychologists Robert Emmons of the University of California at Davis, and Michael Mc-Cullough at the University of Miami. They have collaborated on at least seven different studies published by the American Psychological Association's *Journal of Personality and Social Psychology*. In aggregate, these studies demonstrate that practicing gratitude increases happiness and well-being, improves relationships, enhances overall spirituality, and reduces materialistic attitudes and negative emotions such as envy. Furthermore, it works with a wide range of the population—from students, to businessmen, to the elderly—and for every personality type, from extroverts to introverts.

In perhaps the most interesting of the studies, Emmons and McCullough enrolled people suffering from one of three neuromuscular diseases (NMDs). All the participants were living with a difficult, even traumatic, incurable chronic illness. After practicing gratitude, subjects reported greater overall life satisfaction, had more optimism about the immediate future, and felt more connected with others. When the subjects' spouses and significant others were interviewed separately, they confirmed the reported levels of improvement. This study is especially notable because this group had valid reasons *not* to feel gratitude: the members' lives were painful and difficult, and their long-term prognosis was universally negative. Yet even this most challenged group reported tremendous benefits.

In 2009 psychologist Richard Wiseman of the University of Hertfordshire, England, conducted a study that is striking for both its size and specific conclusions. The study enrolled twenty-six thousand people—an enormous sample that leaves little room for doubt. Wiseman had participants do quick and simple practices such as taking a few seconds to remember something good that happened to them in the last twenty-four hours or to remember something or someone for whom they felt gratitude. It didn't have to be important: even trivial things such as being grateful for a good cup of coffee or an enjoyable movie counted. Of course, people could choose more important things such as a promotion at work or a wonderful relationship.

Two key points emerged: (1) Participants showed a rapid and dramatic upward swing in their happiness. It didn't take long for the positive effects to become noticeable; gratitude works *fast*. (2) The tasks were quick and easy. They didn't require hours of intensive work or any kind of advanced skills. The subjects didn't even have to focus on something vitally important.

It's important to understand that as quick and easy as it is, gratitude is also surprisingly powerful. A 2002 study conducted at the University of Michigan showed that expressing gratitude helped students who witnessed the September 11, 2001, terrorist attacks to recover emotionally more quickly, as well as show greater psychological resilience and a higher capacity for postcrisis emotional growth. Gratitude practitioners were also less likely to develop depressive symptoms. It wasn't that the practitioners of gratitude didn't experience negative emotions relating to September 11. They experienced the full range of grief, fear, anger, and the like. The researchers theorized that the difference is that practicing gratitude added genuine, *truthful* positivity to their viewpoints, thereby preventing the practitioners from becoming wholly consumed by exclusively negative emotions. Gratitude reminded people of the *complete* range of human capabilities and ideals, including our positive traits. It counteracted our bias toward emphasizing, dwelling on, or remembering the negative.

Finally, research published in the journal *Emotion* revealed that gratitude helps us behave less selfishly and more cooperatively. Gratitude practitioners are more likely to help strangers in need, regardless of whether they will receive a reciprocal benefit in return.

The Spirit

No matter our personality, what we've seen or survived, our level of experience, or how much time we have, practicing gratitude is something that we can do. It's a quick, simple, and effective way to pour fresh, clean water into our muddy mind rivers.

I had heard about gratitude for years before trying it. It wasn't until I stumbled across these statements from Elie Wiesel, Holocaust survivor and author of *Night*, that I took it seriously. On one occasion, Wiesel wrote, "No one is as capable of gratitude as one who has emerged from the kingdom of night." He also said, "When a person doesn't have gratitude, something is missing in his or her humanity . . . to this day, the words that come most frequently from my lips are *thank you*."

I realized then that expressing gratitude isn't a practice for the weak, foolish, or those who've led a charmed life. Few people in existence have lived the horror that Wiesel has—yet he emerged from that more certain than ever that gratitude is an essential practice. This, combined with how quick and easy it is, makes it one of the highest priority practices we can do.

What Is Gratitude?

Put simply, gratitude is the conscious remembrance of something positive that we either experienced in the past or are experiencing now. That's pretty much it. We reflect on our lives and make an effort to remember what's going right or has gone right. It can be something good that's happened, a positive quality of ours or someone we know, an enjoyable experience we've had, or something interesting, beautiful, helpful, or positive happening in this now-moment.

Gratitude transforms our negative passivity into positive activity; it awakens and uplifts our consciousness. Too often we drift through our lives as if in a reverie. Things happen all around us, but we barely notice. We become so acclimated to our jobs, material objects, relationships, and situations that we cease to focus on or enjoy them. We take our lives—and everything and everyone in them—for granted.

Gratitude, then, is about bolstering our awareness, sensitivity, and attention. Earlier, in our discussion of awareness and being fully present in the moment, we explored how awareness, when understood and approached properly, leads to a positive fullness, as opposed to a dispiriting emptiness. When we are positively centered in the moment, gratitude is often the dominant feeling. We are noticing and filling our conscious awareness with appreciation. This kind of active, positive attentiveness generates a greatly heightened awareness.

There is nothing artificial or false about this. Gratitude is the practice of observing or remembering the *truth*. It isn't a denial or fantasy. If your boyfriend is short, gratitude isn't pretending he's tall. Nor does it require you to deny that his height is a negative (if it is for you, that is). Instead it's remembering to balance this "negative" with his positive qualities. He may be short, but he's handsome, or kind, or smart. Whatever it may be. Practicing gratitude also assists us in contextualizing and diluting negative thoughts—even accurate ones—by drowning them in a sea of positive ones. Gratitude vigorously asserts the fullness of reality by filling our awareness with positive truth.

Gratitude does *not* require denying unpleasant things. Elie Wiesel doesn't practice gratitude by denying the Holocaust. But he makes sure that in his daily life, the grief and horror are contextualized; he never forgets to also remember and even savor all of the good he's experienced. If Wiesel can find reasons to be grateful, then we all can.

Why Gratitude Works

Obviously, gratitude is a form of positive thinking. We already know that it's vital to ensure that our positive thoughts far outnumber our negative ones.

Most important, gratitude effectively resets hedonic adaptation—the tendency to rapidly adjust to new sensory, physiological, or circumstantial changes. Hedonic adaptation is an unconscious process. For example, we eventually tune out the sound of a leaky faucet we can't afford to fix or adjust to living with a minor but chronic ache in our body—all without making any overt attempt to do so. It just happens "naturally." The good side of hedonic adaptation is that it can help us adjust to negative circumstances: even a formally wealthy person, acclimated to the finest things in life, can eventually adjust to a life of poverty. Unfortunately, the inverse is also true: we adapt too quickly to all the good things in our lives, and therefore effectively ignore them. We start looking for a new partner because we've essentially forgotten all the good qualities of the one we have; we seek out new jobs or travel adventures because we've grown too accustomed to our current location; we want shinier, flashier toys, gadgets, clothes, or objects even though the ones we've got are still perfectly useful, perhaps even beautiful.

Practicing gratitude reminds us of the good parts of our lives, partners, jobs, or objects. Hedonic adaptation applies only when we sleepwalk through life, unconsciously allowing ourselves to drift from moment to moment, experience to experience. Sometimes this can be used in a positive way: for example, I have no wish to dwell consciously upon how much physical pain my body is in, but too often this is not so good. It inevitably leads to a seriously sour state of mind. Further, as the studies above suggest, by breaking through our hedonic autopilot, we can easily and naturally curb our endless need to accumulate more and more experiences and objects. We appreciate what we already have so much more. That, in turn, decreases negative emotions such as envy and avarice.

This virtuous cycle helps us live more fully present in the moment. Practicing gratitude allows us to appreciate, savor, and enjoy whatever we're doing or have already done. The ability to notice, appreciate, and savor the elements of life are crucial for boosting our well-being. Just as importantly, it also keeps us from always needing to look forward for that next, future stimulation by curbing our relentless desire. Above all, it helps us lead more mindful lives in the here and now.

Beyond that, gratitude counteracts our innate bias toward dwelling on negative events. Recall the studies on memory discussed in chapter 7, "Releasing the Past." Since we tend to remember adverse and traumatic events more easily than positive or happy ones, we must make a conscious effort to balance this out. If we don't, then we're *choosing* a negatively biased perception of reality. In other words, *not* practicing gratitude is denying reality. An authentic life requires the conscious remembering of all the good things we've experienced.

Finally, gratitude takes us that much closer to bliss. As the English writer G. K. Chesterton wrote in his biography of St. Francis of Assisi, "Gratitude produced . . . the most purely joyful moments that have been known to man." There is something inherently exultant about savoring our positive experiences. As we'll soon see, it's a feeling that leads us ever so gently on the path toward even more elevated states of consciousness.

The Experiment: Giving Thanks

There are several variations for practicing gratitude. Choose the one(s) that work best for you. You can alternate your practice, do all four different variations, or stick with just one.

1. The fastest and easiest method is to make an informal daily commitment to recall at least one positive thing that has happened in the last twenty-four hours or one person, event, quality, or experience for which you feel gratitude. It can be something minor or major, personal or impersonal (such as for a beautiful sunset); whatever occurs to you. It needn't be pegged to a specific time of the day or done as a formal process. Even a few seconds per day is a great start. Just dwell on something for which you feel gratitude, whenever, wherever, and forever how long it occurs to you. Because this variation is so short and quick, it's crucial to commit to doing it at least once per day to maximize effectiveness.

2. A deeper and more formal variation is to set aside a significant block of time—at least ten to thirty minutes once per week—to write in your

Bliss Journal. You can either create a list of all the positive things that you have experienced in the last week—things for which you are grateful right now, in this moment—or you can write a personal letter to someone who has impacted your life positively. That impact need not have occurred in the previous week; it can be from any period. You need not actually send the letter. You are most likely to remember to do this practice if you schedule a specific time for it each week. For example, every Monday evening after dinner or every Saturday morning while having that first cup of coffee.

3. It can be satisfying to express gratitude directly to someone for whom you feel thankful. You may choose to send the letter you wrote. If you haven't written a letter or prefer not to express yourself that way, you can tell the recipient about your positive feelings of gratitude either in person, over the phone, or electronically. Often these interactions can be rewarding for both parties, as you can also see the positive impact your gratitude has on others. Of course, you should do this only if you feel comfortable. Still, imagine a world in which people routinely expressed gratitude to one another!

4. Practice incorporating spontaneous statements of gratitude into as many of your interactions as possible. Make it a point to express appreciation to others whenever it feels appropriate.

You might even try inserting small thoughts or verbal statements of gratitude during difficult moments. For example, short-circuit potentially fraught situations by taking a moment to express, either silently or out loud, appreciation about a quality of the person with whom you're in conflict. Notice how it can help gently nudge the mood, conversation, or circumstance in a more constructive direction.

Online

Additional videos and resources for this chapter are available at www.theblissexperiment.com.

CHAPTER 14

Planting the Seeds of Bliss

If you think you can do a thing or think you can't do a thing, you're right.

—*Henry Ford, American automobile manufacturer (1863–1947)*

Affirmations are positive statements of truth that we aspire to incorporate into our lives.

They share similarities with practices such as awareness, optimism, and gratitude but also at least one crucial difference: they penetrate much deeper, helping us take the next step to bliss.

In the past few chapters, we've discovered several strategies and techniques for purifying our mental river and helping us gain mastery over our conscious mind. These are all effective and essential practices. Nonetheless, by themselves, they aren't enough. While they improve, even outright manifest, regular happiness, they can't connect us directly with pure bliss. This is because everyday happiness, as we call it on the Happiness Scale, stems primarily from cultivating a positive *mental and emotional* state.

Bliss exists on a deeper plane. It is a *spiritual* state far beyond our mind and emotions. Ultimately, bliss is much more than an abundance of happiness. It's a new category of consciousness that exists on a higher octave of human experience. As indispensable as optimism and gratitude are—we wouldn't have made it this far without them—it takes an entirely new set of tools to help us break through to the next level.

The Story

George is a huge, hulking guy. He stands about six foot five and weighs at least 250 pounds. He grew up in Mississippi, then spent nearly a decade in the army. He still wears his hair high and tight. He's tough, blunt, and no-nonsense. His last posting, prior to leaving the army, was Fort Irwin near Barstow, California. Although George hailed from the Deep South, he found that he liked California very much—especially the desert areas—so he chose to stay there after his military discharge. George and I met when he attended one of my meditation workshops.

He was an instantly likeable guy. I particularly appreciated his straightforward, honest demeanor. He said what he thought, no sugarcoating or carefully phrased tiptoeing around his point. Whenever he felt that I'd said something stupid or incomprehensible, he didn't hold back from challenging me. My kind of guy.

After the workshop, before he drove two hours back to the desert, George invited me next door for coffee. He explained that he wanted to learn meditation because he was having difficulties finding and sustaining a good relationship. He realized that at least part of the problem was that he could be a little too aggressive, even wound up, and this tended to scare off or alienate most of the women he'd met. He'd read about meditation and figured it might help mellow him.

Since George is the type that demands results right away and was looking for ways to accelerate his progress, I suggested that he pair his meditation practice with affirmations. After explaining to him how they worked, being sure to mention a few of the more interesting scientific studies, we selected one that seemed particularly suited to his relationship issues. A constant theme in the feedback he'd received from women was that he was a bit insensitive to their needs and feelings. Therefore, we decided that he would work with an affirmation taken from a book that I happened to have in my car.

This was the affirmation George chose:

By sensitivity to others' realities, I keep myself in readiness to perceive the truth no matter what garb it wears.

Two months later, I received an email from George. He told me that he had been practicing it every day. He had even written it down on sticky notes and posted them on his bathroom mirror, the refrigerator, and his car dashboard. Two weeks after he started working with the affirmation, he went out with a woman whom he'd dated the prior year.

He wrote, "The whole date, I kept reminding myself of the affirmation, but I was kinda nervous, so all I could remember of it was *be sensitive to others' realities.* So I just kept saying that in my head the whole night, especially when she gave me that look I get when the ladies are ticked off at something I said. We had a great time and have been seeing each other since. I'm still doing meditating and affirming every day. Thanks a bunch, my friend, your magic voodoo works!"

The Science

While often seen as excessively self-helpy, affirmations are anything but New Age. They are based on the neural operations inside our brain. One of the accepted truths of neurology is "Neurons that fire together wire together," also known as Hebbian theory. Visualize a dry piece of flat land. When it rains, water begins cutting a path through the ground. At first it is a small channel, but as more water runs through it, the deeper the furrow becomes. In turn, this allows more and more water to flow through the same pathway with less resistance.

Affirmations, when practiced correctly, reinforce a chemical pathway in the brain, strengthening the connection between neurons, making them more likely to conduct the same message again. Neurons that are routinely fired in a specific pattern strengthen their bonds, "wiring together" in a complex network that will be automatically set off whenever triggered properly.

There are a number of scientific studies that show the effectiveness of affirmations. A 1998 study published by the American Psychological Association showed that doing affirmations stops the process of rumination that often leads to depression. Affirmations were an effective way for practitioners to gain enough control over their minds that they could then redirect their thought energies in more positive directions. The researchers even speculated that affirmations alone might be powerful enough to reverse depression. (A 2006 European study confirmed that affirmations gave subjects better and more efficient "mental control" compared to those who don't use them.)

Affirmations also improve academic performance. An encouraging study published in *Scientific American* found that African-American school-children who practiced affirming their integrity and self-worth scored higher on tests and received better grades at the end of the semester than those who didn't. The increase was so substantial that it almost eliminated a previously measured performance and grade gap between white students and African-American students attending the same school. Similarly, a study published in the prestigious journal *Science* demonstrated that college-age women who did affirmations closed the traditional math and science performance gap with men.

More good news for women: research published in the *Journal for the Scientific Study of Religion* concluded that affirmations help women improve their body image, which, in turn, helps them to feel better about themselves overall.

Affirmations also have a encouraging effect on our physical health. A study conducted at the University of California at Los Angeles demonstrated that affirmations have a positive effect on breast cancer survivors. Practitioners reported less stress and fewer adverse physical symptoms from the disease and its treatments.

UCLA researchers also conducted a different study on healthy people under ordinary, everyday stress and discovered that affirmations lowered the subjects' subjective feelings of stress *and* the measurable levels of the stress-producing hormone cortisol in their bodies.

Affirmations can even boost business success: according to a study conducted at the Kellogg School of Management at Northwestern University, participants who developed positive self-esteem through affirmation made better business decisions. Specifically, they were more likely to admit when a project or product wasn't working and were faster to reallocate those resources toward more productive avenues.

Affirmations help actualize our potential and greatly bolster the effectiveness of optimistic thinking. A study of two groups of elite athletes with equivalent injury histories and performance measurements found that athletes with a high degree of self-confidence in their abilities sustain fewer injuries than those with lower self-confidence. What's more, those who expressed self-doubt ("I don't know if I can do this" or "I might injure myself here") suffered significantly more injuries than those who told themselves, "I can do this."

The Spirit

Years ago, I loathed affirmations. All I could think of was the *Saturday Night Live* sketch in which Al Franken plays self-help twit Stuart Smalley, host of a TV program called *Daily Affirmation*, crooning such comically cringeworthy sentiments as "I'm good enough, I'm smart enough, and doggone it, people like me!" I couldn't get that out of my head. I felt like a complete idiot every time I was even near someone doing affirmations.

While I still believe that affirmations done incorrectly do indeed have that Stuart Smalley feel, I eventually realized that, done properly, they are powerful and effective. It turns out that affirmations predate the modern self-help movement by about four thousand years; they have long been incorporated into authentic spiritual traditions and are not, thankfully, the invention of 1970s cheesy pseudopsychologists. Additionally, as we saw, there are legitimate scientific theories, based on our understanding of how the brain works, that explain why affirmations work, coupled with a growing body of experimental evidence. Above all, the largest factor in my acceptance of the practice is that, after I got over my hesitation, I found that they actually worked for me.

What Are Affirmations?

Affirmations are positive statements of truth that we aspire to integrate into our lives. This immediately raises an important question: Given that the point of an affirmation is to repeat something to ourselves that is *not* reflective of our current reality, what do we mean when we say they are *true*? Clearly, they can't be true for the person doing the affirming; otherwise it wouldn't be an affirmation, it would be a statement of fact.

An affirmation is a statement of a *universal* truth, not necessarily of local experience. Qualities like love, peace, joy, and wisdom are genuine possibilities for most humans, but that doesn't mean that all seven billion of us currently understand or manifest these qualities equally. They are true in the sense that they are *potentially accessible* to us. It may be a *fact* that I am currently unhappy, but it is a *truth* that I have the potential for happiness, if I could only figure out how to get there.

We might even think of affirmations as the process of setting mental and spiritual goals for ourselves. Just as students in law school are not yet attorneys, in order for them to achieve that, at some point (probably again and again) they had to affirm their interest and then set a concrete plan in motion to make it happen. Nonetheless, at the moment they set that intention, factually speaking, they were *not yet* practicing attorneys. Nor would we expect to them to be.

Our words are extremely powerful, perhaps more so than we realize. What we say to ourselves, and how we say it, is vitally important. They impact *everything*: our worldly success, bodily health, mental well-being, and, above all, our spiritual realization.

Affirmations, then, are the conscious effort to plant positive thoughts and the best-possible outcomes in our mind. The more effectively we can do this, the more likely that's exactly what will happen, just as athletes who fretted that they might get hurt in an upcoming competition, did, and those who told themselves they wouldn't, didn't.

The Bridge to Bliss

Affirmations work on multiple levels. Like optimism and gratitude, they help us exchange negative thoughts for positive ones. Unlike those practices, however, they help us make direct contact with both the subconscious and superconscious minds.

As you may recall, the superconscious mind is the origin of bliss. The subconsciousness is a repository for the thoughts, impressions, and feelings that pass through our conscious mind and are then stored for future use. This is the first way in which affirmations help us. When performed properly, they tunnel down into our subconscious mind, bringing order to the chaos, and effectively replace negative thoughts, habits, feelings, and impressions with positive ones.

Now comes the twist: the reason why affirmations directly connect with bliss. In addition to improving our conscious and subconscious minds, affirmations open us to the highest and rarest form of consciousness, superconsciousness. When we practice affirmations, we make a conscious attempt to notice, feel, and connect with superconsciousness. As we'll see in the following Bliss Experiment, the correct procedure for affirmations includes directly accessing and seeding the superconscious mind.

By themselves, affirmations aren't powerful enough to completely and permanently open superconsciousness for us. But they do provide our first contact with it, like drilling a pilot hole. Later we'll employ more powerful equipment to further open and expand our superconsciousness.

Tips for Working with Affirmations

As I mentioned, affirmations are an ancient practice stretching back over millennia. There is an accumulated body of spiritual wisdom concerning how they should be implemented. The theory may sound complex (and in some cases it is), but for our purposes here, it can be usefully simplified as follows.

Affirmations are most effective when planted in all three levels of consciousness: sub, waking, and super. Each of these has a corresponding eye position. By concentrating on different places while doing them, we can seed the affirmation on all three levels. The eye position associated with everyday waking consciousness is open and looking straight ahead (as you are doing right now as you read this or as you interact with the world in your daily waking life). The eye position that accesses subconsciousness is closed and looking downward, as we do when we sleep, rest, or daydream. The position that accesses superconsciousness is with the eyes closed but looking gently upward toward the point between the eyebrows (sometimes called the third eye or spiritual eye in various literatures). This is the seat of superconsciousness.

The first step is to choose the appropriate affirmation for our goal. As we saw in our review of the scientific literature, affirmations are helpful with just about *everything*, not only happiness or bliss. There are affirmations for success, love, willpower, physical healing, forgiveness, patience, humility, courage, peace, success, creativity—even income or work. For our purposes, we'll focus on affirmations that improve our happiness and directly help us experience bliss. Once we learn the technique, we can use it to improve every aspect of our lives.

Repetition is critical, in two senses. During the session itself, we repeat the affirmation again and again. Secondly, it's important to work with the same affirmation many times over multiple sessions. Remember the adage "Neurons that fire together wire together." The more we repeat it, the more deeply the groove is etched into our mind. Lack of sufficient repetition is one of the main reasons for failure. Work with a single affirmation for at least a month before changing it. Some people use the same one for years.

Great energy and deep concentration are necessary. This practice can't be done on autopilot or while spacing out. Our complete attention, will-power, and interest are required.

To help you remember to do them, it can help to utilize cards, sticky notes, calendars, even an alarm or chime on your mobile phone—whatever cuing system works best for you. Write down the affirmation and place it where you'll see it often, such as on your nightstand, lamp, altar, bathroom mirror, computer, desk, dashboard, or refrigerator.

If you can't say it out loud because people are around you, at least say it mentally with as much energy as possible.

You can do them any time. If you meditate, immediately afterward is a very effective moment, as your mind is awake and receptive. Other conducive times include when you are falling asleep, waking up, doing yoga, walking, exercising, driving, vacuuming, eating, doing the dishes, brushing your teeth, and shaving.

Use affirmations as a defensive weapon. When a negative thought, mood, or situation crops up, a positive affirmation can be used to counteract it. Think of it like playing an inner video game, using the positive affirmation to conquer the forces of negativity.

Finding or Writing Your Affirmations

In the practice session below, I will give you two affirmations: one for happiness, the other for bliss. There are many resources for finding affirmations written by experienced, knowledgeable people. You can find additional affirmations and recommended collections on the companion website for this book.

We can also write our own. If we choose this route, it's essential to construct affirmations correctly. Otherwise they might not only be ineffective, they could even provoke the opposite response. Some guidelines:

- Keep them short and specific. They will be easier to say and remember. They'll also have greater impact without extraneous elements and if they zero in on the precise seed-thought that we are planting.
- Make them positive. Avoid negative phrasing. Affirm what you want, not what you *don't* want. For example, don't say, "I am no longer depressed." Your mind will hear the word *depressed*. Instead affirm, "I am joyful." This reinforces your goal and doesn't confuse your subconscious mind.
- Phrase them in the present tense: for example; "I am in bliss" instead of "I am going to feel bliss." Remember, an affirmation is not a fact but a truth.

The Experiment: Affirming Happiness and Bliss

Here are two sample affirmations. Instructions for use are below.

For happiness: "I am even-minded and cheerful at all times. Joy is my birthright. I radiate happiness to all."

For bliss: "Behind my thoughts and feelings, infinite joy awaits me. The ocean of eternal bliss flows through me, now and forever."

Choose one of the above for this experiment. Later you can find others or write your own. The process:

1. Sit somewhere quiet, where you can focus without distraction.
2. Close your eyes. Keep your spine erect, chest high. Relax completely. Take deep breaths and exhale thrice. Keep your body as motionless as possible. Empty the mind of all restless thoughts, and withdraw it from all sensations of bodily weight, temperature, and sounds.
3. Fill your mind with compassion, determination, and willpower. Cast away anxiety, distrust, and worry. Surrender doubt or disbelief; these are negative affirmations that will undermine your practice.

4. Look straight ahead with your eyes opened or closed. (Keep them open if you have trouble "looking" straight ahead with your eyelids closed.) Say the affirmation out loud in a clear, strong voice and with enthusiastic energy. If circumstances allow, your voice should be louder than your regular speaking volume. Not necessarily shouting but as loud and energetic as you can muster. Repeat it a minimum of three times—but you can do it as many times as you feel.

5. While continuing to repeat the affirmation out loud, slowly begin lowering your voice, making it softer with each repetition. Say it in your normal speaking voice at least once, then whisper it at least once. This quieting process brings it into your subconscious mind.

6. With your eyes closed (if they weren't already), now repeat it *silently*, or mentally only. Behind closed eyelids, have your eyes pointed down, as they would be when you are resting or sleeping. Visualize the affirmation being planted deep into your subconscious. Repeat at least once like this, but you can do it more if you want.

7. Now, still behind close eyelids, raise your eyes so that they are gazing gently upward at the point between the eyebrows. There should be no tension or "scrunching," as if you were looking at a distant mountain peak. Once again, *silently* repeat the affirmation while looking upward. This plants the affirmation in the superconscious mind.

Online

Scan the Microsoft Tag above to view a brief video, "Affirmations," or go to youtube.com/seanmeshorer.

PART 4

Broadening Our Domain

Now that we've come to understand, relate to, and work with our mind in a new way, it's essential that we learn how to properly reinhabit the world around us.

Although bliss is primarily an inward experience, our lives unfold as part of a broad tapestry that weaves together every atom and being in the universe. We can't ignore the outer world; neither should we want to. A negative relationship with the outer world leads to either a solipsistic self-centeredness or an agitated, fearful loneliness, both of which lead us away from our deepest yearnings and Highest Self. We must learn to relate to the external world in the right spirit.

Our outer world, our environment, and the people with whom we come into contact are vehicles for furthering our self-understanding and excavating the hidden bliss within. We can learn to expand our sense of self to include every object, event, and person in the universe, without losing our balance or inward orientation toward our Highest Self. This redefines and reinterprets the traditional distinctions between the internal and external. In so doing, we skillfully dissolve the false barrier between our inner and outer worlds, allowing the possibility for unity, wholeness, and completeness. Every moment becomes an opportunity for the discovery of bliss.

CHAPTER 15

Environment, Vibration, and Inspiration

Environment is stronger than willpower.

—*Paramhansa Yogananda*

It can be easy to overlook the obvious: we live in and act through our physical environments. We don't have thoughts, feelings, and experiences in a vacuum; they happen while we're interacting with the world around us. Our environment includes *everything* in our physical surroundings: objects, sights, sounds, smells, designs, and, above all, people. It includes where we live, the space in which we work, the music we listen to, the movies we watch, the objects we own, and even the clothes we wear. We are greatly influenced by our surroundings, whether we're consciously aware of it or not. It makes sense, then, that the environments we choose for ourselves go a long way toward influencing our happiness.

Paying better attention to our physical environment—weeding out the negative before it impacts us—pays quick dividends, mentally and spiritually. Learning to see our environment as vibrations of consciousness assists us in breaking our hypnotic spell of material objects and instills in us the powerful spiritual insight essential for bliss.

The Story

Hal, who is divorced and in his sixties, has been meditating and doing gentle yoga for two years. He is enthusiastically committed. He organizes his daily life around these practices, making sure to leave enough time in the early morning before work and in the late evening before bed for meditation and attending a neighborhood yoga class geared toward seniors at least three times per week. He also participates in spiritual groups and events on a regular basis. For all his effort, Hal felt like he wasn't making enough progress. He was lonely and depressed.

He and I spent many hours talking, going over the details of his practice, what was going on in his personal life, his job—everything. We met after events I led or for coffee in the afternoon. Hal mostly seemed together. He had a solid grasp of the underlying principles and did the practices correctly, though he did jump around a lot in our conversations. I chalked it up to enthusiasm combined with inarticulateness. As ideas popped into his head, he couldn't help but blurt them out. There didn't seem to be anything "wrong" with him. We all have our personality quirks.

I thought that Hal mostly needed to relax. My guess was that his feeling of stagnation was largely due to overconscientiousness and being too hard on himself. I wondered if he wasn't making himself depressed by constantly comparing himself to others or some idealized end goal. I had to admit, however, that for all our discussions, I couldn't quite put my finger on the problem—until he invited me over for dinner.

From the second I walked into his condo, I was shocked. It looked like a bomb had exploded. Magazines, newspapers, clothes, and dirty dishes were everywhere. The furniture was ratty and run-down. (Hal made decent money; he wasn't wealthy, but he definitely wasn't poor.) His bed was unmade; books, towels, and debris were scattered across it. Used pots with half-eaten food were piled in the sink. A dozen empty CD cases were open next to his stereo. *Every* picture on the wall hung crookedly. The whole scene looked like it could have doubled as a movie set for a gross-out comedy. It was so ridiculous that I kept wondering if I was being Punk'd or if he'd forgotten to tell me had been robbed last night. Yet Hal conversed as if it were all perfectly normal, even as he casually pushed a pile of crap off his couch and straight onto the floor to make room for me to sit.

I saw Hal's struggles in a new light. It occurred to me that he was always slightly disheveled when I saw him. Then there was the way his mind kept jumping from topic to topic. Anyone content to live in this cluttered environment had to have a cluttered mind. If I lived in that environment, I'd be depressed too! Not to mention why he was lonely: I could barely stand to be there, even though I was his friend and committed to helping. I can't imagine that any date who came over would want a repeat engagement. No friend would willingly choose to hang out there, either. My primary concern, however, wasn't the effect this environment had on others; it was the impact it had on him.

The experience in his apartment made me curious about other environments where he spent his time. Hal worked in the local branch of a midsized insurance agency. Though he had only a desk in an open room there—which, he assured me, was sufficiently public that it didn't look anything like his condo—he did tell me that business was suffering lately. Due to the economy, people were carrying only the minimum amounts of insurance. Additionally, some of major corporations had launched national advertising and branding campaigns that had taken a lot of his company's business. There had been layoffs the previous eighteen months, and his boss was replaced recently. The new guy was cold, driven, and unfeeling. The workplace was tense. Hal no longer enjoyed his work at all, although he didn't think he could afford to retire just yet.

It was clear that Hal's environments were not helping him. No wonder he felt as he did.

The Science

From the macro perspective, evolution is the ultimate environmental influence. Every form of life—homo sapiens being only the most recent—is continually influenced by and even created by our environment. Everything about us: our body, its shape, our brain, how the body functions—just *everything*—is the result of adaptation and natural selection. We're all the direct effect of inconceivably ancient, massive, and utterly pervasive environmental shaping.

At the human scale, science has demonstrated innumerable ways in which we are deeply affected by our environments. A few examples out of thousands:

- There is an entire (somewhat evil) science dedicated to figuring out how to prod shoppers into spending more. Certain types of music prompt us to linger longer or leave more quickly. How stores are designed and where merchandise is displayed greatly influences our buying decisions.
- Even color schemes are used to manipulate us: blue creates feelings of serenity and trustworthiness, while red is associated with power and warmth. Yellow stimulates and energizes.

Sounds of all kinds, especially music, hugely influence us. We all know that certain songs impact whether we feel happy or sad, mellow or hyper. That's just the tip of the iceberg:

- There is evidence that one way to combat depression might be to regulate the music we listen to, ensuring that it is happy and positive.
- Another study found that when pregnant women listened to soothing music, it lessened feelings of stress, depression, or anxiety.
- Amusingly, a town in Nevada blasts hard rock music every night in April. This is the most effective way they've found—better than pesticides—to defend against an annual invasion of a nasty species of crickets. Fittingly, this species, called "Mormon Crickets," hates rock music so much they won't enter the town while it plays!

The things we watch and take in visually impact us greatly, too:

- Psychologists found that watching negative images like the September 11 attacks not only induces depression but also profoundly affects performance. Subjects who watched a short video filled with September 11 imagery were given a math test immediately after. They scored significantly worse than those who watched cartoons.
- In a different study, the *Journal of Broadcasting & Electronic Media* found that watching too much television news exacerbates depression.
- A meta-review of virtually every published study on the effects of video games found that people who spend a lot of time playing violent games exhibit more aggression and less kindly behavior in daily life. They also exhibit a higher incidence of aggressive thoughts and feelings.

- Laughing at funny movies decreases stress, whereas watching tense movies increases it. The results linger for hours, sometimes days.

The good news is that numerous studies demonstrate that merely looking at or (even better) immersing oneself in a natural environment greatly improves our moods, performance, and health:

- Subjects who spent time in nature compared to those confined to urban environments reported higher levels of happiness and well-being.
- A different study found that stressed individuals don't need to immerse themselves in nature physically to feel better. Just *looking at* nature scenes boosted their feelings of affection, friendliness, playfulness, and elation. Those subjected to ugly urban scenes showed higher levels of stress and fear.
- Numerous studies have found that our geographical location, including climate, environment, and setting (for example, urban versus rural) greatly affect our happiness.

Even when confined to "unnatural" environments, as many of us are, the details of our man-made surroundings have a major impact on our well-being:

- The type of workplace lighting has an enormous impact on productivity and well-being. High-flicker fluorescent lighting systems lower productivity, generate fatigue, and lead to more health complaints from employees.
- Subterranean environments with little exposure to natural sunlight negatively change our hormonal balance and brain chemistry over the course of a year.
- Numerous studies prove the benefits of light therapy (exposure to artificial light) for mental health, especially depression. There is even a medically recognized illness: seasonal affective disorder, or SAD.
- Researchers in Geneva, Switzerland, found that flashing test subjects with different colors of light for short periods created major shifts in the subjects emotional responses to vocal recordings.

A critically important study, published in *Gerontologist*, tied together many disparate aspects. Researchers found that we can radically improve the happiness of nursing home residents—especially those who are agitated or dissatisfied—by refining the visual, sound, and olfactory environments, including offering access outdoors. These small, low-cost changes quickly and dramatically boosted seniors' levels of well-being.

The Spirit

There is no *I* that exists independently. The boundaries between "us" and "the world" aren't as firm and clear as we think. Our lives require constantly—every second—inhaling air from outside, circulating it, and then exhaling it. We need food, water, and sunlight to survive; perhaps light most fundamentally of all. The entire ecosystem and food chain are based on photosynthesis, the process of converting light into energy. Without light, there could be no Earth. Moreover, our bodies also directly need it to manufacture vitamin D, without which they deteriorate. Most of our culture is based on seeing. Sight requires light. That's the *definition* of seeing. While it's true that a single individual can survive without seeing, that's only because the majority help that person compensate. If *none* of us had light to see, civilization would disintegrate, and we would rapidly become extinct. Sounds, smells—these too are equally necessary to survive, let alone thrive. As biologists might say, we are an open system. The atoms that constitute the world around us continually flow into, around, and back out of us, circulating millions of time per *second*. We are our environment, and our environment is us. It's one giant, merged system.

It's an inescapable fact, then, that our environment massively affects our consciousness. We've all been in places, situations, or around people that have left us feeling sad or happy, fearful or safe, calm or agitated. What we may not realize is just how easily influenced we are on a daily basis even by seemingly innocuous things. It's essential that we pay attention to this, just as we pay attention to our inner thoughts and feelings.

Good Vibrations

Because our surroundings are so important, it's critical that they be as uplifting as possible. While not every aspect of this is under our control—often we have no choice but to cope with suboptimal situations—there is also a great deal that we can do, perhaps more than we realize.

The key to evaluating and improving our immediate environment is to learn to see past the surfaces and tune into the underlying vibrations. Every sight, sound, smell, taste, object, and person is really a vibrational pattern. As physics teaches, even objects that *appear* solid—a rock or the floor—aren't really solid at all. They are mostly empty space that seems solid because the particles inside the atoms are whizzing around at break-neck speeds, giving the illusion of fullness, just as a ceiling fan or helicopter blade spinning at maximum velocity appears to form a continuous, solid surface. Our entire world is in motion. With motion comes vibration. Everything and everyone is constantly creating and emanating vibrations. Different patterns, frequencies, and speeds create the illusions of different objects.

Relating to our outer environment not in terms of the surface but the underlying vibration is another way of *shedding* externalities. By looking beneath the surface of things—whether objects or people—we enhance our ability to feel what's really going on, what something really means, what effect it's really having on us. Seeing our environment as a series of vibrations, surrounding and filling us, helps us develop sensitivity and awareness.

This is an important spiritual practice in its own right, as it helps us tune into the world as vibrations of consciousness, requiring that we develop our deepest, intuitive faculties. We finally learn to see everything—the entire "material" world—not as something grossly physical but rather as condensed pulsations of consciousness. When we do, our own consciousness shifts in remarkable ways: the world takes on deeper resonance, becoming unimaginably vibrant and alive. We have transcended the material realm and journeyed into the spiritual.

Inspiration Is Everywhere

Once we relate to the world as vibrations of consciousness, new under-standings and possibilities emerge. Importantly, we finally gain a real un-derstanding of not only how our environments affect us but also what must be done to improve them.

Because negative, harmful vibrations are so disturbing and disruptive, often it is easier to sense them above all else. We might suddenly realize just how much negativity surrounds us. The good news is that positive, uplifting vibrations are also everywhere. Beauty, simplicity, creative genius, peacefulness, clarity, harmony, loving kindness: these are all indications of positive vibrations of consciousness. Wherever these qualities exist, uplift-ment follows. We need only to seek them out.

This kind of positive vibration is far from being the exclusive domain of the natural world. In fact, the highest vibrations are human generated. To a certain extent, the beauty and wonder of the natural world pales in comparison to what humans can achieve. Humanity, at its best, is closer to God, Spirit, Pure Consciousness—however we want to put it—than any-thing in creation. Only humanity has the capability of connecting directly and consciously to the highest planes of existence.

This is actually what genius is: when humanity makes direct connec-tion with the Divine, becoming a channel for expressing the highest and best in that one area, or for that moment in time.

When we see the world in this way, inspiration and spiritual upliftment are everywhere. I've had meals created by genius chefs that were as inspir-ing as any Sunday sermon ever preached. Eating their food was like ingest-ing their passion, creativity, and inspiration. The great paintings, music, architectural masterpieces—even certain jewelry, clothing, and cars—all can be Divinity in material form. They represent human beings reaching upward, making contact with the highest consciousness and then bringing that experience back to us so that we can all feel it.

Making It Real

If the above seems too vague or lofty, here's a concrete example:

I recently met a horologist (an expert in time and time-keeping devices). Like many people, I don't often wear a watch, instead relying on my mobile phone. Showing my ignorance, I asked why anyone would buy insanely expensive watches; many over $20,000, some over $100,000. He admitted that it was sometimes silly: some watches are mass-produced crap slapped with fancy brand names, peddled to status-seeking people through slick marketing campaigns. However, there are many expensive watches that are handmade—filled with *thousands* of tiny components and intricate moving parts—by genuine artisans. It can take three to twelve months to build a single watch! Those watchmakers have poured their hearts and souls into it. Their creativity, passion, patience, love of beauty, and attention to detail are astounding. Therefore, wearing such a timepiece is a celebration of genius. As the horologist explained to me, those kinds of watches aren't about knowing the time—a mere *fact*—they are about one's *relationship* with time.

My point isn't that we should own expensive watches; I still don't often wear one. The point is that *everything* in our environment emanates a vibration. By learning to tune into and become aware of those vibrations, we can positively impact our happiness.

One can live in a very simple place with simple tastes and few possessions and be perfectly blissful. Most of the spiritual geniuses in history live in just such a way. However, even Jesus or Buddha didn't live in disheveled environments, eating rotten foods, and wearing unkempt rags draped on their unwashed bodies. Calm, peaceful environments make a difference. Excessively dirty, disheveled, disorganized, haphazard surroundings harm us. Clutter and having too much stuff pull us down. Better to have fewer things with a high vibration than lots of junk. Tune into objects or media that convey creativity, love, genius, or upliftment. Beware of books, music, film, television, or video games that exude negative vibrations.

The Experiment: Tuning into Vibrations

Understanding the vibrations of consciousness that objects, people, media, and environments emanate requires practice.

Part A

1. Look around your current environment, wherever you are right now. Identify one item—an object, song, painting, person; anything that captures your attention—and focus on it with complete concentration.

2. Can you feel or describe the vibrations it emanates beneath the surface? Does it uplift or depress you? Does it emit positive vibrations such as peacefulness, beauty, and harmony, or negative ones such as agitation, ugliness, and disharmony?

3. Identify a second item in your environment that emanates the opposite vibrations of the first. If you first focused on something positive, look around and see if you can find something negative, and vice versa. The goal is to develop your discernment and understanding by noticing the contrasts between things.

Part B

1. Make it a goal and habit to continually evaluate the vibrations of consciousness from both your macro environments and the specific items within it. Try to make it second nature to see beneath the surface of every object and environment, feeling it as a vibratory pattern of consciousness, not as something physical or material.

2. Make a conscious effort to weed out negative objects, media, and environments as much as possible. Replace them with positive, higher vibration ones. Be sure to evaluate all of the places, media, and objects with which you spend significant time.

Online

Scan the Microsoft Tag above to view a brief video, "Positive and Negative Environments," or go to youtube.com/seanmeshorer.

CHAPTER 16

People, Relationships, and Kindness

The best portion of a good man's life is his little, nameless, unremembered acts of kindness and love.
—*William Wordsworth, English poet (1770–1850)*

In the last chapter, we focused mostly on the nonhuman vibrations of consciousness intrinsic to our environment. However, our environment encompasses much more than our physical location or the objects around us—most important, it includes all the people with whom we interact.

Earlier, we explored why romantic relationships and the soul-mate model of love are not only unfulfilling but also often counterproductive. That doesn't mean that human relationships are unimportant. Far from it. As Aristotle said, "Man is by nature a social animal"; as such, our relationships are extraordinarily important in our quest for meaning, happiness, and bliss. By relationships, however, I don't exclusively mean our romantic or sexual ones. We'll explore the entire spectrum, including family, friends, children, coworkers, life partners, pets, and even the casual relationships we have with acquaintances and strangers. Learning to cultivate strong, positive relationships is vastly important for genuine happiness. If we don't understand the value of friendship, most especially how to be a friend to others, we are missing an essential human experience.

There's more to it as well. While it's true that we receive a great deal from our relationships—most of all a big boost in happiness—from the perspective of bliss, our motivations are loftier. The paradox of bliss is that while it's a wholly inner experience (therefore not dependent on receiving *anything* from anyone or anything), the ability to emanate kindness and develop positive relationships is a key indicator of our ability to attain and experience bliss.

Bliss requires us to surrender our selfish desires, including the mistaken need for external rewards. Learning how to cultivate kindness and warm relationships helps us practice this by providing a vehicle through which we give fully of ourselves. In turn, we deepen our feeling of connectedness, not only to one another but also to the very fabric of the universe. Of course, the ultimate irony is that when we learn to give without the need for or expectation of anything in return, the inevitable by-product is that we're certain to attract a large number of friends—and all the attendant benefits.

The Story

Aleksei immigrated to the United States with a green card procured for him by a technology company in California's Silicon Valley. Aleksei has extraordinary computer programming skills, the kind that gains one employment anywhere. He had always dreamed of living in America and couldn't wait to leave Russia, which he found dreary and depressing. Although moving to the States fulfilled a long-standing goal, it came with a price. He had to leave everything behind in Russia, including his mother, father, two brothers, a lifetime of friends, and even his West Siberian laika, a small hunting dog.

Aleksei never regretted his decision to leave Russia, but it wasn't long before he felt lonely. He never built much of a social life, spending most of his time working. After five years, when his contract came up for renewal, Aleksei decided to move to West Hollywood, an area known for having a large Russian population. He felt it might provide him the best of both worlds: a familiar Russian community where he'd find fellow expatriates and the opportunity to live in the middle of iconic and dynamic Hollywood.

Unfortunately, once Aleksei arrived in LA, he discovered that he had little in common with the Russian community there. Many of the expats were older and seemed stuck in the traditional ways of thinking, almost as if they were trying to re-create their Russian village lives. Aleksei, still young and thoroughly Americanized, couldn't relate. The other problem is that LA can be a lonely city. It's spread out geographically and mentally; for introverts, it can feel isolating. Aleksei was anything but outgoing by nature, or at least by habit, since he had spent most of his life interacting more with his computer than with other humans.

Somewhere along the way, Aleksei stumbled across *Autobiography of a Yogi* by Paramhansa Yogananda. The book electrified him. He saw that I was teaching a meditation class based on Yogananda's techniques at the Bodhi Tree Bookstore in West Hollywood and decided to attend. A few weeks later, we met for coffee. Aleksei shared how alone he felt. He was more than a little depressed too, perhaps even beyond the common Russian dourness. I observed that Aleksei was also quite brusque, even rude, to people and exuded a kind of arrogance. I seldom saw him act kindly or charitably toward others unless he wanted something from them.

Even in Russia, he'd had few friends. Aleksei met plenty of people, but the relationships never developed. He had never really been in love, although over the years, he'd had several unrequited crushes. He'd had only one semiserious relationship, but even that, he felt, had been based more on convenience and mutual loneliness than on a deep-seated bond.

Recently, he had started hanging out with a guy named Gerry, whom he met through work. (Aleksei was working as an independent contractor for Gerry's employer.) They went to a bar together after work, saw a comedy show on the Sunset Strip another time, played Xbox at Gerry's house every now and then, and seemed on their way to forming a friendship. One day they discussed politics. Aleksei apparently didn't appreciate Gerry's liberal attitudes. As an expatriate Russian, he was highly sensitive to any viewpoints that struck him as overly "socialist," although Gerry wasn't socialist, just a Democrat. He also took offense when Gerry said he didn't feel like he was in a position to go to his boss and recommend a raise for Aleksei. Based on these minor offenses, Aleksei stopped returning Gerry's calls, ending their burgeoning friendship.

Aleksei returned to feeling alone. It was clear that he didn't have the first clue about friendship, respect, and even basic kindness. He approached friendship with a great many superficial conditions and expectations. We talked about some of the general principles of friendship and how to be a friend. I directed him to a wonderful book that Yogananda wrote on the topic.

While he never did rekindle his friendship with Gerry, over the next six months, Aleksei spent more and more of his time with our extended spiritual community in LA. It was gratifying to see that he did indeed develop some genuine friendships. He made a concerted effort to be nicer to people, to overlook the small quirks and flaws that we all have, and, most important, to create meaningful, warm relationships with others. The change in his demeanor was noticeable: he was more relaxed, smiled a lot more, and generally felt like a heavy energy around him had lifted.

The Science

The scientific evidence that friendship, strong interpersonal relationships, and social support are key components of happiness and well-being is legion.

Because the United States has erected Supermax prisons designed to hold prisoners in extreme isolation for long periods of times, researchers now have concrete evidence as to the effects of largely forgoing human contact:

- Studies suggest that lack of contact with other human beings engenders extreme mental illness in most people. We become catatonic, hallucinate, and generally lose the ability to function.
- A 1992 study of fifty-seven prisoners of war who endured six months of isolation, on average, were examined using tests similar to an electroencephalogram (EEG). Subjects developed mental abnormalities not unlike what doctors see in patients who have sustained a traumatic brain injury.

Of course, although most of us require human contact, the quality of that contact is essential. Numerous studies have demonstrated that we "catch" emotions from one another. Spending time around sad people tends to make us sad, while being around happy people cheers us up, hanging with angry people can provoke us to anger, and so forth. Moods and emotions are constantly transmitted back and forth. Scientists publishing in the journal *Psychiatric Research* discovered that we can catch someone else's emotions in as little as *one second*. And the stronger the mood, emotion, or disposition we're exposed to (say, extreme sadness or anger at one end, or jubilation and peacefulness at the other), the more deeply we are affected.

Proof that our relationships matter a great deal comes from the gold standard of scientific studies: the previously mentioned long-term study that has tracked the life progress of 268 subjects since 1937:

- Those who spent too much time alone or had a poor quality of interpersonal relationships struggled emotionally, regardless of whether they were wealthy, famous, or powerful.
- The happiest subjects were those who sustained meaningful, healthy relationships with friends and family.
- A parallel study found that those with strong relationships of all kinds were much happier than those who didn't have them, even if the members of the "loner" group were far richer and had abundant resources to distract themselves.

Researchers went to Bangladesh, one of the poorest and most densely populated countries in the world, but where reported levels of happiness are higher than those found in many developed countries. They wanted to understand why this could be. The most salient explanation was their strong and abundant social relationships. The people were poor, but their relationships were rich. They put an enormous amount of time and effort into cultivating positive interpersonal, romantic, intergenerational, and intergroup relationships—far more than the average Westerner.

Similarly, inhabitants of Okinawa, Japan, are known for exceptionally long life spans. Okinawans have unusually close relationships, and their society has built strong systems for social support. That and a healthy diet are the two variables that explain not only the length of their lives but also the high levels of happiness.

Traditional scientific studies conducted in Western laboratories demonstrate this truth from another perspective. According to the re-search:

- Very happy people are highly social and have stronger social relationships, more friends, and wider social networks compared to unhappy people.
- Those with abundant social relationships are physically healthier.
- People with strong social networks are generally more successful in busi-ness and at attaining life goals than those without.
- Happiness and friendship form a virtuous circle: being happy magnetizes friends to us; the more friends and warm relationships that we have, the greater our happiness.

The Spirit

There is no question that warm, loving relationships do wonders for our happiness and peace of mind. Our ancestors quickly discovered that com-munities of people working in concert have a much greater chance of survival than working apart. Without the help of others, we'd have to grow our own food, make our clothes, build our shelter, create and manufacture our own technologies, and generally entertain and amuse ourselves. There would be no advanced technology whatsoever: no car, computers, mobile phones, planes, or iPads. For that matter, no leisure activities, no fun, no anything. Life would be unbelievably hard and unimaginably dreary. There wouldn't be any time for personal development or spiritual growth, either.

There are far more benefits to good relationships than mere survival or to prevent mental deterioration. We need one another to flourish. Positive social bonds help us in times of distress and trauma. Often just having someone we trust to confide in automatically helps us feel better. Relationships, too, provide the opportunity to receive varied opinions; the outlooks, ideas, and feedback of others help us gain perspective, learn, and grow. And, of course, because we do pick up emotions from one another, strong, positive relationships infuse us with warmth, security, laughter, companionship, and joy: the gamut of positive emotions.

Positive relationships aren't subject to hedonic adaptation. While we occasionally end up taking a specific person for granted, more generally, we don't acclimate to people in the same way that we do a smell or shiny new object. Most relationships contain a great deal of intrinsic variation that prevents hedonic adaptation from taking root. Many are episodic; people come to the foreground of our lives and then recede to the background in unpredictable ways. We see someone, have a good time, and then don't see him or her for a while. There's also a huge variation in activities and topics discussed. Even the same activity experienced with different people at different times produces different reactions and interactions. Of course, this is by no means universal. For example, we already know that romantic relationships are the most prone to falling into a predictable background rhythm, which likely accounts for their high rate of dissolution.

Relationships Are an Opportunity

We need to be as vigilant about the people around us as we are with everything in our environment. Really, much more so, since the vibratory consciousness emanating from our fellow humans is even more powerful than most landscape, objects, or environments. Negative people and negative relationships can pull us down very quickly.

Of course, it's not always possible to eliminate contact with negative people. Most of us have obligations—familial, work related, or even with certain friends—that preclude total separation. Still, we can try to reduce those contacts as much as possible.

Fortunately, we can affect others through our own vibrations and consciousness. In this sense, fraught relationships are a blessing: they provide an opportunity for positive transformation for ourselves and the other person. Relationships—good and bad—provide us with a vehicle for practicing emanating uplifted vibrations.

We accomplish this by treating everyone with kindness and friendship whenever possible. Not only does this make most of our interactions much more pleasant, it's a great way to help us conquer selfishness and break down false barriers between the world and ourselves. Practicing friendship and kindness—even to strangers (perhaps *especially* to strangers)—helps us cast aside our ego and infuse our lives with warmth and heartfulness. This also allows us to concentrate much more on what we're giving to others and to the world rather than on what we're receiving. We'll also effortlessly magnetize countless numbers of genuine friends.

Most important, especially for the realization of bliss, positive relationships, consciously cultivated, reinforce our fundamental interconnectedness. Though it may not seem so on the surface, the underlying reality is that everyone is an extension of us. If he or she is happy, we are happy. Treating others with kindness is treating ourselves with kindness. The more we play into the illusion that we are all separate, disconnected beings competing with one another, the more alone and isolated we feel. The more we strive to break down superficial barriers, the greater the feeling of unity and wholeness.

Whenever I find myself being mean or thoughtless to someone, invariably my own negativity rebounds against me. Not only do I feel badly inside but also my behavior usually provokes tangible actions from others that makes things worse. Moreover, if we want the world to be a better place, we have to embody that hope. We can't expect a world free of war, intolerance, and hatred if we ourselves are acting like jerks. On a more personal level, why should we expect people to be nice to us if we aren't nice to them? Just remembering to smile at people and act courteously and considerately make a difference. Every time I make a conscious effort to do this, I'm always surprised to discover all over again how wonderfully people respond. Even if someone occasionally does cop an attitude, I've found that if I don't react negatively but respond with kindness and understanding, it usually dissipates. Even if it doesn't, that's their problem, not yours.

When we fully develop the capacities for kindness, heartfulness, and—above all—giving to others more than worrying about what we receive in return, we take another important step toward bliss. I've never met a single person who's been able to feel bliss consciously (as opposed to someone who occasionally falls into it without understanding how or why it happened) who wasn't also a kindhearted person capable of befriending virtually anyone.

The Experiment

Part A: Be a Friend to Everyone

1. Over the next day, beam warm, positive, kindly energy toward everyone you encounter. Visualize positive vibrations of consciousness flowing from you, enveloping everyone you meet. Smile. Behave like everyone is your friend. If someone is rude to you, respond with extra kindness and understanding. Concentrate on giving your friendship to everyone, regardless of what you receive in return.

2. Afterward, evaluate how you felt doing this and the effect that you had on others. How do you feel internally? What kind of responses did you elicit? Did it enhance or detract from your life?

Part B: Evaluating People Around You

1. Think about the people in your life, especially those with whom you interact the most. Taking everything into account, are they mostly positive, negative, or neutral in their influences upon you?

2. For those that you deem to be negative influences, is there anything that you can do to help them become more positive? Do you wish to try? Practice beaming them with warmth, kindness, friendship, and love, and notice the response.

Online

Additional videos and resources for this chapter are available at www.theblissexperiment.com.

CHAPTER 17

Found in Sixty Seconds

If you want others to be happy, practice compassion. If you want
to be happy, practice compassion.
— *His Holiness the Dalai Lama (b. 1935)*

We've been exploring our relationship to the world around us. In the last
chapter, we looked at the general importance of kindness and cultivating
warm relationships. We learned that kindness and friendship are more
about what we give than receive. While we can treat everyone we meet
as friends, we can develop warm relationships with only a few. There simply isn't enough time or energy to form deep friendships with everyone.
However, one attitude that we *can* cultivate toward all—whether friends,
strangers, or even enemies—is compassion.

In Latin, *compassion* means "cosuffering." It begins with empathy: the
capacity to recognize and share the feelings that another is experiencing.
Compassion is the more vigorous cousin of empathy. Empathy is *understanding* another's feelings, especially sad or negative ones; compassion is
actively wanting to help that person in some way. Compassion is when we
energetically wish that others be free from all suffering.

Compassion is its own distinct feeling, different from distress, sadness,
or even love. Knowing this helps us understand why we must practice
and develop compassion separately from kindness, friendship, and love.
If we cannot feel compassion for another and do not wish to alleviate
that person's suffering, then we are lacking a key ingredient for lasting
happiness and bliss. Compassion gently guides us away from self-centered
behavior and teaches us that genuine happiness cannot unfold while being

indifferent to the suffering of our fellow sentient beings. We simply cannot reach the fullness of our human potential without cultivating this latent capacity.

We can learn compassion quickly and feel its benefits—both for us and for the recipient—in less than sixty seconds. It's *that* simple and powerful.

The Story

Lori is half Native American by ethnicity, though nearly 100 percent by self-identification. Her mother is a full-blooded Native American, her father a "Texican" (slang for a US citizen whose family has lived in Texas for generations but traces his or her ancestry to Mexico). Her grandparents on her mother's side grew up on a reservation, as her mom did until she was a young adult. Her mother met her father when she left the reservation and moved to Texas.

Lori still carried with her a great deal of bitterness about what happened to her people generations ago. White settlers unabashedly stole Native American land. Many tribes were also victimized in countless other ways, including, at times, slaughtered wholesale. Particularly galling to Lori was that infamous period in American history during which the Cherokee, trying to find a peaceful resolution and not enter into yet another war against white America, chose to cooperate with the US legal system. They took two lawsuits to the Supreme Court, both of which they won. Not only did President Andrew Jackson shamefully refuse to enforce the Cherokee victories, he encouraged even more vigorous attacks. For many Native Americans, this was especially bitter, as they had been repeatedly assured of the virtuous nature of the American justice system. Yet their entire nation was forced to move at gunpoint—the notorious Trail of Tears—as they vacated their ancestral lands and were pushed westward into smaller, unfamiliar territory.

Refusing to forget these and other indignities, Lori became extremely hard-hearted about other people's sufferings, especially those she perceived as "mainstream" Americans. A litany of horrific tragedies such as the 1995 Oklahoma City bombing, the 9/11 attacks, and even Hurricane Katrina in 2005 elicited no sympathy from her. If anything, she seemed gleeful, frequently reciting variations of "Payback is a bitch." She saw these, and similar events, as "deserved" punishments for our long list of transgressions. She was downright cheerful when discussing things that particularly devastated white, wealthy people such as Wall Street financial scandals.

This began to change one day as she watched *The Daily Show* with Jon Stewart. He interviewed a group of 9/11 first responders—including people from the police, fire, and heavy equipment departments—all of whom were white. They were also all extremely ill, in pain, and several of whom were dying from their heroic efforts in the immediate aftermath of the attack on the World Trade Center in Lower Manhattan. Incredibly, our government was resisting efforts to provide these deserving heroes the health care and financial support they need. This struck Lori. She saw that these people—traditional, white, "pro-American" authority types—of whom she was generally suspicious, were also being screwed over by our government, in ways not dissimilar to what had happened to her forbearers.

Not long after, she had an unplanned lunch with a coworker—a woman known for her conservative and anti-immigration beliefs. Lori found this offensive, partly because of her father's Texican background. Remembering *The Daily Show*, she uncharacteristically found herself speaking calmly and kindly to this woman. They talked about a wide range of things, including how the woman's family was struggling financially. Her husband had been laid off and couldn't find work. They lived in a high-crime, lower-middle-class neighborhood with their two children. They also talked of their mutual hopes, fears, and challenges. Though Lori certainly didn't exit that lunch agreeing with the woman's political views, she realized that her coworker wasn't malicious. She was just trying to get by as best she could. At one point in their conversation, the woman told her, "You're the first Indian I've talked to." Lori saw that although this person, through no real fault of her own, didn't understand much about her people's background, she was open to dialogue and learning. It helped a lot that Lori behaved with kindness and civility. This simple, unexceptional conversation had a profoundly humanizing effect on both of them.

Lori began to notice her own prejudices. No one alive today had anything to do with what had happened to her people. More importantly, she saw that she could have meaningful conversations with people who held opinions she didn't agree with. They were still human beings, trying to work through their own fears, challenges, and needs. As she thought about it, she realized that her own lack of compassion made her similar to those she railed against: thoughtless, indifferent, and even cruel. Without mutual understanding, the ugliest parts of history were doomed to repeat themselves. Lori vowed to do her best to prevent this, starting with transforming herself.

The Science

Empathy and compassion are objective, provable capacities. It is a widely held misconception—even within the scientific community—that British naturalist Charles Darwin claimed that human nature is competitive, ruthless, and selfish. To the contrary, the father of evolution wrote extensively about empathy and compassion, especially in his books *The Descent of Man* and *The Expression of the Emotions in Man and Animals*. He pinpointed those qualities as widespread and essential behavior found throughout the animal kingdom and the human realm. He even posited that compassion and kindness—*not* ruthless competition—would prove to be the driving forces of natural selection and the basis for individual and communal flourishing.

More recently, Darwin's observations have been confirmed by people like renowned primatologist Frans de Waal, whose research catalogues myriad examples of empathetic behavior throughout the animal kingdom—from mice, to elephants, to chimpanzees. That empathy is deeply ingrained and found in many species is an important discovery, if for no other reason than to counteract the benighted claim that humans are like so many other animals: calculating, competitive, and violent. This false "observation" is often used to rationalize our worst behaviors and justify why there is little hope, or even desirability, for positive change among Homo sapiens. If we insist on looking backward to our animal ancestors (of which I'm not in favor) for behavioral—let alone moral—guidance, there are abundant positive examples that must also be considered.

The science of compassion is being notably furthered at Stanford University's Center for Compassion and Altruism Research and Education.

Research from the center demonstrates that compassion is not only a genuine human capacity but also distinct from emotions such as distress, sadness, and even love. Compassion bolsters our happiness, stimulates the brain's pleasure/reward centers, helps us cope with stress and decreases anxiety, and even increases our immune function. What's more, it can be learned by *anyone*.

Researchers at the University of Haifa in Israel have discovered that there is a strong correlation between the inability to feel compassion and certain types of mental illness. In fact, they posit that a psychopath can be defined as someone entirely devoid of basic levels of compassion.

A critically important 2010 study published in the *Journal of Happiness Studies* found that compassionate behavior can improve the life of the practitioner in as little as *one week*. 719 people were followed for six months. They were broken into two groups. The control group was asked to regularly engage in a neutral writing exercise. The second was instructed to take compassionate actions. Practitioners in the compassionate group showed almost immediate and significant increases in their happiness and self-esteem, while their anxiety and depression declined markedly. No such benefits were found in the control group.

Another study, this one from the pages of the *Journal of Clinical Oncology*, demonstrated the effect that compassion can have on others: doctors who showed as little as *forty seconds* of compassion toward their cancer patients could dramatically alleviate the patients' anxiety levels.

One reason that compassion has lasting effects is that it appears to positively change our brain structure. This was the conclusion of a study that looked at subjects' brains using a scanning technology called functional magnetic resonance imaging (fMRI). Importantly, this same study found that people of all age ranges—from children to the elderly—could learn and practice it.

Additional studies demonstrate that compassion has a variety of practical benefits, including in the workplace, on the athletic field, and in a therapeutic setting:

- Compassionate action by both managers and co-workers boosts employee performance and productivity.

- Empathy and compassion are more effective motivational strategies than criticism and anger.
- Compassionate people engage in more prosocial behaviors such as helping and cooperating with others, and responding to people in distress.

The Spirit

Compassion is essential for bliss. Each of us has suffered, is suffering now, or will suffer in the future. Suffering and our response to suffering are two of the defining qualities of the human experience. Compassion is our ability to recognize suffering in another, coupled with a heartfelt yearning to alleviate that suffering. When compassionate people encounter pain or distress in another, they, too, experience the person's distress and feel compelled to act (or at least have the desire to act) to reduce that person's misery. They know that by doing so, they'll reduce their own suffering.

Lack of empathy and compassion toward others permits us to do monstrous things to one another. To feel compassion is to deemphasize our small, self-centered life and to admit that we can't pursue our own well-being at the expense of others. It's a giant step toward breaking down the artificial barrier between the world and us. It is to conquer, or at least loosen, the bonds of narcissistic self-identity and our fears of others.

Despite the centrality of suffering to the human experience, empathy and compassion are poorly understood and frequently underemphasized. This begs the question, If compassion is not only universal but also quick and easy, why is not more widespread?

Barriers and Misunderstandings

There is a false tendency to believe that we're either innately compassionate or not; we're either born with it or without it. The reality is that we are *all* born with the latent capacity for compassion. It can be learned and practiced. It comes down to a choice: some of us choose to access it more than others.

Additionally, there is a tendency to believe that many people don't "deserve" our compassion. We falsely imagine that withholding compassion is an effective response to abhorrent behavior. Unfortunately, as demonstrated by the research from the University of Haifa, the less compassion we cultivate in ourselves, the more our *own* behavior becomes psychopathic. Worse, this attitude perpetuates the cycle of anger, anxiety, depression, and violence.

Sometimes, too, we encounter (especially in men) the belief that compassion is cowardly or weak. It's also frightening because it requires us to enter into the subjective essence of another human being. To feel compassion is intrinsically intimate. We allow ourselves to feel what they feel, see what they see, and understand what they understand. Doing so opens the possibility that our own worldviews might be challenged, even flipped upside down. Above all, it means we might be forced to acknowledge that someone we dislike or hate is not so different from us. This can be enormously threatening to our egos.

Lori, for example, had tightly constructed her identity around her Cherokee heritage and an unshakeable belief in how her people were wronged and that vengeance against an entire race was richly deserved. To allow herself to feel compassion meant loosening the bonds of identity and surrendering long-cherished beliefs. Empathy also requires surrendering our desire to see others wallow in misery, pain, fear, and endless sorrow. It's no wonder that we all struggle with this.

Compassion doesn't lead to weakness or allow evil to run rampant. Evil must be resisted and fair punishments applied. We can beam all the compassion we can summon onto a violent criminal, but as we're doing so, we'd better also be doing something to stop him. In fact, we might well have to send him our compassion *while* he's safely behind bars. We can even strive to be compassionate soldiers, doing our best to fight and arrest evil without surrendering the need to intervene—even kill—to stop violence, aggression, and hatred.

Benefits of Compassion

No matter our outward duties, what's essential is our interior attitude. If we *wish* suffering upon or derive personal pleasure from those who are clearly suffering greatly then we become nearly as callous and unfeeling as they are. Only suffering people commit terrible crimes. Moreover, we virtually guarantee that the cycles of violence continue, even escalate. Compassion means to understand—however wrongly (even monstrously, disgustingly) someone has come to see, feel, and act—that the only lasting, abiding solution is that his suffering *ceases*, not increases. The less we suffer, the more we learn to access our own highest and noblest feelings. In turn, the better the world around us becomes.

Of course, most suffering isn't so extreme. Most of our fellow humans are not monsters, and their misfortunes don't always affect us directly. If extreme compassion in the most egregious cases seems impossible, we can at least begin by practicing routine compassion toward those who are no threat. Each and every day, we encounter fellow humans who are suffering in small, quiet ways.

Compassion inherently creates connection and bonding, while pulling us outside our own solipsistic, self-centered worries. Anxiety and depression are almost entirely the result of ruminating about our pasts or worrying about the future. Specifically, *our* pasts and *our* futures. Compassion yanks us out of this. We put the focus on others, not ourselves. It breaks the hypnotic spell we cast on ourselves by constantly dwelling on our own problems.

Moreover, compassion reinforces and heightens our feeling of connection to the world around us. It breaks down the barriers that manufacture loneliness.

Being compassionate doesn't require acknowledgment or even understanding from another. We can be compassionate toward another without wanting, needing, or expecting his or her appreciation. It is its own reward.

This means that we can be compassionate no matter what we are doing outwardly. We can be compassionate bosses, nurses, ship captains, teachers, coaches, even soldiers—whatever our occupation or situation. It's an internal state of consciousness wholly under our control. Not a day goes by without there being manifold opportunities to infuse our work, relationships, and encounters with empathy and compassion.

The Experiment (1):
Compassion in Everyday Life

This simple practice is derived from the scientific research that showed how quickly the benefits of compassion are realized.

1. Today or tomorrow, make a conscious decision to act compassionately toward someone for as little as five to fifteen minutes.
2. Actively help or interact with someone in a supportive and considerate way. Examples include (but are not limited to): talking to a homeless person, being more loving to those around you, being kind and supportive to someone you encounter "having a bad day," or interacting positively with store clerks.
3. Make note what you did, how you felt while doing it and in the aftermath, and what kinds of responses it engendered.
4. Make a vow to act compassionately toward others as much as you can as frequently as possible.

The Experiment (2): Visualization

The following guided meditation can be done in conjunction with an ongoing meditation practice (if you don't have one, you will learn it in later chapters) or can be done independently.

1. Begin by sitting in a comfortable position with your eyes closes. Sit with your spine erect, without straining or arching your back.
2. Take a few deep breaths, relaxing your mind and body. Try to feel centered and present here and now, in this room, at this moment.
3. Direct compassionate thoughts to yourself. You can create your own spontaneous phrases—things that you wish most deeply for yourself, or you can use the following: "May I live in safety. May I be happy. May I be healthy. May I live with peace and joy."
4. Gently repeat this phrase—or your customized phrase—to yourself for a few minutes. If your mind wanders, pull it back to this process, without anger, recrimination or shame.

5. Now call to mind someone that you care about: a friend, family member, loved one, someone who's helped you, someone who inspires you. Visualize that person; say his name to yourself. Get a feeling for his presence, and then direct the above phrases toward him. "May *you* live in safety. May *you* be happy. May *you* be healthy. May *you* live with peace and joy." Repeat this several times.

6. Call to mind someone you know but with whom you're having conflict or difficulty. They needn't be close to you; anyone you know, even just a little bit. It may help to select someone who's experienced a loss, a painful feeling, or a difficult situation. Imagine her sitting in front of you. Visualize her; say her name to yourself. Get a feeling for her presence, and then direct the above phrases toward her. "May you live in safety. May you be happy. May you be healthy. May you live with peace and joy."

7. Think of someone who plays a minor role in your life, preferably someone for whom you have neither strongly positive nor negative feelings. Perhaps your pharmacist, banker, or hairstylist—anyone that you see occasionally but *don't* know very well. Imagine the person sitting in front of you. Visualize him; say his name to yourself. Get a feeling for his presence, and then direct the above phrases toward him. "May you live in safety. May you be happy. May you be healthy. May you live with peace and joy."

8. Finally, visualize the entire world, including all the creatures within it. Say to everyone, "May all beings live in safety. May all beings be happy. May all beings be healthy. May all beings live with peace and joy."

9. When you are ready, open your eyes. See if you can bring this compassionate attitude with you throughout your day.

Online

Additional videos and resources for this chapter are available at www.theblissexperiment.com.

CHAPTER 18

Selfless Service

One thing I do know: the only ones among you who will be really happy are those who have sought and found how to serve.
—*Dr. Albert Schweitzer, Nobel Peace Prize-winner (1875–1965)*

Selfless service is compassion in action. It is the conscious, outward projection of empathy into the world, performed without any expectation of result or reward for the person performing it. Happiness and bliss are impossible without rendering selfless service to humanity.

The inward truth of service is found not in its outward form but in the manner in which we serve. There is no "right" way—no occupation, method, or area of focus more important than another. Neither must it be on a grand scale. Small, private acts done with the right consciousness can be far more valuable to the doer—and even to humanity—than huge, public, grandiose projects done for the wrong reasons. Anything and everything we are doing can become our vehicle for selfless service. The key is to focus on what's happening inside us as we do it.

The Story

Mark came to Hollywood, as many do, to become a professional musician. He dreamt of forming a band, writing music, singing, playing lead guitar, and following in the glorious footsteps of the famous bands that got their start playing live on the Sunset Strip.

Unfortunately, soon after Mark arrived in Los Angeles, he discovered that unlike in his small West Virginia hometown, fantastically talented musicians are on every corner. Although Mark looked the part—curly bleached blond hair, tattoos everywhere, chains over black jeans—he realized that he wasn't as talented or polished as he'd thought. Even at entry-level open-mike nights, he didn't stand out. Not surprisingly, this depressed Mark greatly. His dreams were dashed, but the last thing he wanted to do was move home to West Virginia.

Mark discovered that he did have one exceptional talent: a hardy constitution capable of ingesting more drugs than just about anyone. It didn't take long before he stopped gigging and instead concentrated on partying. He got a job working in a guitar shop that provided just enough steady income to develop one hell of a drug habit.

At first it was incredibly fun. Mark may not have made the big leagues as a musician, but he definitely made the big leagues of partying. He began mostly drinking and smoking marijuana, but it didn't take long for him to stumble onto cocaine. One day a "friend" of Mark's offered him a speedball, an injected mixture of cocaine and heroin (the same concoction that killed actors John Belushi, River Phoenix, and Chris Farley, two of whom died within a couple miles of where Mark got his first taste). It wasn't long before Mark had a full-blown smack addiction. With it came the usual: all he could think about was scoring his next high, he started missing work, became less social, holed up in his apartment, shot up, and drooled on himself for hours at a time.

Mark was soon fired from the guitar shop. Not long after that, he was evicted from his small studio apartment. He found himself living on the streets, behind alleys near Hollywood Boulevard. He was a homeless junkie. It was only a matter of time before he was in jail or dead.

Then he got lucky. Because Mark's story is far from unusual in Hollywood, there are a number of organizations—and the good people who work for them—who keep an eye out for people like Mark. One evening someone approached him on the street, told Mark that he once had an addiction as well, and handed him a card with a nearby address where Mark could get help if he wanted it. That began Mark's first attempt at recovery. There were many.

Mark tried a variety of groups and sponsors, doing his best to kick the habit. It was especially hard because he couldn't afford the intensive monthlong inpatient treatment programs that seemed to have better results than outpatient rehabilitation. He eventually told his parents what was happening, and they found a low-cost program and paid to send him there. While that helped for a while, eventually he relapsed.

After a rocky three years of on-and-off use, he tried a new facility. This one had a different approach. It required anyone who had been in recovery for over a year—even if not always successfully—to sponsor a newer member. Mark had never sponsored anyone, since he felt like he was the one still needing help. Though he balked at first, largely because he was afraid he'd pull someone down with him, the program insisted.

Something interesting happened. Mark found that his sponsoring another person gave *him* strength, especially every time he thought about using. He visualized the kid he was sponsoring—how devastating his relapse might be to this younger guy who was desperately trying to stay clean—and resisted the temptation. Now, more than five years later, Mark hasn't had a single relapse. He knows, without a doubt, that his decision to help others actively was the key turning point in his own struggle.

Though he has long since abandoned his dreams of being a rock star, Mark is happier than he's ever been. He has found his true calling: helping others like himself get and stay clean. By doing so, he feels connected, compassionate, loving, and uplifted in a way that he'd never felt before. He told me, "I can give these kids something we all need: understanding, no judgments, just honest kindness. They get that and respond to it just as I did when that guy first reached out to me. I know I can't and won't fail in my own sobriety. I have to stay clean for them as much as for me. Besides, I feel so awesome, so clear, and so full when I'm doing this work. It's better than the greatest high."

The Science

People often wonder if genuinely selfless, altruistic behavior is possible. If doing good confers benefits on the doer, can this be classified as altruistic? There is a great deal of confusion, even cynicism, surrounding this. Fortunately, recent scientific research is bringing clarity to the issue.

Daniel Batson, professor of social psychology at the University of

Kansas, is one of the leading experts on altruism. Several of his studies have demonstrated that altruistic behavior among humans exists in
abundance. According to Batson, authentic altruism is distinguished and
driven by empathy above all other possible reasons or motivations, and
those with the most keenly developed capacity for compassion are the
most altruistic.

Other researchers have found emphasis of altruistic behavior in chimpanzees and human infants, suggesting that altruism is both widespread and
innate. Altruistic behaviors in infant children are particularly interesting
because they have no reason or expectation to receive anything in return.
They are too young to have learned concepts like reciprocal gain ("I'll
scratch your back if you scratch mine").

Some of the specific benefits of acting altruistically include:

- enhanced feelings of well-being, happiness, joyfulness, emotional resilience, and vigor, and reduced feelings of isolation;
- improved psychological health, even to the point of diminishing both minor
  and serious mental illnesses; and
- enhanced physical health, and even longevity.

Merely remembering the helping act can generate feelings of happiness
that linger for hours, even days, after the service has been completed. A
separate study, conducted in part by Carolyn Schwartz in the Department
of Psychiatry at Harvard Medical School, found that those who help others
showed pronounced improvement in their confidence, self-awareness, self-
esteem, depression, and role functioning.

A study conducted at the world-renowned Wharton School of Business
found that those whose jobs focus explicitly on serving others experience
less stress and have lower burnout rates than those who don't have service-
oriented occupations. A different study compared those who spend most
of their time and effort engaging in personal pleasure-seeking versus those
who engage in more meaningful activities. Those focused on less selfish
activities were far happier than the self-focused ones.

Mark, the subject of our story above, would agree with the Brown
University study on addiction relapse rates, which concluded, "Those who

were helping were significantly less likely to relapse in the year following treatment, independent of the number of AA (Alcoholics Anonymous) meetings attended."

Earlier in this book, we learned that money couldn't buy happiness. It's time to amend that statement slightly. There *is* one way in which money can boost our happiness: giving it away. According to one study, people who spent the entirety of an unexpected work bonus on themselves saw no boost in their happiness, whereas those who gave away at least some of it, either to charity or to spending directly on others, saw large boosts in their happiness.

One caveat about engaging in altruistic behaviors: doing so with the explicit goal of gaining something for ourselves in return is counterproductive. One study showed that when people give to causes with the explicit expectation of gaining something concrete in return, the act of giving has *no* impact on their happiness.

The Spirit

There are some pressing issues we must explore. First, despite the mountain of scientific evidence, the existence of altruism and selfless service remains controversial in some quarters. At best, doubters assert that behaviors labeled as "altruistic" are really done because they provide a simultaneous payoff for the doer. Secondly, even if altruism exists, it appears to be relatively uncommon and thus of little practical interest in our daily lives.

Both of these issues rest on fundamental misunderstandings. Detractors fail to account for the existence of empathy and compassion: the ability to feel another's suffering as our own. When we feel this kind of interconnectivity, the suffering of another is all the motivation we need. The existence of compassion—not in scientific or spiritual doubt—leads inextricably to genuinely altruistic behavior.

The standard definition of altruism fabricated by social scientists is that an altruistic act must have a cost to the doer greater than the benefit. From the bliss perspective, this is incoherent and nonsensical. We are one, united in wholeness. Enlightened self-interest is based on maintaining a sharp distinction between "the world" and "me." We've seen—and will continue to see in later chapters—that this isn't real; the fantasy of a sepa-rate *I* is an illusion. If there is no *I*, then the very notion of acting selfishly can't arise, at least not once we have graduated to the higher levels of bliss consciousness. Put another way: helping others isn't selfish—enlightened or otherwise—just because we gain from it. *Of course*, we gain from it. We are they; they are we.

This leads to the resolution of our second problem. While the idea of selfless service might conjure images of working for a nonprofit organiza-tion, being a medical professional, a firefighter, or caring for the poor, in truth, anything we do—no matter its outward nature—can be transmuted into service. *Anything and everything,* when done from bliss consciousness, *is* selfless service, large and small acts alike. Every action, such as our jobs, caring for our families, and even running errands, can be infused with an attitude of selfless service. Altruism isn't an outward, external act, it's an inward state of consciousness.

In yoga philosophy, there is a wonderful concept called *nishkam karma*. It translates as "desireless action," or action without desire for the benefits of action. It means giving up the need to achieve any specific goal and focusing instead on the process itself. That, in turn, means doing an activ-ity with the right consciousness and the right motivations, not because we must have a particular end result. Put another way, as the cliché goes, "It's not whether you win or lose, it's how you play the game." This means to engage in our activities always with full enthusiasm, energy, concentration, and compassion, and with only the highest ideals and motivations, while surrendering any personal needs or outcomes.

It even means surrendering the need for our service to help others in the way we desire. Sometimes—often—things don't work out quite the way we wanted or envisioned. If we can't let this go, we are doomed to gen-erate negative thoughts and emotions such as "I failed" or "I feel ashamed, inadequate," "I'm useless," "Those people don't like me now or think badly of me," or even "Those people or this world sucks."

Infusing our every activity with bliss consciousness is all that we can do. The world is simply too big, too complex, with too many variables, to guarantee any particular outcome.

Nishkam karma is not, however, an excuse for apathy. It's the opposite.

Desireless action means learning to do everything for the right reasons with the right attitude, feelings, orientation, and consciousness—and with our full energy, concentration, reasoning abilities, and intuition—and then let it go. Apathy and laziness are easy. *Nishkam karma* requires immense energy, awareness, and self-control. It's the ultimate recognition that our inward attitude is what matters most.

Transmuting Work into Service

Hard work by itself, even for a good cause, is not enough. What's important is the attitude and consciousness we bring to it. Thus, even if we seemingly have a serviceful job, if our inner attitude isn't correct, it's no better for us than doing something apparently less grand but for the right reasons with the right consciousness. Inwardly, we must infuse our work with compassion, calmness, concentration, and even freedom.

If we can break free from the hypnotism that we're going to "work" or have a "job," we can retrain ourselves to see everything as a vehicle for service. Each day provides opportunities to help others and purify our hearts and consciousness. We can surrender our old motives—getting rich, gaining power, even the sheer delight in outwitting an opponent—and instead focus on authentically helping the people with whom we come into contact.

The point is that whatever we do—construction, investment banking, gardening, computer programming, real estate, engineering, politics, science, teaching, retailing, working as an actor or talent agent—it doesn't matter. The spirit of selfless service can be infused into almost anything. (Okay, perhaps not for certain "professions" such as drug dealing, bank robbing, or murder for hire. If we're doing something for which there is no way to maintain a positive inward attitude authentically, it's time for a career change.)

Service and Bliss

Selfless service allows us to forget our self-centered lives and egoic desires, instead devoting ourselves to the advancement of the whole. Service gives us a vehicle through which we can practice compassion and develop our capacity for unconditional love.

Selfless service reinforces the enduring truth that we're each a small drop of water floating in an ocean of infinite consciousness. We cease thinking about ourselves at all. *Nishkam karma*, working without desire for a particular outcome, creates genuine freedom. We free ourselves from the bonds of needing anything at all for ourselves outwardly. With this freedom comes bliss.

Finally, by learning to serve without personal desire for outcomes, we live not in the past or future but in the timeless now-moment. We are present, fully and completely. We realize that our outward actions, even effective ones, aren't nearly as important as how we channel and express the pure, uplifted consciousness of bliss. We feel the divine power of the universe flowing through us, becoming beacons and transmitters of bliss. In so doing, everyone we touch is transformed.

The Experiment: Small Acts of Service

1. Look for a small opportunity to offer selfless service to another. Choose an activity in which you don't stand to gain much for yourself directly. For example, run an errand for a coworker, help an elderly person load her groceries, clean up or repair something for someone, let a stranger go ahead of you in a line, donate blood, volunteer for a small task that isn't being done. It can be anything, and it needn't be major or time consuming.

2. Be sure to do this act with the right attitude and feeling. Tune into your compassion and understanding. Allow yourself to feel the underlying connection to the beneficiaries of this task, whether it's one specific person or an abstract group of people. For example, picking up litter may not help one person you know or see but all of humanity by cleaning the earth, or at least thousands of strangers that will pass by.

3. Concentrate on performing this act of service not for any particular outcome but as a process and opportunity in itself. Be sure to enjoy it, be in the present moment with it, and surrender any hope for personal gain other than a generally uplifted consciousness.

4. Note how this act of service made you feel and what you experienced while doing it. Reflect on ways that you can bring a serviceful attitude to the work you do.

5. Vow to bring an outlook of selfless service into all of your daily activities. Look for opportunities to serve others as much as possible, even in small ways. Reflect, too, on whether pursuing larger opportunities for direct selfless service—through volunteering or even changing jobs—is the right thing for you.

Online

Additional videos and resources for this chapter are available at www.theblissexperiment.com.

CHAPTER 19

Love Without Reason

Love the animals, love the plants, love everything. If you love everything, you will perceive the divine mystery in things. Once you perceive it, you will begin to comprehend it better every day. And you will come at last to love the whole world with an all-embracing love.

—*Fyodor Dostoyevsky, Russian novelist (1821–81)*

At the heart of all warm relationships is kindness and friendship. At the heart of kindness is compassion. At the heart of compassion is unconditional love. Put another way: kindness, friendship, and compassion are aspects of love. But unconditional love is something even greater: it encompasses, expands upon, and extends all of these qualities—and more. Developing our facility for kindness, warm relationships, friendship, empathy, and compassion are vitally important steps toward feeling and expressing unconditional love.

The ability to feel and radiate unconditional love is deeply, profoundly, and inextricably tied to bliss. If we can't understand, let alone exude, this highest form of love, without question we haven't yet developed our capacity for bliss. I dare say that never in history has there been a single being who felt true bliss without knowing and feeling unconditional love.

We've mostly forgotten the true meaning of love. Yes, to one degree or another, we've all felt it. But only partially. We allow our love to stop at the boundary of a single relationship or a small family. Genuine love is a universal force without boundary, condition, or limitation. Tapping into unconditional love isn't so much a process of active development as it is learning how not to interfere or needlessly constrict its natural tendency. It is the highest and purest form of love, one that requires no reason for being.

The Story

Olivia is one of the least obvious Texans I've met. Bright, wisecracking, and sarcastic, she seems more at home on the East Coast than in an affluent suburb of Dallas. She was adopted into a wealthy and powerful family. She has never met her birth parents and is disinterested in doing so. Unfortunately, Olivia's adoptive parents divorced, rather messily, while she was still young. Her mother is the more high-powered and successful of her parents. The father is a bit of a wandering ne'er-do-well, having spent years working as a session guitarist for low- and mid-tier blues and country acts. While her mother played the role of responsible provider—it was her side of the family that belonged to established Dallas society—Olivia's father popped in and out of her life.

Olivia was not what we might call a heartful person. As she readily admitted, even relished, there was an edge to her. Her romantic relationships had a very passionate but thoroughly volatile quality. Mostly she preferred men who were as callous, even mean, as she was. The more emotionally troubled they were, the more she liked them. This might sound strange, but part of the reason she liked her relationships this way was due to her own innate romanticism. Not a flowers-and-chocolate kind of romantic but the more dangerous kind; she was heavily influenced by a *Wuthering Heights*–style Heathcliff and Catherine sensibility, and very much attracted to the Byronic hero archetype. She coupled this with a contemporary cynicism bordering on existential angst.

Olivia so embraced this viewpoint that she once dumped a boyfriend who had (much to her approval) started out moody, even unkind, but who had, perplexingly, grown "too nice" as their relationship progressed. She felt it was a sign of weakness and emotional inauthenticity.

The turning point came when Olivia, now in her early thirties and unmarried, got pregnant by mistake. She decided to keep the child, a beautiful baby girl, though she had no interest in marrying the father, who to this day maintains only a distant relationship. Something amazing happened: from the moment of her child's birth, Olivia felt a kind of unconditional love toward her baby that she had never before experienced. She had never *wanted* to experience.

After a few years of raising her child and continually being awestruck by the sheer love she felt for this being, Olivia found her innately curious mind unable to resist exploring the meaning and nature of this love. She told me, "I started to think that if this is how I feel toward my kid, and I like it, why couldn't I feel it with my boyfriend, family, or friends? Maybe that's not revolutionary for others, but for me that was a revelation that got me interested in the real meaning of love."

Being a self-aware person and aided by the stark contrast with how she used to see the world, Olivia noticed that once she allowed herself to feel love for her child, she started naturally feeling love toward other people and in many different circumstances. In fact, she found that she had to make a concerted, even draining, effort to maintain her long-cherished acerbic personality.

She stumbled across a local Buddhist teacher and started practicing a form of Buddhist meditation, developing her understanding of loving kindness. While meditating one day, Olivia had a remarkable experience. She felt like she was floating in a sea of love, that love was all around her and inside her, her child, everyone. She knew that she didn't generate that love; it had always been there. She felt immensely grateful to her child, too, for opening her to this much broader love. It was all the same: what she felt for her child, her family, her friends, her teacher, and even the strangers on the street. There is only one eternal love. She couldn't believe that she'd waited so many years to feel it.

The Science

Scientists have found remarkable evidence that there exists a type of love—what we call unconditional—that is physiologically different from romantic or familial love. Unconditional love is the ability to feel love for another person regardless of that person's beliefs, actions, or responses toward us. This was first demonstrated spectacularly in a 2009 experiment conducted by Professor Mario Beauregard of the University of Montreal. He placed subjects in a functional magnetic resonance imaging machine (fMRI) and looked at their brain activity as they were induced to feel different types of love. When patients were instructed to feel unconditional love toward strangers with intellectual disabilities, entirely different neural networks and areas of their brains lit up than when they experienced other types of love. All told, seven distinct areas of the brain lit up, in both hemispheres and in both the primitive and advanced parts of the brain.

Though the idea of studying unconditional love in the laboratory is new, there are some other studies worth examining. Avi Assor and Guy Roth, a team of researchers based at Israel's Ben-Gurion University of the Negev, along with Edward Deci at the University of Rochester (New York), have collaborated on researching the tremendous difference in outcomes between conditional love and unconditional love. Their early efforts have concentrated on comparing two groups of children and young adults: those who were raised with a sense that their parents' love was conditional versus those children who received unconditional love, no matter their behavior or accomplishments.

The scientists discovered that parents who grant their love conditionally can indeed get their children to behave in certain ways in the short term. However, it comes at enormous cost.

Not only are conditionally loved children more likely to resent their parents, eventually they are much more likely to rebel. Conditional love shatters a child's self-esteem and sabotages his or her long-term capacity for happiness.

A study sponsored by the Institute of Noetic Sciences, a nonprofit organization cofounded by Apollo astronaut Edgar Mitchell, recruited thirty-six long-term, loving couples as participants. The goal was to see if two partners could transmit their strong feelings for each other when apart. The man and woman in each couple were separated from each other—isolated in sealed, double-steel-walled chambers—so that they couldn't see or hear each other. Electrodes capable of monitoring five physiological variables were attached to each subject. One of the partners was designated the "sender"; the other, the "receiver." The receiver was told that at random intervals, the sender would be viewing live video of him or her from a distant location for an unspecified length of time, and that during each of these periods, the sender would attempt to connect with him or her mentally.

The findings? When one person focused her thoughts on her partner, the partner's blood flow and perspiration rose dramatically within *two seconds*. The odds of this happening by chance were one in eleven thousand. Interestingly, no fewer than three dozen double-blind, randomized studies by such respected institutions as the University of Washington and Scotland's University of Edinburgh have reported similar results, seeming to prove that loving people can "feel" each other even at a distance.

The Spirit

From the perspective of everyday happiness, developing warm, loving relationships is critically important for our own well-being, as both the studies demonstrate and our intuition confirms. Unconditional love, on the other hand, is more properly understood as a component of bliss. As such, neither bliss nor unconditional love strictly requires relationships of any kind. How can love not require another person? That may seem a startling claim.

We must remember that bliss—and its attendant aspects—are *inward* feelings, accessible to us even if we were locked alone in a black box. Technically, one could be eternally alone, never having met another human being, yet still feel unconditional love and pure bliss. For example, there are cloistered Catholic monks and nuns who are voluntarily locked into cells inside monasteries or yogis in the Himalayas who find a private, isolated cave and never leave it for the duration of their lives. Many of these people still reach the very pinnacle of self-realization. If we had an opportunity to meet them, we'd be overwhelmed by the love they emanate, though they seemingly have had no firsthand experience.

How is this possible?

Unconditional love means love without limits, conditions, or reasons. This type of love has no boundaries; it is infinite and all pervasive. Love that *requires* another person is necessarily confined to that person or that relationship. Confinement is a limiting boundary. In this sense, love and bliss are impersonal. Usually we take *impersonal* to mean "without feeling."

That's *not* the meaning here. Instead I mean that unconditional love isn't something that we create or must wait for others to create. It's not contingent upon anyone else for its existence. Rather it already exists: inside, outside and all around us. We need only make the *internal choice* to tap into it and experience it.

Love Is the Universal Power of Attraction

Just because love is universal and impersonal doesn't mean that it's always manifest. Paramhansa Yogananda coined a striking definition of love, one that I've found to be profoundly true. He said that *love is the universal divine power of attraction in creation that harmonizes, unites, and binds together.* The opposite of love, then, is repulsion, division, differentiation, and disharmony.

Seen in this light, we can better understand why love is not a human-generated emotion but a pervasive cosmic force. Love is the glue that holds together our universe. This is a useful antidote to our more conventional understandings, particularly the emphasis on experiencing it as an intensely personal emotion that by the nature of its intimacy is impossible to experience beyond a small circle of interactions. Broadening our understanding of love beyond the domain of fickle human emotion creates a monumental shift in understanding. Suddenly we realize that the potential for love is everywhere.

We are continually surrounded—one might say bathed—in harmonious vibrations of pure love and bliss, though, of course, we often don't realize it. *Wherever* there is positive attraction, harmony, and cooperation, there is unconditional love. Instead of love being something that we generate, it's akin to something that we *tune into*, just like dialing in a signal on your radio. Or perhaps we can think of love more vividly as the sun's warming rays, evenly shining down upon the whole of Earth. We need only orient ourselves correctly and then step into the sunlight. Immediately we feel its luminous, healing, and joyful radiance. Whenever we choose harmony and unity rather than disharmony and division, we have oriented ourselves toward unconditional love.

The flip side is also true. The more we insist that love can be felt *only* for certain people—our partner, family, or friends—or in certain situations, the more we cut ourselves off from its full majesty. To love unconditionally doesn't require us to love our partner, family, or friends less; it means only that we don't confine our lovingness to them alone. We acknowledge that as important as these personal relationships are, these designated few haven't exhausted our reservoir of love. Love is not something that should ever feel depleting. The highest form of love is energizing, invigorating, and infinite. To place limits on our capacity to love diminishes us and introduces disharmony into our consciousness. It's like willfully choosing to set our radio dial halfway between two stations, mixing beautiful music with static, or exposing only one small part of our body to direct sunlight, while keeping the rest cloaked in shadow.

A Starting Place

Cultivating unconditional love requires conscious effort. As strange as it may sound, we must *practice* loving fully. Love is neither an accident that we stumble into nor a passive state that happens to us.

In a certain sense, learning to love unconditionally is the process of *un*learning much of what we've been taught and internalized through unconscious habit. We've hypnotized ourselves into believing that love exists only between people who are intimate with each other; it is only for special people in certain circumstances.

Few of us are ready to make a quantum leap into impersonal yet unconditional love. Nor does the isolated route of cloistered monks or cave-dwelling yogis seem appealing. Most of us still feel a strong pull, perhaps even a need, for loving relationships with just a few other people. This is a wonderful place to start. Our existing relationships are an essential vehicle through which we can learn unconditional love. Not only needn't we turn our back on conventional relationships, we can embrace them for their transformative potential.

When approached with the right attitude, relationships can teach us how to give, express, and receive love, just as Olivia used the unconditional love she feels for her daughter as a launching pad to expand her capacity for love to an ever-widening circle of humanity. The only alteration we make is that we no longer assume that these few relationships are the *exclusive* vehicles through which we can give, receive, or otherwise express love. Instead we slowly begin expanding our heart ever more widely, including more and more people and situations.

Over time, we come to see that love doesn't *require* specific individuals. Of course, it's a wonderful feeling to receive love from a mother, a lover, a child, or a friend. But there is a vast difference between appreciating them and *needing* or requiring that they do so. We can learn that love is everywhere. Tuning into this love is to understand, see, and experience the cosmic force of harmonious attraction everywhere and in every moment of our lives.

Everywhere we encounter harmony, unity, beauty, attraction, or coherence is an opportunity to tune into unconditional love. In this sense, too, we can even come to love every atom and molecule of creation. After all, atoms are a collection of harmoniously bound subparticles: neutrons, protons, and electrons working in concert. Molecules are collections of atoms united together in precise formulations. *Anywhere* there is coherence—which is to say practically everywhere in our universe, every physical and biological system—you'll find the binding power of love.

Equally important, we must do more than just feel all-pervasive love. We must become active retransmitters of it. Again we return to our radio analogy. Radios work by first being tuned to receive a signal and then amplifying that signal into the local space surrounding it. Without that second step of amplification, the best we could say is that radio is incomplete; we might even conclude it was useless or broken.

So, too, it is with us. We mustn't keep the love we feel bottled up inside. The love that flows into us must also be amplified and expressed outwardly to everyone we meet. We can't be a dead end or cul-de-sac for love: to complete our circuit, we must augment it and then rebroadcast it to the world. The more and better we can do this, the purer the channel we become.

The Experiment (1):
Feeling Unconditional Love

1. Find a place to sit comfortably, with your spine straight and eyes closed.

2. Think of someone you dislike: whether a true "enemy" or just someone you're having a hard time with at the moment. This can be anyone: a family member, acquaintance, coworker, or even someone you don't know personally but feel extremely negative about (a politician, public figure, corporate CEO, and so forth).

3. Visualize your dislike of this person as a cord of negative energy binding the two of you together like a heavy, blackened rope made of lead. This negative connection between you is weighing you *both* down, preventing you from feeling light, free, and joyful.

4. Visualize mentally cutting that cord, so that whatever created that tension disappears. See the heavy metal cord disintegrate upon severing. Feel yourself no longer negatively affected, but light, free, uplifted, loving, and joyful—regardless of what that person says, does, or believes now and in the future.

5. Now concentrate on your own heart area. See a bubble of loving, healing light emanating from your heart center.

6. Understand that the past difficulty between the two of you is because of ignorance and misunderstanding. It might be mostly his/hers or mostly yours or a combination of both. It doesn't matter.

7. Feel or see that the person is suffering greatly, if only internally, because of his/her own hatred, ignorance, or misunderstandings. Make a conscious effort to wish your adversary well, hoping or praying that he/she overcomes whatever delusions are fueling such suffering.

8. Visualize the pure light of illumination emanating from your heart and enveloping this person, so that you are both inside the bubble of unconditional love together. See him/her completely surrounded and infused with this light of unconditional love. As it encompasses the person, his/her veil of ignorance is lifted. See the person floating in this light, smiling, happy, and free from all suffering.

9. Hold that image for as long as you wish. Again end by silently wishing the person well. Open your eyes when you're ready.

The Experiment (2):
Affirmation for Unconditional Love

1. You can also do an affirmation for unconditional love. You can write your own, use the resources on my website, or try this: "I love others as extensions of my own Highest Self. Pure love surrounds us both, uniting us in uplifted consciousness."

Online

Scan the Microsoft Tag above to view a brief video, "Love and Compassion," or go to youtube.com/seanmeshorer.

CHAPTER 20

Discovering Meaning, Finding Purpose

> Many people have the wrong idea of what constitutes happiness.
> It is not attained through self-gratification, but through fidelity
> to a worthy purpose.
> —Helen Keller, American deaf and blind advocate (1880–1968)

I've never met anyone who simultaneously believes that life is meaningless yet remains truly happy. We can perform all the happiness practices in the world, but if we don't believe that anything truly *matters*, we undermine their effectiveness.

There is a tight interconnectedness between happiness, meaning, and purpose. Experiencing bliss is the most intrinsically meaningful thing we can do; it reveals the highest and deepest mysteries of our existence. To set bliss as our goal—and all that it encompasses—is the highest, noblest purpose to which we can aspire.

Meaning, like bliss, is not something we *create*. It already surrounds us and pulsates through us. It is here with us right now, lurking behind every thought, feeling, and action. Ours is an inherently purposeful universe; our individual purpose clarifies and unfolds as we relate to and interact with the world around us. Meaning is present within every atom of creation—we need only learn how to see it.

The Story

Mike is a veteran reporter who has worked for newspapers and print publications his entire thirty-plus-year career. He has covered local, national, and international news, politics, and current events. He's now in his mid-to-late fifties.

Mike is a throwback kind of guy. He is a skeptic by nature and by training. He was raised in a working-class, pro-union, Democratic family. He wasn't religious, although his parents were nominally Episcopalian. He's covered mostly hard news and is disdainful toward softer features and human-interest stories, which he thinks of as pure fluff, not real reporting. H. L. Mencken and Ernest Hemingway are two of his heroes. After years of covering politics—everything from school board elections to presidential elections—Mike had a jaundiced view of human nature. In his experience, people routinely lied or manipulated facts to suit their own purposes.

Mike had strained and limited contact with his three grown daughters from a failed marriage. He's not a bad man or a bad father, but his ex-wife gained full custody when the children were young and subsequently remarried. His daughters spent more time with their stepfather than with Mike. He had never remarried, although he had dated off and on. Twice he had serious live-in girlfriends, though he was now single and mostly alone. He admitted, without embarrassment, that he sometimes "rented" company for a few hours.

Mike wasn't a happy man. He drank fairly heavily, although he didn't consider himself an alcoholic. He was never a fall-down drunk, nor did his work ever suffer. As time progressed, he fell deeper into despair. Life didn't seem particularly meaningful. He couldn't really name anything that mattered. He loved his children but didn't feel like they needed him. After more than three decades of reporting, his job was starting to bore him. It was an extremely stressful environment, even more so in recent years now that newspapers are under extreme financial pressure. He started having suicidal thoughts. His mind kept returning to Hemingway, who committed suicide in 1961—a shotgun blast to the head. Mike started wondering if he maybe he should emulate the author one last time.

Fortunately for Mike, his health insurance had a generous allowance for mental health services, as his editor (and friend) pointed out to him none too subtly one day. He decided he would at least try a few sessions with a therapist.

It took all of one session for the therapist to tell Mike that he was suffering from "existential malaise." Mike said to me, "That sounds better than saying I'm depressed like every other loser, so what the hell, let's go with that." Over the course of a few sessions, it became abundantly clear that Mike felt life was utterly pointless: just a lot of selfish people doing crappy things to one another in order to get what they wanted, all for no cosmic reason.

Not long after he began therapy, his employer offered him a generous early retirement buyout. He figured he might as well take it, not only because he was sick of reporting but also because the paper might not last much longer anyway.

His therapist, meanwhile, had taught Mike how to meditate, which was helping him feel considerably less stressed and angry. He was also gently prodding Mike to see if he could find, create, or unearth any kind of meaning. Mike eventually decided to travel, especially to Europe, where he particularly wanted to visit many of Hemingway's favorite haunts.

While traveling, Mike had an inspiration. After returning home, he began working on a book. He wants to explain to the general public how journalism really works and why it's so important in a democracy. He feels that there is so much hatred toward journalists these days, a sort of anti-media frenzy.

Talking with Mike, his excitement about this project is palpable. His eyes are bright. He's focused, almost ebullient. He's clearly more engaged with life than he's been in years. He found a way to use his wisdom and experience to help make a difference. Combined with his new meditation practice, he's calmer, lighter, and happier than he's ever been. He told me, "This is the best I've ever felt. I'm working for myself, doing what I want the way I've always wanted. I'm not reacting or reporting or following other people and their agendas. Now *I'm* setting the agenda!"

The Science

The notion of studying meaning and purpose in a laboratory setting is a relatively recent development. Nevertheless, there have been some critically important findings.

A study published in the *Journal of Personality and Social Psychology* found that prior attempts to measure happiness or life satisfaction *without* accounting for purpose in life and the potential for personal growth were incomplete. Happiness cannot properly be understood without exploring meaning as well. Additional research has found that people who have a greater sense of life's meaning and purpose fare much better over the course of a lifetime, both psychologically and physically, than those who don't. In fact, meaning is one of the *strongest predictors* of future well-being. According to another study, an effective way to treat mental illness is to help patients find meaningful activities. Doing so mitigated and lessened symptoms.

Meaning makes a huge difference on the physical level, too. For example, AIDS patients who'd recently lost their partner to AIDS but found meaning in their loss and their own illness reported positive health outcomes. Fewer died, and they generally were of more robust health than those who found no meaning in their loss. Meaning also directly boosted their immune systems.

More startling is the finding of a different study that over a seven-year period, those reporting a diminished sense of purpose in life were more than *twice as likely* to develop Alzheimer's disease compared with those reporting a greater purpose in life. Additionally, among this same group of almost one thousand elderly men, researchers found that those with a higher sense of meaning and purpose were less likely to be cognitively impaired; had better physical dexterity and mobility; and were better able to carry out basic living skills such as housekeeping and managing money. Furthermore, they were *significantly less* likely to die—by almost 60 percent—than those without a strong sense of purpose.

There is a tight correlation between happiness and meaning. While "everyday happiness" is to some degree a by-product of meaning, that's not to imply that it is unimportant. Meaning and happiness are synergistic. Six different studies conducted by a team of researchers led by Laura King at the University of Missouri found that happiness helps people find meaning in their lives and that positive life outlooks predispose us to feel that life is meaningful. In a related finding, happier, more positive people are more sensitive to seeing or discovering the meaning in difficult situations.

The Spirit

The kind of meaning we're exploring here is *meaning* in its largest sense. We all broadly understand a phrase like "the meaning of life." It's the attempt to identify the overarching context and justification for our beliefs, feelings, and actions. We want to know *why* we do what we do, and to what end, goal, or standard we relate. Though we all have the drive for meaning, it's an open question as to whether a single answer can possibly satisfy all people or even all life situations for one person.

Because we're unsure whether or not life has an external, enduring meaning, we often try to convince ourselves that we can *create* our own meaning sui generis. The difficulty is that claiming that each of us *invents* our own meaning is really saying there is no Meaning (with a capital M). It's to make the implicit claim that life is meaningless while trying to hold a middle ground that, while there is no Larger Purpose, we can at least find smaller things that make life tolerable, interesting, and perhaps even enjoyable.

This seldom works for long. It's like building our dream house on sand. The foundation can't hold. This viewpoint is okay as a stopgap measure, as long as we realize its inherent instability and continue working toward uncovering a larger, objectively true, and more grounded worldview.

I'd like to propose that meaning isn't a personal choice, like deciding whether to have waffles or eggs for breakfast. It *must* correspond to some essential framework or structure of the universe. And that framework is bliss itself. Once we are in contact with it, bliss authentically serves as our universal bedrock of meaning, an unbreakable foundation upon which we can construct an enduringly successful, satisfying, and complete life. This book, then, is one large argument for understanding the meaning of life. As we continue forward in our journey toward bliss, this will become increasingly clear.

Meaning Versus Purpose

Meaning and purpose are not synonymous. While the word *meaning* alludes to a comprehensive framework of objective truth, *purpose* can be thought of as the specific way in which each of us fits into this larger framework. Meaning is universal, purpose is specific.

Meaning precedes purpose. Within the context of universal meaning, we strive to find and understand our own specific purpose. Purpose is the way in which the universe's meaning unfolds for us. We each have our own, unique life purpose. While we all share a single all-encompassing meaning and framework, no two people share exactly the same purpose. My purpose is following my own unique pathway to bliss.

Because purpose is unique and individual, finding our life purpose can't be achieved by following others or doing what society tells us to do. It's primarily internal. We can look to others for understanding life's *meaning* but only we can discern our *purpose*. (Of course, others can help us, chiefly by suggesting the most effective tools necessary to conduct a successful search).

Finding Your Purpose

The better we know ourselves, the more clarity we have in seeing our unique purpose and personal pathway to bliss. In most cases—though there are exceptions—purpose reveals itself most clearly to those who know themselves best.

Our life's purpose is being and doing whatever creates a seamless fit between our internal selves and our external environment. Purpose is when we are in perfect harmony, internally and externally. This is why purpose is unique to everyone. We have different challenges, outlooks, needs, skills, levels of understanding, and lessons to be learned. And we all inhabit different external geographies, social strata, demographics, and the like. The permutations are infinite.

This is why I can't tell you—and you can't tell me—what your specific life purpose is. We each must take all of our internal and external variables and decide that for ourself. What I *can* do is give you the tools necessary.

Though, of course, much more could be written about how to find ones purpose (it's a whole book unto itself), the bottom line is that the ideas and practices in this book *are* those tools. The greater our awareness, the more clearly we discern our life's purpose.

The Meaning of Life

Happiness is dependent on meaning. We may not yet realize it, but bliss *is* that meaning. To find bliss is to find everything. It is to know everything, feel everything, understand everything, experience everything. Permanent bliss is total self-realization. It is to have the mysteries of the universe unveiled. In this sense, the purpose of life is to find bliss, though the specifics of that that journey are unique for each for us.

Because meaning and bliss are synonymous, meaning is everywhere, just as bliss is everywhere. It is inside us, all around us, it permeates our being. Meaning is pregnant in every molecule of the universe, everything we do, say, think, feel, and experience. We need only tune into it. It is always here for us, quietly and patiently waiting for us to understand.

The above isn't intended as an objectively deducible statement that can be known independent of direct experience. We can't truly comprehend this until we make contact with bliss for ourselves. This is why it's so essential that you don't take my word for it.

The Experiment: Finding Your Life's Purpose

Here are two different variations for finding your life's purpose. Most people resonate more with one or the other, depending on their personality. The first is more free-form and intuitive; the second, more structured and deliberate. Choose whichever one calls to you. You can do both if you want.

You will need something in which to record your thoughts: your Bliss Journal, loose paper, or a computer. This experiment is less effective when done mentally only.

Find a place where you can be alone, quiet, and uninterrupted. Turn off your phone, television, or anything else that distracts you.

Method A

1. Write down, "What is my life purpose?"
2. Write any and every answer that pops into your head. Complete sentences aren't necessary; bullet points or fragments are fine. So too are drawings and images.
3. Keep writing every possible idea or answer until you generate something that deeply resonates with you. You'll know if you feel a great sense of joy or total peace sweep over you, find yourself crying, feel a surge of positive excitement, or if your mind keeps returning again and again to the same thing or a variation of it.
4. Often it takes writing at least twenty to fifty thoughts before something strikes a deep chord. I've known it sometimes to take two hundred to five hundred attempts before something truly clicks. Even if this exercise takes two hours, it could be two of the most important hours of your life. It will pay dividends for years.
5. Everyone is different: sometimes we immediately hit upon the key thing for us, other times (especially if you think this exercise sounds idiotic) it takes five to ten minutes to relax and allow yourself to get into it.
6. Expect that at least some of what you write is false. It'll be what *other people* want your life purpose to be. Or what you *used* to want but no longer truly do. Keep going to get the real answer.
7. It's okay if many of your answers are similar or repetitive. Sometimes changing a word or two in each variation ends up sparking a whole new tangent or direction.
8. You might experience a minirevelation, but it doesn't feel complete or full. This might be a sign that you're on the right track but haven't quite nailed it. Start riffing on and refining these partial hits.
9. Don't quit, even if you've written fifty or one hundred answers yet feel like nothing is jelling. This is normal. Push past any resistance and keep writing. Discouraged or negative feelings will pass. Feel free, however, to write down those negative feelings—it helps to release them. Even if you're thinking, "I have no purpose," write it down and keep going.
10. If you're feeling antsy or concerned that you're not getting anywhere, you can take *brief* minibreaks, no more than a minute or two. Close your eyes, relax, and center yourself. *Do not* stop completely, leave the area

(stretching is okay), or do anything that breaks the mood. After you feel refreshed, continue onward.

Method B

Some people do better with a more structured approach. Here are concrete questions you can ask yourself. Write down the first answer that pops into your head. Don't think too long or hard—spend no more than thirty to sixty seconds of reflection—for each question. Be honest. Remember, nobody is going to read this but you.

Answer the following:

1. What makes you smile (activities, people, events, hobbies, projects, and so on)?
2. What were your favorite things to do in the past? What about right now?
3. What activities make you lose track of time?
4. What makes you feel good about yourself?
5. Who inspires you most? List as many people as you feel inclined (This can be anyone, whether you know the person or not: family, friends, authors, artists, political leaders, spiritual teachers, and so on.) What is it about them that inspires you?
6. What are you naturally good at (skills, abilities, gifts, talents, and so on)?
7. In what areas do people typically ask you for help?
8. If you had to teach something, what would you teach?
9. If you were on your deathbed right now, reviewing your life, what would you regret not having done, experienced, possessed, or tried?
10. Pretend that you are still on your deathbed but have lived a long life with no regrets. Everything went perfectly. You are lying there, filled with bliss, reflecting back on your blessed and wonderful life. What would a regret-free life look like for you? Pretend you're conducting a life review of this perfect fantasy life, including all that you've experienced, achieved, acquired, all the places you've been, people you've known, close relationships developed, services rendered, and so forth. What matters to you most? For what are you most grateful? What was it that made your life so blissfully perfect?
11. What do you value the most *right now*?

12. What were some challenges, difficulties, and hardships you've overcome or are in the process of overcoming? How did you do it?
13. What causes do you believe in most strongly?
14. If you were speaking to a large group of people on the topic of your choice, but it had to be something important to you that you wanted to share, what would your topic/message be? To what group of people would you want to deliver it?
15. Look again at the talents, interests, and values you've written down. Write down as many ways as you can think of to put these to good use. What ways can you serve others or make some kind of positive contribution, while also being true to your own nature?
16. What has emerged as a clear direction or concrete purpose?

Online

Additional videos and resources for this chapter are available at www.theblissexperiment.com.

CHAPTER 21

Embracing Your Spiritual Self

Christian, Jew, Muslim, shaman, Zoroastrian, stone, ground,
mountain, river, each has a secret way of being with the mystery,
unique and not to be judged.

—*Rumi, thirteenth-century Persian poet*

By and large, we've so far avoided much direct mention of religion, religious terminology, specific doctrines or beliefs—even God. This is intentional. Whether we are Christian or atheist, Jewish or Muslim, Hindu or Wiccan, Buddhist or Native American, bliss is in harmony with all of the world's great wisdom traditions. Not only is it a universal experience found in all religions, it is actually the highest attainment and loftiest end goal for which each religion aspires. It is only the differences in terminology that prevent some from seeing this. As such, religion can play a vital role in the bliss process and experience.

Still, there are important differences between spirituality and religion. Whether we are traditionally religious or not is less important than having a general spiritual orientation. Learning how to inhabit and relate to our world through a broadly spiritual perspective is essential. Spirituality unifies and integrates all of the disparate topics and practices we've examined so far. Without that, our world remains fractured.

Bliss has little to do with our *beliefs* but everything to do with our *experience*. This experience—and the practices required to induce it—is the distillation of the highest and most effective practices found in each of the world's religions.

The Story

Jacob is a nice kid from a liberal, open-minded family. His great-grandparents on his father's side, who grew up in Missouri, had been on the leading edge of the mid-twentieth-century Evangelical Christian revival. His grandparents were a little looser but still conservative. His father broke away and dabbled in Eastern spirituality, ultimately gravitating to a liberal Christian church.

When Jacob was in his midteens, he got into drugs, had a few minor scrapes with the law, and did poorly in school. Partly out of his own choice, he was sent to a military boarding school for troubled kids. At twenty, he decided to enroll in the military.

He had no clearly defined religious or spiritual beliefs. He considered himself agnostic and disinterested. Jacob suffered from low-grade anxiety and depression, occasionally punctuated by panic attacks. He carefully hid this information from his military recruiter because he was concerned that it would disqualify him. Once he got through basic training, he was assigned to a job in electronics and mechanical engineering at a Midwestern base.

There he met Ava, a devout evangelical Christian from a conservative Indiana family. She attended a Christian college before enrolling in the military. Her beliefs could fairly be characterized as fundamentalist: she believed in the literal and inerrant truth of Scripture, that Christ's death was in atonement for our sins, that we must profess faith in Christ alone as our Lord and Savior or risk eternal damnation, and that most of modern culture is evil, godless, and to be avoided—unless one sees an opportunity to convert a lost soul to the righteous path.

Jacob and Ava eventually fell in love and got married. Perhaps due to his grandparents' background, Jacob had little difficulty accepting Ava's faith. He decided to be baptized in her church. Jacob's depression and anxiety lessened, his panic attacks decreased. He felt sure that this was a sign from the Lord that he was on the right track.

Several years later, with one child born and another on the way, Jacob was transferred to work at a base in California. (Ava didn't reenlist after their marriage, in order to stay at home and raise the kids.) They looked for a church to join. Their initial choice fit well with Ava's background and beliefs, but they decided they didn't much care for the head minister.

Jacob found a more moderate, even liberal, church that had a charismatic minister. Though his newfound faith was the centerpiece of his life, once away from Ava's family and in an environment with more options, Jacob confessed that he'd been slightly uncomfortable with the more extreme, dogmatic positions of their previous church. Ava admitted reluctantly that she too preferred this more moderate pastor and congregation, so they decided to join.

This church had a much less fundamentalist view of Christianity and other faiths. The congregants didn't believe that nonbelievers automatically went to hell. They also accepted that the Bible wasn't intended literally and was far more tolerant on social issues. They placed a strong emphasis on one's own spiritual practice, communing directly with God and Christ through prayer, contemplation, and Christian meditation.

After a year in this church, both Jacob and Ava saw the definite contrast with their old one. They realized how tense and unpeaceful that church really was: they felt like they had been at war with the people and culture around them. Jacob realized that although his depression and anxiety had eased at first, as they stayed in the old church, the symptoms had slowly been returning.

In their new church, the couple felt happier and closer to God than ever. They immersed themselves in contemplative practices, which helped them feel more peaceful, compassionate, and grounded. For the first time in years, Jacob no longer had any trace of anxiety or depression. Ava felt like she finally had "room to breathe." They were excited to share their revitalized faith with their family and the world.

The Science

Dr. Harold G. Koenig is the clear leader in this field. He's the founder and former director of Duke University's Center for the Study of Religion, Spirituality, and Health, and the current director of Duke's Center for

Spirituality, Theology, and Health. Through his own research and meta-analyses of hundreds of findings by other scientists, he's brought great clarity to this subject.

One of the most surprising discoveries for some—especially those skeptically inclined or who have a traditional training in psychotherapy—is that religio-spiritual beliefs and practices actually *improve* our mental health. This is a startling reversal of the traditional view. Beginning with Sigmund Freud, psychology has often claimed that religious believers are neurotic, delusional, or generally unstable.

Compared to nonreligious people, religious believers have greater life satisfaction, lower rates of depression and anxiety, and fewer overall mental health problems. A more astonishing finding, published in the mainstream and bellwether *American Journal of Psychiatry*, was that religiosity actually *decreases* our lifetime risk of experiencing mental disorders. (Freud is rolling in his grave.) This study enrolled over 2,600 twins. Religiosity *reduced* the risk for a wide range of mental disorders, including major depression, phobias, generalized anxiety disorder, bulimia nervosa, substance abuse, and antisocial behaviors.

Koenig published a separate review of studies done on the physical health benefits of religiosity. He found ample evidence that religious and/or spiritual beliefs correlate to decreased risks of pain, disability, infection, cancer, and cardiovascular disease; enhanced immunity and neuroendocrine function; and longer life spans.

Of course, religious people get sick too. When they do, according to the research, spirituality lessens their anxiety and provides an effective coping mechanism. For instance, one study showed that among recovering cardiac arrest patients, those that embrace spirituality have better recovery rates than those who don't. Additionally, religious people are *less* likely to commit suicide, become juvenile delinquents, smoke or drink to excess, and get divorced.

For those that do develop alcoholism, spirituality aids in their recovery. Multiple studies show that those with higher religiosity have lower relapse rates. Moreover, nonreligious people who entered AA and then reported a subsequent "spiritual awakening" were nearly four times more likely to be abstinent after three years than individuals who didn't.

Here are a few more of the many pro-religious/spirituality findings researchers have uncovered:

- Recently widowed religious believers report more joy than widowed nonbelievers do.
- Mothers of developmentally disabled children with deep faith are less prone to depression than those without.
- People of faith recover more quickly after traumatic events such as divorce, unemployment, serious illness, or bereavement.
- Religious older adults report higher life satisfaction.

Perhaps needless to say, religious and/or spiritual people are also happier. A study published in the *Journal of Contemporary Religion* found that the happiest people are the most religious.

I'd like to call attention to two recent studies that specifically drew a distinction between spirituality and religiosity. A fascinating study compared and contrasted them in a population of Iranian Muslim students attending the University of Tehran. The study categorized students in three ways: nonreligious, spiritual but not heavily religious, and traditionally religious. Results showed that both the spiritual and religious groups reported higher levels of well-being than the nonreligious group. However, the spiritual group showed that *spirituality alone* was a much stronger predictor of overall well-being than mere religiousness.

A study in the *Annals of Behavioral Medicine* showed that those who engage in some level of *daily spiritual practice or experience*, as distinct from claimed religious affiliation or traditional "religious" activities such as merely attending church, report a much higher quality of life, and even a boost in social status, over those without a daily spiritual practice.

The Spirit

Bliss is always a spiritual pursuit, sometimes a religious one.

At the heart of all spirituality is sacredness: the sensation that the world itself is miraculous, and crucially connected to and revealing of our essential being, and is therefore deserving of our concentrated, reverent attention. This quality of perception and concentration is fundamental to virtually all traditions of spiritual striving. It is to wonder and marvel at the mystery of existence; to feel awe in the face of the Infinite. It is an openness and enthusiasm for exploring our highest potentials, whatever they may be and wherever they may lead.

In my philosophical training, the most elementary question we grappled with was, *Why is there something rather than nothing?* This is the foundation of all mystery. As Albert Einstein said, "There are two ways to live: you can live as if nothing is a miracle; you can live as if everything is a miracle." At its most fundamental, spirituality is choosing to live as if everything is a miracle.

While this captures an essential aspect of spirituality, it's not quite complete. The one key missing ingredient? Ourselves. Specifically, our understanding of who we are and how we relate to the miracle of creation. A better definition might be: *Spirituality is the inner-directed practice of self-transcendence.*

Being inner-directed means taking responsibility for our own understanding and growth, through awareness and diligent practice of our transformational techniques. We acknowledge that real progress comes only when we penetrate to the deepest levels of our being. Beliefs, dogmas, and rituals, while not unimportant, are always secondary to authentic inner work. Most important, whenever we encounter a challenge or difficulty, we look inwardly at ourselves first before trying to change the world around us. Self-transcendence means to be both inwardly oriented and self-aware, while keenly interested in broadening our personal, egoistic perspective. It's to replace the personal with the universal. It's the recognition of our untapped potential and the fervent commitment to explore and develop it. Above all, it is to prioritize the expansion and elevation of our consciousness until we attain exaltedness. In doing so, we not only transform ourselves but the world.

It is important to acknowledge that all the world's major religions incorporate elements of this basic spiritual outlook. As an expert on comparative religion—both intellectually and practically—I've discovered that bliss is either the implicit or explicit goal of them all. As such, we needn't renounce our particular religious beliefs to discover bliss.

On the flip side, nor must we acquire any. Atheists and agnostics can pursue and attain bliss as well as anyone. We need only maintain a *positive* form of disbelief, which we might call "enchanted agnosticism." This requires only three things: (1) orienting ourselves toward the world as Einstein did and seeing everything as a miracle; (2) knowing or at least believing that we have untapped potentials; and (3) actually *doing the practices* in this book. The rest takes care of itself.

No one religion holds a monopoly on truth or bliss. There are universal truths embedded not only in all religions but also in every form of human aspiration. Whether we are Christian or Hindu, Jewish or Muslim, Buddhist or atheist, Wiccan or animist, Taoist or Native American, bliss forever remains available. In all religions, bliss *is* the end goal, although the terminology varies. Self-realization, enlightenment, union with Christ; *fana* in Islam; *samadhi* in Hinduism; *yehidah* in Judaism; nirvana in Buddhism; gnosis in various wisdom traditions; harmony with *Wakan Tanka* in the Native American tradition—just a few examples—are *all* ways of pointing to the *same* underlying experience of pure bliss.

Religions at their best offer us a clear and proven map and pathway toward bliss. They provide us with premade forms and well-marked charts designed to ensure a relatively safe pathway to self-transcendence. They are a collection of beliefs, practices, and rituals that, when actually performed, yield genuine results. Just as importantly, they offer us a community of fellow travelers who understand and support one another on our journey.

The dogmas, practices, rituals, and community that form a religion carve a single pathway up an infinite mountain. However effective that particular pathway may be, it's still only *one* way to the summit. There are *many* other trails. Further, within each religion, there are faster and slower lanes on that pathway. A precious few dive deep into all that their religion offers, verily sprinting upward. Others dawdle, take breaks, wander off the trail, even quit and descend back to base. Still others jump constantly from one path to another, always moving perpendicular to the mountaintop, never sticking with one path long enough to reach the summit.

Religions are a *vehicle* to transport us up to the mountaintop. The trick is that once we arrive, we must remember to disembark. Too often we become so habituated, even enamored with, our conveyance, we lose track of our original goal. Using our map analogy, we forget that our specific religion is just the map that helped us navigate the territory. As they say in India, "It is very good karma to be born into a religion, but very bad karma to die in one."

The goal in any case, whether or not we associate with a particular religion, is to avoid the dogmatism that comes from being too set in our ways to question our choices and satisfactions.

It's impossible to live without at least *some* beliefs. By "beliefs," I mean that which we accept as true though we don't (yet) have definitive proof. Everyone—including atheists, agnostics, scientists, and empiricists—holds beliefs of some sort; usually a large number of them. Scientists, for example, believe a great many scientific theories and "facts" outside of their own fields even though they have never personally run the experiments that confirm them. Atheists, in their clear statement that God doesn't exist or religion is false, are, in fact, expressing a *belief,* since no one could claim that "God" or "religion X" has been *proven* untrue.

There is nothing wrong with this. It's the *only* way it can be. The world is an infinite place, while we are finite people. We don't have the capacity to experience everything directly. None of us is omniscient and omnipresent. While we can't escape having beliefs, we *can* have the proper understanding and attitude toward them. First and foremost, we must be honest with ourselves. Do we *know* something is true or do we just *believe* (or hope) it to be?

We are best served when we adhere to our beliefs only provisionally, like a scientist would a hypothesis. Most scientists undertake an experiment—or even dedicate their life to a field of study—because they *believe* that their area of inquiry might yield interesting truths. The belief propels them forward, generating enough enthusiasm to prod them into conducting the experiment. Still, as much as they might *hope* that their experiment (or lifelong pursuit) will yield something true, a good scientist will admit it if the results don't validate the starting belief/hypothesis. He will then further reflect as to whether the failure can be rectified through adjustments or the theory should be abandoned.

Genuine spirituality requires total honesty. Once we find ourselves protecting beliefs that we know (or strongly suspect) are untrue, we've taken

238 | The Bliss Experiment

a step off the path and perhaps even lost our way. This only delays our ascendancy.

Once we have found a kindred path, bliss requires steady effort. This is not dogmatism but diligence: assiduous practice over time and a "religious" commitment to finding our way forward. The goal is not to dabble in the anthology of spiritual delights but to immerse ourselves in an appropriate practice that helps lead us to the pinnacle of realization and transcendence.

Many of us are well served by riding one of the extant vehicles up the mountain. This means finding an existing religion—and denomination or expression within that religion—to join. Of course, we often don't give this much thought. We go along with whatever religion we were born into. Or, if we decide to reject our birth religion, it doesn't occur to us that alternatives exist apart from nothingness.

It is vitally important not to be a dilettante, aimlessly flitting from religion to religion, group to group, pathway to pathway. In the beginning, exploration of different approaches is not only acceptable but also desirable. It helps us find the right fit for us. Different religions and denominations—or teachers within a religion—really do fit some of us better than others.

At some point, though, it's time to choose a particular pathway and get climbing. All pathways will have difficult stretches. It's imperative not to quickly abandon our chosen path because it's temporarily arduous or we're bored. None of the world's great religions surrenders its deepest truths to dilettantes. There are *always* tests and challenges. The spiritual path is not for cowards or weaklings. Occasionally a change is justified, especially if we are *certain* that our initial choice was mistaken. If, however, we find ourselves frequently changing religions, we can be sure that the real problem is our inner attitude, not the discarded pathways.

Regardless of the path we choose—including trying to blaze our own—the teachings and practices in this book are essential. They are the universal keys for finding the blissful state at the summit.

The Experiment: Sanctify Everything

This is very simple. Following the guidance of Albert Einstein himself, this experiment requires only making a conscious effort to see everything we encounter in the next day as a miracle. Make a conscious effort to feel wonder, excitement, and awe.

1. You can look at the landscape, a sunset, or any natural phenomenon: trees, hills, rivers, oceans, vistas, animals—anything and everything in creation. See the phenomenal complexity, harmony, and mystery behind it. Also look at our fellow humans. So many shapes, sizes, colors, interests, behaviors, outlooks! It's incredible.

2. Look, too, at the objects around you. The technology: computers, cell phones, televisions, the Internet, your bathroom, kitchen appliances. Furniture, fabrics, bedding. All of your food choices, both in your home and at the supermarket. All of the myriad expressions of human creativity and ingenuity. Clothes, cars, watches—even basic things like lighting and air-conditioning.

3. Look at the miracle and mystery of your own body. Even if you are not perfectly well, think how many things are going right in your body. (More things must be going right than wrong, or else you'd be dead!) For that matter, think of the mystery of death. That we come into existence on this plane and then vanish. Where do we go? It's all just so incredible. What an amazing journey.

4. Take an opportunity to feel the wondrous awe and delight in everything you experience. The more you can bring this attitude into every moment, the more attuned you will be to the miracles that surround us and inhabit us, to the miracle that we are, just by dint of being here at all.

Online

Additional videos and resources for this chapter are available at www.theblissexperiment.com.

PART 5

Making Direct Contact

We now come to the heart of this book. It's time to explore bliss directly and deeply. We've been slowly working ourselves up the Happiness Scale toward higher realms of consciousness. We've examined our relationship to our external world, the inner world of our mind, and the best ways to understand and interact with people and our environment. All of this has created a broad context and solid foundation for bliss. Now that the foundation is built, in this section, we'll concentrate exclusively on bliss itself and its attendant practices.

CHAPTER 22

The Nature of Bliss

It's good to be just plain happy, it's a little better to know that
you're happy; but to understand that you're happy and to know
why and how and still be happy, be happy in the being and the
knowing, well that is beyond happiness, that is bliss.

—Henry Miller, *American author*
(1891–1980)

Bliss is difficult to describe. Like most profound experiences, it transcends
language. It has an ineffable quality that literally leaves one speechless. It's
not that bliss itself is a vague or hazy experience. Quite the opposite, it represents the very pinnacle of clarity available. We truly ascend to a cosmic
perspective of ourselves, our environment, of every atom in creation. But
how does one capture such an experience in words?

It's not easy. Language by nature is limiting, proscribed, and literally,
definite. All words have a definition. To *define* means to state or describe
exactly the nature, scope, or meaning of something. It also means to mark
out the boundaries or limits. Yet bliss is an intrinsically infinite experience.
It's the complete antithesis of "defined." Not because it's inchoate, fuzzy,
dreamy, blurred, or ambiguous but because it is so vast, boundless, and im-
measurable that it encompasses every possible word or definition ever in-
vented—and then some. This is, of course, why we continue to stress that
bliss must be personally experienced, not just discussed.

With this caveat and understanding established, let's now take our
deepest, most refined look at the nature of bliss itself.

The Story

Katie grew up in a suburb of San Diego. One day around dusk, when she was a teenager, she was sitting on a bluff overlooking the ocean. She looked out at the seemingly endless water and found herself wondering, "Why is this all here? Why am I here?" Suddenly she felt weightless, free, and unburdened. She had a sense of a veil being lifted on creation. She felt a joyful oneness, as if she (but not the "she" of her ego, more like the world of which she was a part) had answers to everything, all of life's mysteries were solved, that she knew everything had a divine meaning.

Katie didn't know how long that feeling lingered, as she lost track of time. But it was clear when it ended: all of her weight, her mental and bodily tension, came crashing back into her. The veil had closed. She felt peaceful but also a little confined, as if the experience were her true reality and most of her life was unreal.

She desperately wanted to get back to that place but had no idea how. For months she returned to the same spot and tried to re-create her thoughts at just that moment, but it never came. She was confused, even a touch despondent, but also persistent. The young woman felt a strong connection to the ocean, so she took up surfing and scuba diving. She especially enjoyed diving. Although it never provided anything quite like that initial experience, she loved the peacefulness, beauty, and harmony of floating in the deep. Katie traveled the world, sampling all the best dive locations.

While she was diving in Belize, she met a man on the dive boat. He was considerably older. Their relationship wasn't romantic, just a natural friendship. He, too, found diving to be an almost mystical experience. He told Katie that he had learned to meditate in an ashram in India and that it helped him appreciate his diving experiences. He taught her the technique he learned, although she didn't really have the time or space to do it much on that trip. After she returned from Belize, she made a concerted effort to practice.

About a week later, Katie was sitting in her room doing this simple technique when she felt the weight leave her body, just as it had years ago. This time, however, it wasn't so much a feeling of oneness as it was an intense, almost pleasurable feeling (though she said that wasn't quite the right word). Her body pulsated with waves of energy that moved from below her waist up to the top of her head. It was so powerful, she wondered if she might burst. It was almost too much for her nervous system to handle. In an instant—just as her mind was pondering if this might be too much of a good thing—the sensation vanished as quickly as it had appeared.

Katie was left with a profound feeling of calmness and joy. Though the experience had been almost too intense, it was a good kind of intensity. She felt happier, more complete than she had ever felt before. She didn't have the vocabulary for it at the time, but Katie had indeed experienced her first glimpse of pure bliss. In just those few moments, her life was transformed forever.

The Science

Bliss is a genuine state of consciousness different from both "normal, everyday" consciousness and mental illness. It's natural to wonder if these profoundly positive experiences are really just a form of psychosis or insanity. Fortunately, the research proves that nothing could be further from the truth. At least a half dozen studies demonstrate this from a variety of approaches.

The journal *Psychological Reports* published a study that evaluated 118 people who had claimed some sort of mystical or exalted experience. After subjecting them to a battery of tests, the researchers concluded that *all* of the subjects had a stable personality, with no signs of mental illness. In fact, they exhibited high levels of functioning.

A separate study conducted by researchers at the Southern Virginia Mental Health Institute compared three groups: (1) "mystical contemplatives," as they called them; (2) "normal," healthy people; and (3) psychotics. They found that it was *easy* to distinguish among all three groups. There was little overlap in their behaviors or personality traits..

Similar studies, including one published in *Schizophrenia Bulletin*, have found that those reporting mystic experiences show no signs of either neurotic or psychotic behavior and what's more, that schizophrenia and mystical experience are unrelated, share no significant characteristics, and are *easily* discernable to any mental health professional. Surprisingly, these mainstream researchers suggested that while extreme mental illness is relatively uncommon, they suspect that "the human capacity for mystical experience may in fact be widespread."

Now that we can be certain that those who have mystical experiences aren't insane—or even neurotic—it brings up the question, exactly what *is* going on in the brain of a mystic?

While this area of research is new, a few highly intriguing studies provide some insight. Neuroscientists Mario Beauregard and Vincent Paquette from the University of Montreal published the seminal study in the journal *Neuroscience Letters*. They received permission to study the brain functions of Carmelite (Catholic) nuns *while* the nuns were having mystical experiences—including while they claimed to be in a state of "union with God." The nuns were hooked up to fMRI machines. From this study, Dr. Beauregard drew some important conclusions:

- Mystical experience does not come from one brain region. There is no single "God spot." These experiences, he wrote, "are complex and multidimensional and mediated by a number of brain regions normally implicated in perception, cognition, emotion, body representation, and self-consciousness. This conclusion correlates well with subjects' descriptions of [their experiences] as complex and multidimensional."
- There was a large spike in theta brain waves while the nuns were in the mystical condition, which is different from our normal, everyday brain state. Theta is commonly associated with REM sleep, hypnosis, and lucid dreaming. When accessed while in a conscious state, theta waves improve our learning, healing, and spiritual growth.
- The abundance of theta activity during the mystical experiences demonstrated a clear change in the nuns' consciousness.
- This same theta state has also been observed in studies of Zen Buddhists and of subjects doing a type of *Kriya yoga* meditation in which the practitioner reports being in a "blissful state."

Richard Davidson, director of the Laboratory for Affective Neuroscience at the University of Wisconsin, has made studying the brain states of spiritual practitioners a primary focus. In collaboration with the Dalai Lama, Dr. Davidson gained the cooperation of a number of long-time Tibetan Buddhist monks to come to America and participate in a study.

These advanced meditators went into higher states of consciousness while undergoing brain-imaging scans. The researchers concluded that longtime spiritual adepts have completely different brain wave patterns while meditating. The scans revealed not only elevated theta activity but also clear bursts of gamma waves—much more activity than had ever been seen in a "normal" person. Gamma brain waves are the brain state of hyperalertness, perception, integration of sensory input, and along with theta, most closely associated with spiritual experience and growth. In addition, the monks' brains showed high levels of synchrony, or coordination, with the nerve cells firing in an unusually rhythmic, coherent manner suggesting deep harmony. The longer the monks had practiced meditation, the higher their levels of these positive gamma waves. This indicates that the brain can be trained and physically modified in positive ways that most experts hadn't realized was possible.

These states of consciousness are not only *different* from those of psychotics and "normal" people, they are objectively *better*. Studies have shown that people who can access these states of consciousness are:

- more likely to have higher moral development and hold positive values;
- more at peace with death and dying;
- less likely to commit suicide;
- less likely to relapse into addiction;
- less tense and stressed;
- more successful and able to outperform those who don't have such experiences in everyday real-world tasks; and
- happier, better adjusted, and have a stronger sense of life's meaning and personal purpose.

The Spirit

If bliss is all around us, why so do few of us see, feel, or experience it?

Like so many aspects of life, bliss is not readily apparent to our senses. Because bliss is not an object or a thing, our faculties of sight, hearing, touch, taste, and smell are not designed to detect it. Our senses, as wonderful as they may be, are designed only to process certain kinds of experiences, especially the external world of things. This renders them wholly ineffective at discovering bliss.

The notion that our unaided senses are limited in their capabilities is hardly revolutionary. Almost *every* scientific and technological discovery of the past four hundred years required some kind of addition or modification to our basic faculties. Our unaided senses detect only a small portion of the actual world. Astronomers need telescopes, biologists peer through microscopes, and physicists rely on calculus to do their jobs. We've had to create *millions* of tools in order to extend our innate facilities.

Sometimes, too, something is so pervasive that's it difficult to comprehend. Gravity didn't come into existence when the English physicist and mathematician Isaac Newton discovered it in 1686. It existed since the beginning of the universe; we just didn't understand what we were experiencing until Newton explained it. This is what the great spiritual adepts from the world's religions do for bliss: they "discover" it and then report to the rest of us what they've found so that we can understand it ourselves.

Discovering gravity—proving it, that is, and not just theorizing about it—required much more than watching an apple fall from a tree. Newton had to use a variety of mathematical tools, some of which he had to create himself, in the form of calculus. Without the assistance of mathematics and other apparatus, we couldn't see, grasp, or understand gravity, despite having been surrounded by it since the dawn of existence.

Bliss, too, requires certain tools. Unlike scientific tools—which can mostly be understood as methods for extending our senses—spiritual tools enhance a different set of our faculties. Some of those tools have already been presented. The most powerful tools will be introduced in subsequent chapters, including learning the specific techniques used by the Carmelite nuns and Tibetan Buddhist monks, among others.

The Illusion of Duality

In order to discover all-pervading bliss, we must first quell duality. Duality is the constant vibration of the universe that creates the illusion of separateness. Think of a chair. It supports our weight when we sit on it, and it seems relatively hard and permanent in that it doesn't disappear from one minute or day to the next. At another level of reality, however, chairs aren't remotely firm, let alone permanent. If we look closely enough at a wooden chair, we find that it's nothing but a compilation of atoms—in turn, a collection of subatomic particles—moving *really* fast in a specific pattern. Believe it or not, 99.99 percent of every atom is empty space! Yet we don't fall through the chair when we sit on it. That doesn't change the fact that, at the microscopic level, the solidity of the chair *doesn't exist*. "Hardness" is a quality that emerges from certain perspectives but is nonexistent at others.

Patterns of vibration manifest more than just physical objects. Our minds manufacture a mental duality through the everyday process of making distinctions and seeing differences. It is the act of comparison, relativity, and differentiation. Hot or cold. Pleasure or pain. Up or down. Right or wrong. In or out. Positive or negative. Black or white. Success or failure. Even good or bad. These sets of opposites vibrate together to create the illusion of separateness from each other. Every person, thought, feeling, and object vibrates in a different pattern and at a different speed.

Duality is created by our sense of ego, "*I*-ness," and our inner mind river—that voice within us that we think of as "me." Our egos are always labeling, judging, commenting, comparing, and making distinctions. This continually reinforces our feeling that this inner-me dialogue is "who I am." Yet it is real only from a certain level of consciousness, just as a chair appears firm from one perspective. Our ego is real in a certain sense but unreal in the highest sense, just as our dreams during sleep are real enough while we're in sleep consciousness but vanish when we awake. Resolving duality wakes us from the slumber of our everyday lives; when that happens, our ego simply vanishes like our dreams.

Bliss requires damming our mind river or at least penetrating its illusory, dreamlike nature. We can't simultaneously be *invested* in our egoic mind river self and experience bliss. To cling to our ego is to insist upon on differentiation, judgment, and disconnectedness. Our everyday consciousness—even a happy one—*creates* separation, like cutting up the world into millions of distinct pieces of a jigsaw puzzle. When we resolve the delusion of duality, we reassemble the puzzle. One seamless and complete picture emerges. This is bliss consciousness.

The Experience of Bliss

Bliss is what remains after the world of things dissolves. In bliss consciousness we feel our narrow individuality transformed. The wave patterns generating the illusion of duality resolve into oneness. We're overwhelmed with a feeling of expansiveness and unconditional love. It is a feeling without a center. In this state, there is no "I, me, or mine"—our ego. It's an experience without an experiencer, an infinite continuity of wholeness. Bliss simply *is*.

As Paramhansa Yogananda wrote, "It is a transcendental state of superior calm including within itself the consciousness of a great expansion and that of 'all in One and One in all.'" Buddhists often describe this state as nothingness. What they mean—at least the realized adepts—is not emptiness but *no-thing-ness*. "Things" come into being when we differentiate and make distinctions between this and that. In a state of unbroken wholeness, there can't be separate things.

Because all boundaries have dissolved, in bliss we can see, feel, and know things that don't seem humanly possible to see, feel, and know. We can experience the world not only through ourselves but also through others. One time, while I was lying in bed with the curtains drawn in a dark room, writhing in pain—these were my darkest times—I heard my neighbor's children outside playing, although I couldn't see them. They were two sisters, perhaps six and ten years old. I could hear their shrieks of delight and laughter. Putting aside my own pain for a moment, I concentrated deeply on *their* joy. Suddenly I found myself feeling the laughter, joy, and innocent freedom that they were experiencing. My pain evaporated. I was flooded with a weightless, connected, superconscious bliss.

We can experience this at any moment, in any situation, and through any channel because we live in a sea of pure conscious awareness. Bliss flows around us, through us, in every atom in the universe.

Bliss is not something we create, invent, or produce. It is something to which we attune ourselves. This makes sense only if we have the proper model of consciousness. Some people *believe* (there is no proof) that consciousness is created *inside* our brains, as if our minds are a secretion, even a side effect, of the approximately three pounds of brain matter residing in our heads. A more useful model might be to think of our brains as radios and consciousness as radio waves.

Radios don't *create* the programming that we hear. They capture it out of the air and then amplify it. The different levels of consciousness that we each embody are akin to the different stations we choose to tune into. Some stations play heavy, depressing music; others, light and uplifting music. We can change the vibration of what's flowing through us by learning how to change the channels of our consciousness. Looking for bliss consciousness inside our brains is like trying to open our car radio to see where the Rolling Stones, or Howard Stern, or Terry Gross live inside our dashboard. They aren't there, and we won't find them no matter how hard we look.

Tuning into bliss requires a specialized set of tools, plus the instruction and experience in their use. Once we acquire this, we'll find that the all-pervading joy of bliss permeates our existence, quietly awaiting our discovery.

The Experiment:
An Experience of Cosmic Consciousness

In 1929, Paramhansa Yogananda wrote a poem called "Samadhi" that captures the experience of pure bliss. This poem is special because Yogananda wrote it *while in a state of bliss*. This isn't an "after report" or distant memory. It's an attempt to communicate bliss as it's unfolding.

Samadhi is a Sanskrit word meaning "oneness of human consciousness with cosmic consciousness." Just as the wave melts into the sea, so too does the human soul become spirit.

The experiment for today is to read and visualize the poem. Take your time. Try to feel it, see it, and absorb it. It will help you better understand what bliss is and inspire you to experience it for yourself.

"Samadhi"

Vanished the veils of light and shade,
Lifted every vapor of sorrow,
Sailed away all dawns of fleeting joy,
Gone the dim sensory mirage.
Love, hate, health, disease, life, death,
Perished these false shadows on the screen of duality.
Waves of laughter, scyllas of sarcasm, melancholic whirlpools,
Melting in the vast sea of bliss.
The storm of maya stilled
By magic wand of intuition deep.
The Universe, forgotten dream, subconsciously lurks,
Ready to invade my newly wakened memory divine.
I live without the cosmic shadow,
But it is not, bereft of me;
As the sea exists without the waves,
But they breathe not without the sea.
Dreams, wakings, states of deep turiya sleep,
Present, past, future, no more for me,
But ever-present, all-flowing I, I, everywhere.
Planets, stars, stardust, earth,
Volcanic bursts of doomsday cataclysms,
Creation's molding furnace,
Glaciers of silent x-rays, burning electron floods,
Thoughts of all men, past, present, to come,
Every blade of grass, myself, mankind,
Each particle of universal dust,
Anger, greed, good, bad, salvation, lust,
I swallowed, transmuted all
Into a vast ocean of blood of my own one Being!
Smoldering joy, oft-puffed by meditation

Blinding my tearful eyes,
Burst into immortal flames of bliss,
Consumed my tears, my frame, my all.
Thou art I, I am Thou,
Knowing, Knower, Known, as One!
Tranquilled, unbroken thrill, eternally living, ever new peace!
Enjoyable beyond imagination of expectancy, samadhi bliss!
Not a mental chloroform
Or unconscious state without willful return,
Samadhi but extends my conscious realm
Beyond the limits of the mortal frame
To farthest boundary of eternity
Where I, the Cosmic Sea,
Watch the little ego floating in me.
The sparrow, each grain of sand, fall not without my sight.
All space like an iceberg floats within my mental sea.
Colossal Container, I, of all things made.
By deeper, longer, thirsty, guru-given meditation
Comes this celestial samadhi
Mobile murmurs of atoms are heard,
The dark earth, mountains, vales, lo! molten liquid!
Flowing seas change into vapors of nebulae!
Aum blows upon the vapors, opening wondrously their veils,
Oceans stand revealed, shining electrons,
Till, at last sound of the cosmic drum,
Vanish the grosser lights into eternal rays
Of all-pervading bliss.
From joy I came, for joy I live, in sacred joy I melt.
Ocean of mind, I drink all creation's waves.
Four veils of solid, liquid, vapor, light,
Lift aright.
Myself, in everything, enters the Great Myself.
Gone forever, fitful, flickering shadows of mortal memory.
Spotless is my mental sky, below, ahead, and high above.

Eternity and I, one united ray.
A tiny bubble of laughter, I
Am become the Sea of Mirth Itself.

Online

Additional videos and resources for this chapter are available at www.theblissexperiment.com.

CHAPTER 23

Discovering the Bliss Within

The soul's nature is bliss—a lasting, inner state of ever-new, ever-changing joy which eternally entertains, even when one passes through the trials of suffering.

—Paramhansa Yogananda

For this chapter and the next, we'll dive deeply into the practice of meditation, which is the single most important bliss practice. In fact, it's the most important practice of any kind. Meditation is the closest thing to a magic bullet that humanity has ever discovered. Let me put this as succinctly as possible: if you only do one practice in life, meditate.

Meditation helps with our body, mind, and spirit. It works on every level of our being. If you want to be more successful in business, meditate. If you want to live longer and with less stress, meditate. If you want to tap into creativity or intuition, meditate. If you want to find the meaning of life, meditate. If you want to be happy, meditate. If you want to develop your spiritual self fully, meditate. There is nothing that it cannot improve; every other activity, advice, or practice pales in comparison.

Best of all, meditation can be practiced by almost anyone and everyone. It doesn't matter your age, race, mental capacity, religious beliefs, physical fitness, or anything.

The Story

Judy was a cheerleader in high school. She was a naturally happy, bubbly, peppy personality. A natural optimist, she is not prone to depression. She married a man she met during her senior year of college. They had two children, lived in the suburbs, and seemed moderately happy. Her husband was a midlevel executive at a large corporation. After taking many years off from work to raise their children, Judy reentered the workforce part-time as an executive assistant at a food product company.

One day she made a surprise visit to her husband's office during lunchtime. She saw him sitting in his car with a woman coworker. They were kissing and clearly having an intimate conversation. In that moment, Judy knew her marriage was over, though it would take many months before her husband moved out and she filed for divorce.

As Judy began rebuilding her life, she felt both sad and hopeful. Since she was a naturally positive person, she didn't spend a lot of time moping around. To her credit, she saw it mostly as an opportunity for a new life and new adventures. Her husband had given her a stable but—she had to admit—pretty boring life. For the first time in almost twenty years, she was free to do what she wanted, explore her own interests, and become the person she'd always wanted to be.

A couple years prior to her divorce, Judy had begun doing yoga postures at her local gym. She now found herself doing it more and more. She found it really helped her mentally and physically. She switched to a dedicated yoga studio that offered a more intensive practice. One of her new teachers recommended that Judy learn to meditate. Soon after, she attended one of my four-week class series. During the second class, I taught her the meditation technique we'll explore in the next chapter.

At the beginning of the third week's class, participants had the opportunity to share their meditation experiences from the past week; they were supposed to practice every day. Judy told us about an amazing experience she'd had just two days before. While her eyes were closed, she saw a bright white light in her forehead with a shining star in the middle. The deepest feeling of peace she had ever known washed over her. Judy's mind went entirely quiet as she floated in a deep, joyful peace for several minutes. When it ended, tears of happiness were streaming down her cheeks. She said she'd never felt so alive, thankful, calm, and perfectly whole. In her lighthearted way, she exclaimed, "I can't believe it took me this long to meditate!"

Since then, Judy has not only continued to develop her mediation practice but also now leads a small group meditation in her local community. It's a core part of her life. Meditation has changed her life completely. When she runs into friends from her "old" life with her husband, they hardly recognize her. One close friend even asked if she'd had plastic surgery because she looked so different! (She hadn't.) Judy added, "For the first time, I feel like every part of my life is working. Physically, mentally, and spiritually, life has never been better!"

The Science

Meditation is the best-studied practice in this book. There are thousands of published studies examining the efficacy of different aspects and applications of the practice. In this chapter, we'll look at what science has discovered about meditation's effect on the brain. In chapter 22, we'll explore some of the practical results that we can expect to gain from regular practice.

One of the most exciting findings is that meditation can literally reshape the brain. For decades, scientists believed that the adult brain was permanently hardwired and unchangeable—that the shape of the brain at maturity was what you had to work with for life. But we now know that this is false, and that the mature brain changes in all sorts of ways throughout our lives. What is exciting for us is that meditation has been shown to be one of the most effective and direct ways in which we can intentionally reform our own plastic brains. By practicing patterns of concentration, we can actually change our brain structure. This has enormous implications for our health, our concepts of who we can be, and, through the changes we choose to make, for our futures.

Meditation acts positively on our brain in myriad ways. At a basic level, it changes the ratio of activity between the right and left hemispheres. There is evidence that the right hemisphere is associated with negative emotion, while the left side processes happiness. Research conducted by Dr. Richard Davidson, which you read about in the previous chapter, indicates that long-term meditators have much higher levels of left-brained activity than nonmeditators.

Beyond this simple distinction, meditation changes the patterns of electrical waves in our brains. The billions of neurons in our brains constantly emit electrical charges that can be recorded by EEG machines. En masse, our neurons create broad categories of electrical frequencies that correspond to the underlying subjective states that we're feeling. An average, healthy person relaxing with her eyes closed will have a different brain wave frequency than, say, if she fell into deep sleep. An epileptic in the middle of a seizure will show a tremendous, almost chart-busting surge of activity with each convulsion.

Numerous studies show that meditation boosts delta and gamma brain waves. This generates feelings of peacefulness, happiness, and heartfulness; stabilizes awareness and augments our feeling of spaciousness; enhances our ability to tune out unwanted or overwhelming sensory inputs from our environment—which tend to induce anxiety, nervousness, and tension—and sharpens our attention and focus.

Meditation doesn't merely change brain waves. It also permanently alters brain density. (That's a good thing!) The brain's density tends to thin as we age, leading to a variety of difficulties. A team led by Sarah Lazar at Massachusetts General Hospital discovered that in as little as *eight weeks*, meditators developed measurable increases in cortical thickness (the outer layer of the cerebral cortex, composed of folded gray matter and playing an important role in consciousness), especially in the prefrontal regions associated with attention, interoception (sensitivity to stimuli originating inside of the body), and sensory processing, known to be important for learning and memory, and in structures associated with self-awareness, compassion and introspection. Encouragingly, this effect was most pronounced for older meditators, suggesting that meditation might slow or reverse the aging process. Other studies have found that meditation increases activity in the prefrontal cortex, aiding in both cognitive and emotional processing capabilities.

Several studies also suggest that meditation increases blood flow to the brain. Our brain is the body's largest consumer of oxygen, which gets transported throughout the circulatory system by way of red blood cells. Although the brain represents only about 2 percent of our total body mass, it accounts for more than 25 percent of the blood flow. Increased oxygen delivery to the brain improves cognition and concentration and retards the onset of dementia and brain degeneration.

Meditation also affects the neurotransmitters in the brain. A study published in the journal *Cognitive Brain Research* concluded that meditation increases the release of dopamine. Regulation of this brain chemical plays a crucial role in our mental and physical health. It affects brain processes that control movement, emotional response, and the ability to experience pleasure and pain. According to another study, published in the *Journal of Neural Transmission*, meditation also boosts serotonin levels. Serotonin is the primary neurotransmitter acted upon by SSRIs, the most recent generation of antidepressant medications. It is essential for maintaining a feeling of happiness, helps control our moods, aids sleep, calms anxiety, and relieves depression.

Finally (although we could keep going), let's also note that meditation helps with neural stability in the brain, probably by increasing overall coherence and connections. Impaired attention and emotional instability are hallmarks of many forms of mental illness. Meditation can help "stitch together" brain functioning and boost cohesion. It also helps form new connections between neurons and discrete areas within the brain. In addition, it can repair lost or damaged neural pathways associated with aging.

The Spirit

At its heart, meditation is a transformational practice. It transforms our body, mind, and, most of all, spirit. Because it's all encompassing, there are many ways to define or understand it. Here are a few of the definitions that I have found most useful:

* when the mind and body are still, and the heart is open;
* upward relaxation (not just "relaxation"—but *upward* toward expanded, uplifted, superconsciousness);
* remembering who *you* really *are*; and
* a vacation for the mind.

In some ways, I prefer the last definition. Who doesn't want to go on vacation? It's positive and approachable. Best of all, it's the only kind of vacation we can take any time or any place, with no expense, planning, or difficulty. How wonderful is that?

It may also be helpful to understand meditation by knowing what it is *not*: sleeping, daydreaming, spacing out, or being passive. It is an *active* practice. A purposeful, directed attention that lifts the mind upward against the inertia of its continually downward-coursing stream of thought. Meditation as we mean it is an externally silent practice. Though the technique involves mental activity, we won't be using music, guided visualizations, or any other outwardly audible experience. It's also not the same as intercessory prayer. A useful distinction: prayer is *asking* for guidance, meditation is *listening* for the answer.

Meditation and Bliss

By lifting and stilling the mind, meditation allows bliss to break through into the normally distracted and defensive self.

Let's return to our analogy of the mind as a river. Most of the practices we've learned so far can be understood as working with the quality of the "water" flowing through our minds. Practices such as gratitude and optimism take a muddy mind and infuse it with fresh, clear water. Meditation is wholly different. It doesn't merely clean our mental river; it helps it to vanish altogether. It's like building a dam that at first greatly slows, and then, with practice, introduces a complete cessation of our usually endless parade of thoughts, emotions, and images. Remember, too, as we explored in the last chapter, it's this mind river that generates our perception of egoic separateness and individuation; that false sense of "I, me, mine" that masks our deepest and Highest Self. Slowing the mind river's volume allows the underlying bliss to shine forth.

If a mind is like a river, the following diagram helps illustrate the effect of meditation. Think of the unbroken line as our usual stream of thoughts, emotions, and images.

Everyday mind without meditation:

_____

Meditation introduces gaps by damming the mind river:

____ ____ _____ ____ __ __ _____

The more we meditate, the more spaces appear between our thoughts:

____   _____   ___ __ __ __ ___   ____   __ __

Eventually the mind of an advanced meditator looks like this:

__   ___   ___   ___   ___   ___

Without meditation, even a positive mind still feels like an unbroken river of egoic separation. Meditation quiets the mind, enabling moments of bliss to occasionally peak through the gaps. The more we meditate, the quieter our minds become, and the more bliss radiates through.

If we could see the mind of a spiritual master, we'd realize that he has thoughts only when necessary. The rest of the time, he is quietly absorbed in bliss.

One important implication is that bliss is directional. It's not either/or, on/off, yes/no. We can have small experiences of it—as many people report in those moments when their conscious minds quiet for reasons beyond their control—and those experiences can grow in frequency and intensity. Only the most accomplished spiritual geniuses live in pure bliss all the time. Even small amounts of meditation practice produce significant experiences of bliss.

Different Techniques and Styles

Meditation is found in every religion I've encountered. There are Christian, Jewish, Muslim, Hindu, Buddhist, Native American, shamanistic, Jain, Taoist, Confucian, Zoroastrian, and Wiccan variations, to name just a few. Neither does meditation require any specific religious beliefs. That meditation is found in each the world's major religions is yet more testimony to its singular importance. Spiritual aspirants and adepts of every tradition have independently discovered the efficacy of this practice.

There are hundreds of specific meditation techniques. Most of these, in turn, can be classified according to a few broad groups. The four main categories are: mantra, awareness/listening, movement, and breath manipulation.

Mantra techniques use the silent repetition of a word or phrase in our mind, often (but not always) synchronized with the inhalations and exhalations of the breath. Awareness and listening techniques require paying attention to something: our mind river as it drifts along, external sounds in our environment, or an inner experience deep inside our mind. Movement meditation uses the body, often synchronized with breathing, to elevate our consciousness. Breathing techniques consciously manipulate our breath in certain ways.

I've personally used techniques from every category and religious tradition. In my own daily practice, I use at least one from three of the four main categories.

As with religions, we sometimes encounter dogmatic partisans of a particular school or technique who claims that theirs is the "best." I don't listen to these meditation dogmatists any more than I do religious fanatics. Both scientifically and spiritually, it's been demonstrated conclusively that the main techniques are equally effective. As with religion, we may discover a preference for one over another, but it's essential to recognize that it is a personal decision.

In the next chapter, we will learn a good, basic beginner's meditation technique that has been researched in over seven hundred scientific studies. I chose this one because I know it's effective, easy to learn, and relatively simple. If you feel drawn to a different technique that falls within the guidelines of this chapter, feel free to use it instead.

The Experiment: Learning to Breathe

Meditation is made more effective by beginning with transitional breathing exercises. These practices are not meditation techniques themselves. Rather they help prime us for meditation. They create a buffer between whatever was happening immediately prior to meditating and the practice itself. More importantly, these techniques begin the process of quieting the mind, and bringing a sense of inner peace and receptiveness that enhance meditation's effectiveness.

The following two practices are done immediately prior to meditation. They can also be used on their own, throughout the course of the day, whenever we need to induce a state of relaxation quickly.

Breathing Technique 1: Double Breathing

This is *very* fast and easy. If you are using this as a transition to meditation, do it in a seated position. If you are using it independent of meditation, you can do it from any comfortable position, including standing or lying down.

1. Begin by taking a few deep breaths, becoming aware of your lungs and the rhythm of your breathing.
2. Next, do a two-part inhalation, through your nose, while consciously bringing tension into the muscles of the body. The first inhalation is short and sharp, immediately followed by a long, strong inhalation that fills the lungs completely.
3. Then, without pause, exhale through your mouth: again, first with a short exhalation and then a long exhalation. Release all the tension in your body along with the breath.

The breathing sounds like this on the inhalation through the nose: "*sniff, sniiifffff.*" Yes, the sound really is a bit like when we're sniffing or taking a strong inhalation through our nose. The exhalation through the mouth sounds like this: "*Huh, Huuuhhhh.*" The exhalation throws the breath out of us, in two distinct phases. Both sounds should be audible.

This breath is accompanied by tensing the body from head to toe during the inhalation and rapidly throwing out all bodily tension during the exhalation. Tensing and then relaxing the tension in our muscles allows the body to release any bodily stiffness or anxiety quickly.

Tense and relax the body in conjunction with double breathing three to six times. Each round takes only five to ten seconds, so even six rounds doesn't take long.

Breathing Technique 2: Even-Count Breathing

This practice, also called "measured breathing," is when we inhale, hold the breath, and then exhale for the same duration at each step. Be sure to sit while doing this practice.

1. Close your eyes. Look gently up and out behind closed eyelids.
2. Now inhale through your nose for a count of six seconds.
3. Hold the breath for six seconds.
4. Exhale for six seconds.
5. Immediately begin your next inhalation—do *not* hold the breath out of the lungs.
6. Do this for three to six rounds. When you are done, you can gently open your eyes.

Be sure to begin your next inhalation immediately after completing your exhalation. We do *not* hold our breath for six seconds. You can count silently in your mind or gently tap on your leg six times.

As you inhale, feel the breath first filling your belly and diaphragm area. Make sure that your belly is not constricted by clothing. As the inhalation flows upward from the diaphragm, the rib cage expands outward to the sides and a little in back. Finally, you can expand the air, if you need to, into your chest area.

All three phases should flow together smoothly; there should never be a sense of strain. Exhale in the reverse order.

As you inhale, try to feel the breath flowing up the body. As you exhale, feel the descending breath taking you deeply into inner peace.

You can adjust the count either shorter or longer. Some people can do this only for a count of four, while others can go for counts of eight, ten, or twelve. I know one person who does it for twenty-four seconds! Find the right duration for you, based on your lung capacity, breath control, and comfort. It is *extremely important* to feel no strain as you do this. The point is to induce peacefulness, not compete with anyone or turn yourself blue! Most people use a count between six and ten.

Online

Scan the Microsoft Tag above to view a brief video, "Meditation Positions," or go to youtube.com/seanmeshorer.

CHAPTER 24

The Power of Bliss

Meditation is the answer, the only answer.
—*Sri Chinmoy, Indian spiritual teacher (1931–2007)*

In this chapter, we'll learn a powerful, scientifically and spiritually proven technique called *Hong-Sau*. I've used—and continue to use—many different meditation techniques on a daily basis. *Hong-Sau* is the easiest to learn, grounds us in the fundamentals of meditation, and is enormously effective right away. It takes very little practice and a minimal learning curve to get up and running at full speed. Even now, more than twenty years after I first began meditating, and with a whole arsenal of interesting and advanced techniques at my disposal, I still practice *Hong-Sau* every day. It's something that you can do daily for the rest of your life and continue to learn, grow, and obtain a tremendous depth of wonderful experience.

The Story

Andre is biracial, with a white mother and a black father. He grew up in a conventional Baptist household. Though his family attended church regularly, it never meant very much to Andre. He saw the Bible as a sometimes inspiring, often confusing, and occasionally maddening book. He felt particular concern about how it was used so frequently to justify intolerance, bigotry, and sectarian hairsplitting. He naturally recoiled at what he calls the "holier-than-thou" attitude of so many believers.

Over thirty years ago, Andre's parents started a gourmet grocery and food products business that specializes in importing uncommon items from Europe, Asia, and Africa. Today his parents are retired, and Andre is the CEO.

When he first took the helm, the family business was a mess. Much larger competitors had recently entered the business and were squeezing out most of the smaller entities. In addition, consolidation among retailers—most every major store was now part of a chain—had made it difficult sometimes to even get the attention of a chain's buying staff. In his first two years as CEO, Andre wasn't sure if he was making things better or worse. The company was disorganized, and revenues were declining slightly. Andre worried that he was in over his head.

The stress was starting to get to him. A friend recommended that he learn a nonsectarian form of meditation.

Three years later, his company is thriving. Andre decided to focus on importing Fair Trade goods; this captured the attention of grocers and gourmet markets across North America. Andre has taken a leading position in the industry. He is part of a group developing fair trade guidelines for farmers and artisans around the world. His company invests in local communities on three continents and gives to charities and nonprofit organizations both at home and abroad. Not only does the company now financially support and employ much of his family, it's grown to over one hundred employees and contractors, including sales reps, office staff, warehouse workers, and product buyers. A business magazine recently identified it as one of the fastest-growing small businesses in America.

Andre attributes one thing above all others for this remarkable turnaround: meditation.

He meditates every day at home prior to going to the office and, whenever possible, takes a short meditation break before lunch. He also meditates before important meetings or making critical decisions. Compared to how he felt, thought, and acted prior to learning meditation, Andre knows that the practice has grounded him, induced clarity of mind, sharpened his intuition, helped him see opportunities, and generally guided him in keeping his company going in the right direction.

Andre uses meditation as much more than a business tool. First and foremost, meditation fulfilled his original reason for learning: he feels much less stressed and more balanced. He used to worry that he might go insane. No longer. He is calm, confident, and even-minded.

Most important, meditation has revolutionized his spiritual life. When he began meditating, Andre experienced a life-changing depth of inner peace and joy. He says, "Meditation anchors everything: my business, family relationships, and relationship with God. It's the real deal."

The Science

Andre couldn't be more right. We've already learned how meditation works in the brain and produces a higher state of consciousness. Let's now look at the benefits across a wide range of categories.

Physical Health Benefits

There are two types of studies done on meditation: broad meta-analyses that survey every known study, attempting to draw overall conclusions; and targeted studies, which examine one specific area of concern. Several meta-analyses of meditation have been published in journals such as the *Journal of Psychosomatic Research* and the *Journal of Alternative and Complementary Medicine*. Both systematic, overarching reviews found that meditation had clearly beneficial effects on a wide variety of physical illnesses. In addition to these meta-reviews, numerous individual studies demonstrate benefits for specific illnesses. Meditation has been proven to:

- decrease the risk of stroke and heart disease;
- be more effective than many pharmaceutical drugs for a variety of diseases;
- alleviate chronic physical pain;
- improve recovery from cardiac surgery;
- reduce or eliminate symptoms of premenstrual syndrome (PMS);
- Lower blood pressure;
- improve or eliminate insomnia;
- decrease the frequency of epileptic seizures;
- ease the symptoms of menopause;

- slow the rate of cellular decay, which implies a strong antiaging effect, including extending our quality of life as well as life span; and
- help cancer patients cope emotionally with their disease more effectively.

Psychological and Stress-Related Benefits

Early studies on meditation focused on its effectiveness as a general stress-reduction tool. There are now so many studies demonstrating the so-called relaxation response benefit of meditation that it is not the least bit controversial or in doubt. At least two dozen studies conducted over thirty years, enlisting subjects of every age group and background, prove conclusively its powerful stress-reduction capability. Less well known is that meditation has the following positive psychological benefits in addition to alleviating stress:

- reduces depression (equal to or better than antidepressant medications), anxiety, and panic attacks;
- improves mental cognition and functioning in the elderly;
- alleviates social anxiety disorder;
- improves patients with bipolar disorder.;
- reduces binge eating disorder (bulimia nervosa); and
- decreases addiction and aids in recovery.

Meditation has many important benefits for directly enhancing our happiness. One important study I'd like to highlight was published in the *Journal of Clinical Psychology*. According to this report, meditation boosts the effectiveness "of broad, multitiered happiness enhancement programs." In other words, when performed in conjunction with practices such as gratitude, forgiveness, living in the now, cultivating optimism, and so on, *meditation heightens their effectiveness.*

For what I hope would now be obvious reasons, I cannot stress the importance of this finding enough. By itself, this should be more than enough reason to begin meditating. In addition, meditation bolsters self-esteem, well-being, optimism, and overall happiness, while at the same time helping to control harmful negative emotions.

Workplace and Productivity

Andre is also correct that meditation is an effective workplace tool. Studies show that meditation can increase workers' productivity, efficiency, enthusiasm, decision making, and morale; reduce the number of sick days and absenteeism; and improve group harmony and social cohesion. Interestingly, many successful professional athletes, such as New York Yankees slugger and future Hall of Fame baseball player Alex Rodriguez, now actively employ mental techniques to clear their minds and improve their focus. They firmly believe that doing so helps them achieve greater success than physical training alone.

Spiritual Benefits

Above all, meditation is a tool for self-realization and transcendence. For obvious reasons, spiritual experiences are very difficult to measure and quantify in a laboratory setting, not to mention that comparatively few scientists are interested in exploring them. Nonetheless, there already exists clear scientific evidence indicating its spiritual effectiveness. It has been shown that meditation increases our empathy for others; induces brain states entirely unlike sleep, mental illness, or normal waking consciousness; and is the primary tool being practiced in laboratory settings when practitioners such as Carmelite nuns or Buddhist monks report ecstatic experiences—including overwhelming bliss.

The Spirit

Here is a primer on basic meditation practice. On my website, I have included a series of photos, videos, answers to frequently asked questions, tips for success, and all kinds of supplementary material helpful for fine-tuning all aspects of our practice.

Setting Your Intention and Cultivating the Right Attitude

Meditating with the proper mind-set is crucial for success. Before beginning our practice, it's helpful to remind ourselves of the reasons we meditate. Make a vow to practice faithfully and regularly. It's important to really commit to the time we've set aside for practice. Make a concerted effort to release all thoughts of past or future, fears, worries, and ruminations. Be fully present.

I sometimes visualize placing all of my thoughts, worries, issues, and projects on a shelf prior to starting. I know that they'll still be there later, so if I still feel so inclined, I can reclaim them after I finish. Of course, after meditating, I often decide they are no longer interesting or necessary after all.

Most important, remember that the point of meditating is to feel blissful. Meditation is fun and joyous. It's a positive, relaxing, upward-inspiring vacation for our mind. A thrilling adventure of the highest order that only gets better and easier the more we do it.

An Overview

To get oriented, let's look at the complete overview of a sample meditation practice. I will explain each of these steps in more detail below. The sequence includes:

* finding a comfortable and effective body position;
* transitioning into the practice (how to begin, including the incorporation of the breathing techniques from the last chapter);
* watching the breath;
* working with the mantra;
* sitting in the silence, including adjunct practices;
* ending our session, including optional ideas and techniques; and
* additional tips, suggestions, and resources.

Body Positions

Meditation begins with finding a comfortable, seated position. It's vitally important to meditate with the spine erect in an upright position. Lying down while meditating is strongly discouraged. There are few situations short of being in a full-body cast that justify meditating while lying down.

When we meditate in the prone position, we greatly increase the odds of our mind wandering, spacing out, or, most likely, falling asleep.

Meditation is an active, energetic practice. Meditating while reclining is the opposite of energetic. Despite my having severe chronic pain twenty-four hours a day that's exacerbated by sitting, I *still* sit upright to meditate. No matter what your physical condition or bodily challenges, you can almost always find a comfortable upright position.

There is wide range of acceptable positions. The three most common are (1) sitting in a chair, (2) kneeling on a meditation bench, and (3) sitting on the floor, usually with a cushion.

When sitting in a chair, have your feet flat on your floor. Your knees should be either even with or below your pelvis, never above. This means that your thighs are either parallel to the floor or lightly sloped downward. This requires getting the right chair for your height and body proportions; ideally, one that is adjustable. Cushions can be used to attain the correct position.

Many people enjoy sitting on dedicated meditation benches designed to support the body comfortably. However, their use is discouraged if you have knee problems, since they put pressure in that region. The traditional meditation position is sitting on the floor, with your legs crossed in front of you. There are several variations for leg placement. Find the one most comfortable and natural for you. Usually it's helpful to place a pillow beneath you, both for cushioning and to create a gentle downward slope with your backside slightly higher than the front of your pelvis and legs.

In all three cases, the chin should be parallel to the floor, not pointed down or up.

Your eyes should be closed. The proper eye position behind closed lids is to be gently gazing upward at the point between the eyes. It's a *gentle* upward lifting of your eyes, without scrunching or tension, as if you were gazing at a distant mountaintop. At first this uplifted eye position might feel difficult to hold for long periods, especially if your eyes aren't used to it. Like any muscles, your eye muscles will eventually adapt as you train them. If it feels difficult to keep your eyes upward for long—especially if a sense of strain creeps in—it's okay to lower them to a neutral position: looking straight ahead behind closed eyes. Whenever you feel like resuming, you can gently lift them again and hold them gazing upward as long as it is comfortable. Eventually you will be able to hold them there indefinitely without strain. This can be a gradual process. Be gentle and patient.

Your hands should be open, with the palms facing upward. No fancy hand positions are required.

Starting Our Practice

Many people begin with a prayer, chant, visualization, or ritual. This is optional. Choices vary by our own personal interests, paths, and needs.

Next, to help center and transition ourselves into a meditative mindset, we do the two breathing practices explained in the previous chapter. They are double breathing and even-count breathing. This helps settle the mind and body, preparing us for the heart of our practice.

We begin by "watching" our breath, behind closed eyelids, gently gazing upward. Release all tension in the body and breath diaphragmatically, meaning through your belly not your chest. Try to release all tension, allowing your body to breathe in the most natural, least tense way possible. Sometimes we are so acclimated to holding in our stomachs that it can feel strange to allow our belly to loosen and expand instead of our chest.

Breathe through your nose, not your mouth. Notice your breath going in and out, *without* making any attempt to control it or manipulate it. Allow your body to breathe however it likes, at whatever pace it wants, in whatever rhythm it desires. I sometimes visualize my breath as waves on the seashore, pulling in, then out, in then out. Feel the breath as it passes in and out of your nostrils. As you inhale, the breath is cool; as you exhale, it's warm. Perhaps you feel the inhalation at the tip of your nose, or perhaps at the base, closer to your brain. Just notice. If you can't feel your breath, that's fine. Just be aware of your abdomen or lungs gently moving in and out—all while remembering to stay focused on the point between the eyes.

The Main Meditation Technique

After a few rounds of just watching your breath, it's now time to introduce the mantra.

Hong-Sau is a mantra-based meditation technique. This means that we say words silently to ourselves, in synchronicity with our breathing.

I've found that mantra-based techniques are fabulous for beginners (and experts, too). Not only do they have the largest body of scientific research behind them, in my teaching experience, they are the easiest to understand and learn, leading to the fastest results.

To understand why I advocate the use of a mantra-family technique, you need only consider an elephant. As any elephant trainer will tell you, an elephant's trunk is mischievous. If an elephant were to walk through a public place—imagine a market or bazaar—the trunk would swing from side to side, continually try to pick up objects from the tables, play with people's hair, twist their clothes, and generally get the elephant into as much trouble as possible.

Elephant trainers have learned that if they place a stick in the animal's trunk, the trunk curls around it, and the elephant quietly holds the stick, keeping the trunk down and in front. It stops swinging and probing entirely.

Our minds are like the elephant's trunk, and the *Hong-Sau* mantra is like a stick for the mind. It replaces our wayward thoughts, our mind ceases wandering incessantly, and slowly inner peace, then bliss, emerge. As our thoughts subside, superconsciousness bliss, which has been hiding behind the busy distraction that is our everyday mind, shines through.

I recommend using *Hong-Sau* as your mantra. This is a Sanskrit phrase that roughly translates as "I am spirit." As you inhale, *silently* repeat "*Hong*" (rhymes with "song"). And with each exhalation: "*Sau*" (sounds like "saw").

It is not necessary to use this specific phrase. You can use something in English, such as "A-men" or "I am peace." You can even find a short phrase from a religion or wisdom tradition that inspires you. For example, if you wanted something explicitly Christian, you could use "Hail Mary" or "Jesus." If you felt the need to strip it of every possible spiritual connotation, you could even say "one" on the inhalation and "two" on the exhalation.

The truth is that whatever we say isn't critically important, so long as it's positive. The primary benefit derives from the practice itself, not the meaning of the words. If you'd like to create your own customized mantra, the key is to find short syllables: preferably one syllable for the inhalation and one for the exhalation, and never more than two syllables per inhalation and exhalation. Personally, I prefer *Hong-Sau*, as do the majority of people I've taught. This mantra has been in continual use for thousands of years. It was designed to work perfectly with the rhythm of the breath and is fairly neutral in content and meaning.

After using the mantra for a period of time (more on length below), the next phase is to stop using the mantra but remain meditating. We sit quietly in the silence, relaxing and feeling. Concentrate deeply on the spiritual eye, holding your mind as still as possible. Try to relax and feel the quiet state of peaceful bliss that the mantra practice has generated. Setting aside this time after doing the mantra helps us consciously shift from a "doing" state to a "being" state of consciousness. One experienced teacher put it like this: taking time to sit in the silence is like taking the time to eat the meal after having cooked it. One wouldn't cook a meal just to throw it away—the point is to eat it. So, too, with sitting in the silence after practicing *Hong-Sau*. The technique carries us into a higher state of consciousness. Once we're there, the point is to *be in it* as long as possible.

This period of time should make up at least 25 percent of our meditation. In other words, if we meditated for ten minutes, we'd do the mantra for seven and a half minutes and then sit in the silence for two and a half minutes. The 25 percent is a *minimum*; the longer you can hold this, the better. If you can make it one-third or even one-half of your meditation time, so much the better. On the other hand, we don't want to let our minds drift and spiral out of control. Some people find that the mantra gives them only a certain amount of time before their mind becomes hyperactive again. If they tried to sit in the silence with no mantra for 50 percent of their meditation, by the end, they would have completely lost any semblance of peace and bliss. It's better to use the mantra longer rather than *pretending* to sit in the "silence," when, in fact, your mind is racing. Experiment and see what feels best for you.

Length

If you are new to meditation, start with five to ten minutes, once per day. As you feel more comfortable, you can gradually lengthen your meditations. A nice intermediate goal is to meditate once per day for twenty to thirty minutes.

A more aggressive approach would be to meditate either once per day for an hour, or perhaps two sessions of thirty minutes each. You may also choose to designate one day per week or month for a longer meditation.

Working with Ourselves

The most important part of our practice—other than actually doing it—is to catch our mind as soon as we notice it wandering. Every time you discover that you've stopped doing the mantra and started thinking other thoughts, gently reintroduce the mantra. Any thoughts or images other than the mantra or gazing into the silence mean that we've become distracted. If we're thinking about our day, creating a list of chores, replaying a conversation, trying to solve a problem, or even having a positive or inspirational thought, we've gotten off track.

This happens to everyone. If it didn't, you would already be a spiritual master. Understand that working with the wandering mind *is the practice*. The trick is to gently—without beating yourself up, feeling guilty, or decrying your "failure"—return your mind back to the practice of breath and mantra. Again and again—and again! The more you remember to do this, the more you'll develop focused attention, the deeper you'll go, and the more blissful your experience will be.

Our goal with this practice is gradually to deepen our concentration at the point between the eyes until we are no longer thinking about anything except the flow of the breath. As the mind grows ever calmer, you'll notice that your breathing slows down. Eventually natural spaces between the breaths may occur. This is nothing to be alarmed about; quite the opposite, it's to be enjoyed. This should never be forced. It's vitally important not to control the breath in any way. Allow it to naturally and organically do whatever it wants.

In very deep states of relaxed concentration, amazing experiences might happen. The endless stream of thoughts, emotions, and images might slow to a trickle, even vanish altogether. Or the usual thoughts get replaced by something extraordinary. As our mind and breath slow, we begin to feel the gaps between our thoughts. There is no better way to drive home the point that *we are not our minds*. Complete experiences of inner peace and bliss may wash over you. Some people see lights or colors at the spiritual eye. They even hear beautiful sounds that are not in the physical environment. All kinds of positive and wonderful things *might* happen. Just let them come and go. In the moment, you'll know and understand. Trust me.

The Experiment: A Complete Practice

Here's a routine that you can follow when you sit to meditate.

1. Get in a comfortable seated posture, with your spine erect.
2. Optional: if you feel the need to, offer an opening prayer. This can be based upon your own particular religion or spiritual path. It can be offered to God, a saint, or spiritual master who inspires you, or even to your own Highest Self. You can also do a brief devotional chant.
3. Begin with the transitional breathing techniques, double breathing and even-count breathing. Do at least three to six rounds of each.
4. Begin watching your breath without controlling it, noticing your inhalations and exhalations, while gazing upward behind closed eyes. Perhaps feel the cool currents in your nose as you inhale, and the warm currents as you exhale.
5. After a few rounds of watching your breath, introduce the *Hong-Sau* mantra. Silently say to yourself *"Hong"* as you inhale, *"Sau"* as you exhale.
6. Meditate for however long you feel. At least five to ten minutes is recommended to start.
7. Drop the mantra, leaving between 25 percent and 50 percent of your total meditation time for sitting in the silence. Gaze intensely at the spiritual eye while relaxing and feeling the benefits of your meditation practice.
8. Optional: end your meditation with a silent prayer or visualization for the well-being of others—loved ones, those in need of help or healing—or for the world in general. Pray or visualize that you are a blissful emissary of light.
9. End your practice by gently opening your eyes.

Tip: Time your meditation using a watch or nearby clock, glancing at it as needed. Alternatively, set a timer to chime gently when your session is complete. Many cell phones and watches have this feature, with a wide selection of pleasant tones.

Online

Scan the Microsoft Tag above to view a brief video, "Meditation Routines," or go to youtube.com/seanmeshorer.

CHAPTER 25

The Presence of Bliss

One way to recollect the mind easily in the time of prayer, and preserve it more in tranquility, is not to let it wander too far at other times. You should keep it strictly in the presence of God; and being accustomed to think of Him often, you will find it easy to keep your mind calm in the time of prayer, or at least to recall it from its wanderings.

—*Brother Lawrence, Carmelite monk (ca 1614–91)*

While formal meditation is the single most important bliss practice, it's not enough. Obviously, this must be true, since prior to learning meditation, we explored twenty different practices. In another sense, however, meditation alone *is* sufficient to realize bliss, *if and only if* we understand and employ its deepest meaning.

Meditation isn't something we do only a few minutes or hours per day. Our goal is to make every moment a living meditation. We should *never stop* meditating. By this, I don't mean we ought to sit quietly alone in a room twenty-four hours per day doing *Hong-Sau.* I mean that we should strive to take the practice and experience of meditation with us into *everything* we do. Where meditation and living in the eternal Now intersect is where bliss emerges.

There is a specific family of techniques that helps us accomplish this, without diminishing our attention and functional capacities as we go through our daily lives. In fact, they greatly enhance and enliven each moment of existence. Every spiritual tradition advocates a variation. It's called "practicing the presence." One specific variation that I practice is called *japa*, which is derived from the Sanskrit language root *jap-*, meaning "to utter in a low voice, repeat internally, mutter."

Japa is the simple practice of repeating a phrase silently to oneself as often as possible. It's almost like a continuous chant looping repeatedly in our mind.

It has much in common with the *Hong-Sau* meditation technique but is done in such a way as to allow us to practice while going through every aspect of our day: from buying groceries to performing at work to interacting with our friends and family.

The Story

I first met David when he was twenty. He came with a noticeable intensity and a deep desire to learn meditation. His reason for doing so was clear, focused, and decidedly different from some others I've taught. He said, "I want to know God." David was on fire with a longing for truth and to experience pure bliss.

He was cagey about his background or past. He didn't want to discuss it. From what I could gather, his parents divorced while he was young, and he was raised by his father. He didn't go to college. He isn't intellectual or interested in book learning. David also had no interest in a traditional career. Although he's a Caucasian American, his ideal was to be a modern Western version of a cave-dwelling yogi or wandering mendicant. He wasn't interested in anything but intensive spiritual practice.

He rented a simple studio apartment. I taught him to meditate, and he immediately began meditating eight, sometimes twelve, hours per day. After about a month, David came to me slightly distraught. He was having some wonderful experiences in meditation, but his father, who paid for David's apartment and upkeep, was (unsurprisingly) pressuring David to get a job and become self-sufficient. David found this unreasonable, even devastating. He kept saying, "I just want to meditate!"

While I admired his fervent dedication, I couldn't help but side with his father. If David wanted to meditate all day, every day, in the traditional Eastern fashion, then perhaps he needed to join a contemplative monastery or go to India or another culture with a custom of supporting full-time spiritual seekers. It struck me as more than a little unfair for David to expect his father to support him indefinitely, especially in the middle of a major Californian city known for shock-inducing rents and high cost of living. Given that his father didn't understand or agree with David's life decisions, I thought that his dad had already been more than generous.

The good news is that I could offer David a solution. There are effective ways that one could—and should—bring meditation practice into daily life. In fact, David was making a common mistake: believing that his meditation practice was separate and distinct from the rest of his life. He could achieve all of his spiritual goals no matter what he was doing outwardly. If he didn't think he could, then he was misunderstanding the very essence of what he pursued.

I taught him *japa*. Admittedly, David was skeptical at first. It seemed like a severe compromise, one that he wasn't certain would work. But since he had few choices, he decided to try. He got two part-time, low-intensity jobs, as a restaurant busboy and a clerk at a natural food market. The jobs allowed him to earn just enough to pay for basics but didn't consume all his time and attention, either during or after hours.

After a month, David and I met for lunch at the market where he worked. He seemed relaxed and ebullient. He happily told me his positive experiences with *japa* and admitted that it had worked out for the best. He still meditated as much as possible, especially in the morning and evenings before and after work. Now, though, he also got out of his apartment, met interesting people, supported himself, and generally felt more engaged with life. Most important, he felt that his spiritual experiences were deepening. He felt integrated, balanced, and happier.

After about a year, David decided to return to school to learn graphic design. He now works as a freelance designer for projects including some major national brand advertising campaigns. He met a wonderful, spiritually inclined woman and got married. They are planning on starting a family.

To this day, David continues to meditate daily. But he spends much *more* time doing *japa*. It has allowed him the freedom to live in the world but not be subsumed by it. Most of all, it's helped him to feel ever-increasing bliss throughout his daily life, no matter what's happening around him or what he's required to do.

The Science

Because practicing the presence is a variation and extension of mantra-based meditation techniques, most of that research applies here as well. In fact, *japa* is so closely related to meditation that some of the meditation studies already mentioned included *japa*, possibly without the researchers recognizing the distinction. To date, Western science has tended not to separate out *japa*-like practices from the more familiar forms of meditation. Most of the research specific to *japa* comes out of India, where these techniques are better understood.

Within a *japa*-specific context, the most important study was published in the journal *Nuclear Medicine Communications*. Researchers led by Dr. Dharma Singh Khalsa studied the effect of *japa* practice—referred to as "chanting meditation"—on the brain and compared it to traditional meditation. They concluded that *japa* had exactly the same effect as meditation. This is crucial because it verifies that most, if not all, of the thousands of positive meditation studies apply. A study published in the *Indian Journal of Physiology and Pharmacology* confirmed this finding.

A vitally important study looked at the effects of *japa* on our health. Scientists trained 480 generally healthy subjects between the ages of twenty and forty in the technique, then followed them for one month. The results were extraordinary—and in such a short amount of time! Those trained in *japa* were found to have lower pulse rates, blood pressure, and stress levels; major drops in their levels of anxiety, depression, fatigue, and feelings of guilt; increased, positive brain activity; and a subjective feeling of "being more alive" and filled with vitality. Other studies have shown that *japa*-like practices can reduce the anxiety of patients in the operating room about to undergo major surgical procedures. Comfortingly, it didn't matter whether the patients were "religionists" or atheists—the result was the same.

Tangentially, although this is not a direct study of *japa* itself, there is a great deal of evidence that people, especially children, learn better when they are taught via repetitious chanting of the material rather than merely having it spoken to them. These studies indicate that rhythmic repetition is uniquely penetrating and powerful, and exceeds the effectiveness of other methods.

The Spirit

Japa meditation is a direct reversal of an uncontrolled interior monologue of thoughts. Whereas our usual monologue is associative, frenzied, and often distorted, *japa* is specific, intentional, and chosen for its positive, self-affirming qualities.

Japa works on all three levels of our consciousness: subconsciousness, waking consciousness, and superconsciousness. By substituting the sacred word formula for the usual flotsam and jetsam, two things are accomplished. First, *japa* helps us gain mastery over our mind river. We cease being at the mercy of unwelcome thoughts and feelings. Instead we discover that our mind river is merely a tool that we can learn to control and utilize for our positive benefit.

More importantly, as with formal meditation, *japa* interiorizes our mind, slowing and calming it. This helps us to damn our mind river, creating the gaps necessary for bliss to bubble up into our consciousness. To use our diamond analogy: *japa* cleans off the muck and peels back the layers of grime, polishing our mind so that bliss shines forth in all its radiant abundance.

The more we remember to repeat our sacred word formula at every opportunity throughout the day, the faster we reach a state that yogis call *ajapajapam*. This is when our egoic self dissolves and the mantra essentially "repeats itself" in the mind. There is no longer a distinction among the *I* repeating the mantra, the mantra itself, and the external world. It's a state of grace, of union with Pure Consciousness, of the Divine, of total absorption in oneness.

Anytime, Anyplace

As David discovered, finding bliss must be incorporated into every moment. While it may seem as if bliss demands a great deal of time and effort, this is largely an illusion. Following these practices ultimately frees us from wasting attention and life on unrewarding thoughts and pursuits. *Japa*, perhaps above all others, helps us integrate our pursuit of bliss into the rhythms of ordinary life.

Part of what this means is that *japa* should be practiced anywhere, anytime. It is a profoundly flexible and accessible style of observance. The goal is to keep the mantra going as often as possible, whenever our mind doesn't need to concentrate on something else. We can even do it while holding a conversation—especially ones that don't call for our full attention. Except in moments where total concentration is required (such as typing these sentences), we can always keep a part of ourselves continuously repeating the mantra. In those moments where nothing much is happening and our mind is potentially idle, we can "turn up the volume" on the *japa* mantra, making it the one and only focus of our internal monologue. The mantra weaves in and out of our mind continuously, up and down in volume, cresting and receding, but almost always present—unless we forget. When that happens, as soon as we remember, pick it up again.

It's an especially wonderful practice if we find ourselves submerged in negative thoughts or emotions. *Japa* almost instantaneously lessens the frequency and intensity of negative thoughts, and often helps to eliminate them completely.

As mentioned, the only time that you wouldn't do *japa* is when fully absorbed in another activity, meditation, a creative project, studies, a sporting contest, an important or intense conversation, and so on. In those moments, we ought to be completely engaged and immersed in what we are doing. There is no need for *japa*. Our minds are already fully concentrated and positively occupied.

Japa creates a feeling of flow and total absorption—that quick, miraculous, beautiful passage of time—*all of the time*, including during moments in our lives that seem like "downtime," when nothing much of interest is happening. It's almost shocking to realize how much time we waste on idle thoughts, daydreaming, and unproductive negativity. *Japa* practice means that we no longer must wait for those all-too-rare peak moments or experiences to come our way. *Every moment* becomes a peak experience. *Japa* transforms empty, squandered time into opportunities for bliss.

Japa Compared to Meditation

Japa is as directed and mindful as *Hong-Sau* but considerably less formal, in both time and space.

Unlike formal meditation, we can do it whenever we feel so inclined, for as short or long a time as we want. We do it while walking, talking, standing in line, lying down, taking a shower—whenever. There is no set time of the day. Our body can be in any position, our eyes open or closed. We can use it when sitting around the pool without a care in the world or when we are filled with anxiety and tension. Unlike *Hong-Sau*, no attempt is made to synchronize the mantra with our breathing. We breathe, speak, and act as we normally do. It is a practice with few rules.

Like our practice of *Hong-Sau*, *japa* is a silent practice. If we notice our mind drifting, we gently reintroduce the mantra, without any feelings of shame, guilt, failure, or recrimination. It's a gentle practice, intended for use anytime we remember.

Practicing the Presence in the World's Religions

Choosing an appropriate mantra is an act of identifying what is personally meaningful to us. Effective word formulations can come from any of the world's spiritual traditions or from private sources of inspiration.

Although I've been using Sanskrit words such as *japa* and *mantra*, it's important to understand that this practice is found in each of the world's religious traditions. It's by no means specific to one religion. I use the Sanskrit terminology only because that's the context in which I first learned the practice.

In Catholicism, for example, one finds the use of rosary beads, which are almost identical to a Hindu *mala*. Many Catholics, especially most of the saints, extensively use this practice. Within the Catholic tradition, it's considered a form of contemplative prayer known as "prayer without ceasing." Frequently, the "mantra " is based on the Jesus Prayer, the Hail Mary, or one of the other popular prayers in Christian liturgy. In Islam, the practice is called *dhikr*; most commonly, the "mantras" are derived from the Hadith texts or verses from the Qur'an. In Mahayana schools of Buddhism, the practice is called *nianfo* (Chinese) or *nembutsu* (Japanese); it involves the continuous repetition of a name for the Buddha. In Judaism, adherents often repeat "*Shema Yisrael*" or phrases derived from the Talmud or Zohar (the primary book of Kabbalah). Virtually every wisdom tradition on earth recommends a variation of this practice.

Finding Your Sacred Word Formula

I've used the same Sanskrit mantra for over twenty years. You must find your own word formula that resonates with you. You needn't select just one; feel free to change them as often as you're inclined. The benefit of picking a single phrase and sticking with it is that it becomes a habit. It's easier for the mind to automatically remember and repeat. On the other hand, different sayings have different meanings and vibratory effects. Sometimes our needs or circumstances change.

There are many sources for finding sacred word formulas. I will list a few, but this is far from exhaustive. There are hundreds, if not thousands. And, of course, you can create your own. There are plusses and minuses to this approach. For example, I use a traditional mantra that's been employed for millennia. It's not only particularly meaningful to me but also connects me to a broad, deep, and continuous tradition. On the other hand, you might consciously decide that you *don't* want to feel connected to any religion, path, tradition, or community. There is no one "right" phrase that universally works for everyone.

You can also choose the language of your sacred word formula. The benefit of using words in our native tongue is that, obviously, we clearly understand what we're saying and are more likely to pronounce it correctly. On the other hand, powerful liturgical languages such as Hebrew, Latin, and Sanskrit (among others) imbue the words with sacred vibrations. Again, there is no "right" language. Choose that to which you feel drawn.

If you are creating your own or adapting one from the suggestions below, I recommend keeping it relatively short. It's important that you be able to recite and repeat your phrase without strain. Examples in no particular order:

Judaism

Shema Yisrael Adonai Eloheinu Adonai Ehad: "Hear, O Israel: the Lord is our God, the Lord is One."

Ein Keloheinu: "There is none like our God."

I Am That I Am: English translation of God's response to Moses, found in the Torah, when Moses asked God His name. Used by both Jews and Christians.

Christianity

"Lord Jesus Christ, Son of God, have mercy on me, a sinner" (the Jesus Prayer).

You can also excerpt a passage from the Lord's Prayer or the Hail Mary. (Either one might be too long if used in whole.)

Lord's Prayer: "Father, hallowed be your name. Your kingdom come. Give us each day our daily bread, and forgive us our sins, for we ourselves forgive everyone who is indebted to us. And lead us not into temptation."

Hail Mary: "Hail Mary, full of grace. The Lord is with thee. Blessed art thou amongst women, and blessed is the fruit of thy womb, Jesus. Holy Mary, Mother of God, pray for us sinners, now and at the hour of our death. Amen."

Hinduism

Aum Namo Bhagavate Vasudevaya: "O my Lord, the all-pervading Personality of Godhead, I offer my respectful obeisance unto You."

Sri Ram, Jai Ram, Jai Jai Ram, Aum: "Lord God! Victory to God! Victory, victory to God! *Om*."

Buddhism

Aum Mani Padme Hum: "The jewel in the lotus."

Sabbe Satta Sukhi Hontu: "May all beings be well [or happy]."

Islam

Allahu Akbar: "God is the greatest."

Alhamdulillah: "Praise to God."

Subhan'Allah: "Glorious is God."

Bismillah Ar-Rahman Ar-Raheem: "In the name of God, the gracious, the merciful."

Native American

Hey a-Na-na: "I unite the earth and the sky inside myself."

Chanoon ho-ya: "Wonderful willow tree, your example teaches me."

Nonreligious or Nondenominational

"I am peace," "I am spirit, or "I am bliss."

"Reveal thyself!"

"Peace, wisdom, love, bliss."

There are countless others. If none of the above strikes your fancy, do some research or compose your own.

The Experiment: Practicing *Japa*

1. Choose a sacred word formulation from the above list. (If you already employ a different one, you can use that). You can change or customize your selection later.
2. Right now, in this very moment, practice saying it silently to yourself as many times as you feel. Make sure that you are comfortable with the pronunciation and commit it to memory.
3. Over the course of the next twenty-four hours, make a concerted effort to repeat the mantra silently to yourself *every time you remember, as often as possible*. If you find yourself forgetting or drifting, start up again the moment you catch yourself. Whether that adds up to five minutes or

twenty hours of practice isn't important, so long as you try it with full devotion and intensity.

4. Notice and reflect on the effects the practice had on your mind and consciousness. Did it distract you from negative thoughts or emotions? Did it help quiet your mind, increase your peacefulness, or uncover feelings of joy?

Tip: Many people also use a string of beads, called a *mala* or a rosary, to count each repetition while doing *japa*. This adds a kinetic element to the practice that many people find helpful. You can wear your *mala*/rosary on your wrist or neck so that it's available any time you feel to practice. It also acts as a reminder.

Online

Additional videos and resources for this chapter are available at www.theblissexperiment.com.

CHAPTER 26

Freedom in Bliss

I used to desire many, many things, but now I have just one desire, and that's to get rid of all my other desires.
—*John Cleese, British comic actor (b. 1939)*

We began our journey by looking at several common mistakes that we all make to varying degrees: pursuing wealth, sex, romance, power, fame, and/or beauty. We know that one thing they have in common is their external nature. There is another thing, even more fundamental. They are powerful forms of desire.

Desire is defined by the *Oxford English Dictionary* as "that feeling or emotion which is directed to the attainment of some object from which pleasure or satisfaction is expected." It is wanting something or wishing for something to happen, characterized by a sense of craving. When we desire something, our sense of longing is excited by thoughts of potential enjoyment that we believe we'll experience if we can fulfill it. As such, our desire stimulates us to take whatever actions necessary to achieve our goal.

This may sound benign, even good. Certainly it seems so normal, even stitched into the very fabric of what it means to be human, that many of us couldn't imagine the problem. We believe that our desires animate us; they are what make us unique, even interesting, and will carry us toward the highest fulfillment. In truth, every desire, no matter how commonplace, inhibits us from feeling genuine happiness, purpose, and truth—that is, from discovering the hidden bliss within.

Purposely, I've waited for twenty-six chapters before tackling this broader issue. This notion is so controversial and misunderstood, particularly in the West; we must first lay a great deal of preparatory groundwork. My hope is that by now, given all that we've explored and experienced together, it will be more understandable why desires of all kinds are the enemy of bliss.

The Story

Gemma was getting desperate. She was in her late thirties, had never married, and felt her biological clock ticking toward extinction. She was frantic to meet a man, get hitched, have kids, and settle into her happily-ever-after. Since childhood, she'd been consumed with dreams of romance and family. For reasons she didn't fully understand, none of her relationships went the distance. She was more than a little picky about what constituted the "right man"—she literally kept a list of qualities that he must have: handsome, wealthy, funny, tall, romantic, educated, and successful. Though few met all the criteria, occasionally she found a suitable candidate. Even then, the relationship faltered. The men ended up dumping her, cheating on her, or stringing her along with no intention of popping the question.

Gemma had little insight into why this happened. Though I kept it to myself, it seemed to me that there were some pretty obvious explanations. Not to be unkind, but Gemma was far from the female equivalent of the qualities she demanded from her potential mates. Physically, she was average, perhaps slightly above. She was neither wealthy, successful, nor the recipient of a top-tier education. She didn't have a great sense of humor, nor did she seem especially light and fun. She had no great talents, passions, or interests. She wasn't deeply spiritual or accomplished in any way that I could discern. There was nothing bad or wrong about her but also nothing spectacular, either. Worst of all, she exuded the kind of clinging desperation that men tend to avoid. She smothered and forced her relationships, pushing too hard, too fast.

One day Gemma announced that after much soul-searching—I'm not certain what prompted it—that she had decided to become celibate. She had slowly been growing more interested in the spiritual path and decided that she would forget the man hunting and family building, and focus instead on her spiritual growth. Gemma stopped dating, or even worrying about her appearance. She no longer treated every conversation with a man as a marriage interview. She made a conscious decision to forgo sex, romance, children, beauty, and being taken care of by someone else's wealth. It went beyond even this. More broadly, she decided to abstain from every sort of worldly satisfaction to which she once aspired. She concluded that the whole thing had been a waste of her time and energy, and that none of it would ever give her what she truly wanted.

Two months later, Gemma came to me with a problem. She had recently met a fellow named Daryl who had taken an instant liking to her. She was still celibate and disinterested in relationships, but Daryl kept pursuing her. She had twice declined his invitation to dinner. Part of what made this interesting is that I know Daryl. He embodies many of the qualities that Gemma originally wanted in a man, with the exception of being tall (he was of average height) or wealthy. Though he wasn't yet rich, he had recently started his own business that seemed like it has genuine prospects for success.

Eventually, after two more attempts, Gemma broke down and went out with Daryl. Three months later, they were engaged.

As it turns out, Daryl had (at least) one flaw that concerned her. He was fairly materialistic and status conscious. He definitely liked to acquire things. For example, even though he couldn't afford it, he leased a Porsche with monthly payments higher than many people's rent. He had nice clothes and the latest tech toys. Though his future financial prospects seemed bright, he was clearly living beyond his means for the moment.

Gemma decided that even if it risked their relationship, she needed to confront Daryl about his overspending. Gemma began by forthrightly admitting her own recent issues about relationships, especially how her prior attempts always backfired and made her miserable, and how much better things were after she'd let it go. Daryl confessed that he knew he had been overspending. He was considering ditching the Porsche, among other austerities, but was worried that it would harm his image and, even worse, that Gemma would be disappointed. When Gemma reassured him that she wasn't the least bit interested in the car, Daryl felt relieved.

This conversation strengthened their relationship. It drew them closer and reinforced that they each only wanted the best for the other. Gemma still didn't know if, once married, they would even try to have children. But now she didn't really care. She was sure that it would work out. If she couldn't have them biologically, they could always adopt. Maybe, too, she was now realizing that it didn't really matter either way. She clearly saw that having or not having children was not the determining factor in making her life worth living.

The Science

Most of the research we examined in earlier chapters explores the consequences of striving for specific desires: money, sex, romance, beauty, and power. In every case, we discovered that they failed to make us happy. In aggregate, they form a multipart indictment of desire. Though conclusive, these are still *indirect* ways of examining the issue. What we might call the *direct* science of desire, in the sense of looking at the broad and underlying nature of craving itself, is a relatively new field of inquiry. Still, there are some compelling, even shocking, findings worth noting.

A foundational study, "The Neural Correlates of Desire," used functional Magnetic Resonance Imaging to look at subjects' brains. They showed the volunteers pictures of events, objects, and persons—the three kinds of things humans can desire—in an attempt to determine which parts of our brains are activated in the presence of desire and if different types of things (say, desire for an object, as opposed to a person) triggered different parts of the brain.

According to the results, *all* forms of desire—even those that might appear dissimilar—activated the *same* three areas. That is, there appears to be only one, unified desire system. Likewise, a similar study published in *Cognition and Emotion* found that seemingly very different desires such as for food, alcohol, smoking cigarettes, and playing sports triggered biologically similar mechanisms.

These studies are critically important. They suggest strongly that anything and everything that "lights up" our desire system is likely to produce the same kinds of positive and negative rewards. Secondly, there is no type of desire likely to produce long-term satisfactory outcomes. If we know that one, or a few, desires fail us (such as sex, power, wealth, fame, beauty, and so forth), then it's likely that *all types of desire will fail us*, since they all trigger the same neurological response.

Bolstering this conclusion is a study published in the journal *Nature Neuroscience*. Researchers found that the same brain structures that mediate pleasure and desire also participates in feelings of fear. The neurons flip back and forth, generating either a strong desire *or* an intense fear, depending on the mood at the time the neurons are fired. The amount of stress placed upon subjects determines whether the neurons read the sensation as "positive desire" or "negative fear." In other words, according to study coauthor Kent Berridge, "We experience desire and fear as psychological opposites. But from the brain's point of view, they seem to share a common kernel that can be flexibly used for either one." This means that positive desire and negative emotion *are two sides of the same coin*, sharing the same chemicals and neural pathways. There may not be any way to consistently pursue our desires without frequently triggering negative consequences.

Research published in *Psychological Review* on how desires are formed and processed in our mind leads to some essential discoveries. Desires are *not* driven primarily by uncontrollable, subconscious biological responses. Instead they are produced by our conscious minds when *triggered by external or physiological cues*. Essentially, the "world out there" presents us with an image that intrudes on our consciousness, sparking the conscious creation of that desire. We can then store that image and retrieve it—like any memory—for later rumination and restimulation, even when the original external stimulus is no longer present.

Most important of all, scientists concluded that *all desires are simultaneously rewarding and painful*. At the same moment that we relish our hopes of future fulfillment, we also become acutely aware that we currently lack that thing in our lives. This creates what the researchers called a state of "exquisite torture." Put differently: by highlighting a lack or emptiness inside us, *all desires intrinsically, inexorably produce physical or emotional pain*. There is no such thing as a painless desire.

The Spirit

It's time to emphasize the destructive nature of *all* forms of desire and the beneficial alternative of desirelessness. What does it mean to forgo our desires? Who would ever want to do such a thing? Aren't desires what attach us meaningfully to the world and to other people? Why would we not wish to feel strongly for something or for someone? This is a topic fraught with strong opinions and misunderstandings.

During my senior year at Stanford, I unintentionally found myself in an angry, emotional confrontation with my professor and closest advisor. After class one day, as we chatted over a beer, my professor asked me what I was reading at the moment (in addition to his course materials). Innocently, I mentioned that I had just finished a biography of Gandhi, which I found captivating and inspiring. Shockingly, this incensed him. At first his mind skipped and raced around so much that he barely made sense. After lengthy questioning, a clear thesis emerged: Gandhi was a criminal to humanity because he tried to overcome his worldly desires. To my professor, this was unconscionable because Gandhi had tried to deny all that made life good and worthwhile.

That was the first, but far from the last, time I've encountered strong reactions to the topic of limiting, controlling, or eliminating one's desires. In almost every case, the problem arises from a misunderstanding of what this does—and does not—mean.

The Anatomy of Desire

We constantly create desires, both small and large. We've already explored some of the most common "big desires," including wealth, fame, power, beauty, drugs, and sex. But there are also a virtually infinite number of smaller desires: for a particular food, to go to a certain place, to buy some shoes, to meet a specific person. We generate hundreds, if not thousands, of new desires every day. Some are minor and fleeting: a desire to make it through a yellow light or for a good parking space. Others linger in our consciousness indefinitely.

All desires, whether large or small, long-term or fleeting, are the combination of three things.

1. We feel some kind of lack, incompleteness, or deficiency.
2. We come into contact with an object, person, or event in our external world that triggers a belief that this thing we've come into contact with is the solution to our feeling of lack or deficiency.
3. We form an emotional attachment to this thing—we *want* it. In fact, we often convince ourselves that it's no mere "want," it's a *need*.

Desires can persist even after the trigger is removed from our immediate environment because we store it as a memory. Like any memory, we can recall it at will and then ruminate about it, turning it over and over again in our mind, just as we can with our past negative events, emotions, and traumas.

There is a certain reasonableness and logic to this process. We come into contact with an object, person, or event that prompts our realization of lack. It's natural to assume that it must be this thing itself that is the solution to our emptiness. So we try to acquire or experience it. If we fail, we continue to pine for it, perhaps growing more and more intensely focused on achieving it—even to the point of obsession or other negative emotions. If we succeed, we eventually realize—sometimes right away, sometimes after a delay—that the object, person, or event did *not*, in fact, completely fill our inner emptiness after all.

We conclude, then, that either we are completely mistaken (it wasn't that object, person, or event at all) or partially mistaken (that person, object, or event was a useful addition, just not quite enough by itself; there must be something else needed in conjunction). Either way, the result is that we transfer our attention to acquiring the next object, person, or event that has come into our field of consciousness. On and on the process goes, continuously and endlessly cycling through everything that stimulates a desire, desperately hoping that we eventually stumble across that which will finally and lastingly give us a sense of completion and fullness.

This process creates some enormous problems.

As one of the scientists said so elegantly, desires are "exquisite torture."

To be in a state of desire is to be in pain. The more desires we have, the more pain we feel.

There's more to the pain than just what happens at the moment of desire creation. Should we fail to procure our desire, we've now opened ourselves to some combination of sadness, anger, anxiety, frustration, envy, jealousy, resentment, disappointment, discouragement, and depression. On the other hand, if we succeed in fulfilling it, we'll eventually realize that it didn't pan out in the way we'd hoped. This generates confusion, doubt, hopelessness, and/or despair.

Because desires are triggered by externalities, this means that we are at the mercy of our environment. We surrender our mastery and self-control to the whims of our surroundings and passing sensations. There is something slavish about this. It's why those who claim that they are radically free because they pursue their every desire—regardless of the cost to themselves, others, or society—are, in fact, not free at all. They live in a state of complete bondage: prisoners of desires they cannot control. In act of desperation, they try to convince themselves (and others) that their life sentence was by choice.

Worst of all, the desire-creation process *never* ends. Since no amount of desire satisfaction can *ever* fill our internal emptiness, we are trapped inside an infinite torture chamber.

The Meaning of Desire

We needn't be trapped forever. There is *one* way out of the torture chamber: blissful consciousness.

At some point, most of us realize, however vaguely or tentatively, that the external world is not quite living up to its promise. Instead of continuously bouncing from desire to desire, we wonder if there isn't another solution altogether. Perhaps what's really missing isn't something "out there" but something inside us. That something is what we call bliss.

This realization transforms our understanding of and relationship to the external world. Every desire becomes a reminder that we haven't yet discovered the fullness of bliss within. From this moment forward, the news continues to get better and better.

For it turns out that just as we aren't really "missing" something, neither are we as empty or deficient as we believed. We all possess an infinite reservoir of bliss. It's already here, inside us, right this moment. It's just not activated; we haven't yet made contact with it.

This also gives us insight as to why we so often experience desires as fleeting, transferrable, and mutable. It's not the object, person, or event that we crave, it's the bliss inside. These things are just cues. It's no wonder that we seem to desire so many things. The world is trying to send us a message. Desire after desire after desire pops up, each serving as a reminder that we haven't yet reached the fullness of our inner potential.

From Desire to Bliss

No desire, not even the smallest or most benevolent, can successfully fulfill us, or even connect us to the world in a satisfying way. Desires are intrinsically disconnected from bliss; there is a yawning chasm between them. There is no direct way to leap from desire to bliss; they are too far apart, too radically dissimilar in nature.

There is, however, one exception built into the nature of our consciousness, *one* way, and one way *only*, to bridge the chasm between desire and bliss: to prioritize and promulgate the desire for self-realization.

Paramhansa Yogananda calls this the "desireless desire." It is the desire for spiritual enlightenment and liberation. It's fundamentally different from all others because it's inner directed and transcendent. The desire to find lasting happiness, meaning, and truth is *the* desire that animates our existence.

To pursue the desireless desire for bliss is to reorient toward bliss and bliss alone. It's the refusal to be satisfied, or pretend to be, with the lesser desires of the external world. These are merely layers to be peeled away. It is to be undeterred in our project of cutting away the outer layers of dirt and misshapen rock that separate us from the pure diamond of bliss at the center of our being.

The desireless desire means that we needn't directly renounce the world and its things so much as skillfully use them as reminders and vehicles for our highest attainment. Desire itself can become a tool for gaining our freedom. Every time we notice that an object, person, or event has triggered a desire, we can deftly redirect it inward, as a reminder that we have not yet fully attained our highest aspiration of bliss consciousness, prodding us forward in our inward journey.

Moreover, the very act of consciously navigating the world of desires helps us acquire and practice the skills necessary for bliss. Every object, person, or event—the building blocks of desire—is an opportunity to develop our awareness, release our past, forgive others, reframe the negative, practice optimism, feel gratitude, see the underlying vibration of things rather than their surface, develop our capacity for compassion, selflessly serve others, and love without reason.

All of life, every moment, becomes an efficient vehicle for attaining bliss. We don't have to carve out separate time for our bliss journey; daily life itself, approached with the proper awareness, understanding, and tools, *is* the process of attaining bliss.

Waste and inefficiency creep in only during those moments when we temporarily forget our commitment and goal, drifting back into the old ways of subconscious imprisonment to our desires.

The Fullness of Desirelessness

My professor who was so enraged by Gandhi's experiments with truth, was deathly afraid that if he surrendered his desires, life would become apathetic and boring.

We now see that this isn't the case. It's the opposite. It was *my professor* who was suffering and world-weary. His volatile temper and pugnacious personality were signs of his discontentment. In his angry defense of living a desire-filled life, he missed a simple truth: he was miserable, while Gandhi was filled with joy.

To be desireless is to be fully engaged with life. Every moment becomes an opportunity to either directly experience inner bliss or to take us one step closer to doing so. This fills us with vitality and enthusiasm for every moment. Gandhi himself is an excellent example. He was *far* more engaged with the world than my professor, who lived isolated in an ivory tower, filled with rage and jealousy, living a life of meager accomplishment both outwardly—and much more importantly—inwardly. While my professor threw alcohol-fueled hissy fits, Gandhi led a nonviolent revolution that liberated nearly a billion people and inspired the world. There is nothing apathetic and disengaged about Gandhi's desirelessness.

The further paradox of releasing desire is that in so doing, we gain all that we ever dreamed—and much more. Although externally focused desires are abundant, they are actually limiting. Our mind is too flawed, too finite, too filled with harmful thoughts and emotions to ever see the full gamut of possibilities. Desire causes tension and pain. Pain creates tunnel vision, it locks us down, squeezes us like a vice, consumes our attention. Life narrows down to a battle for survival. We can't see the big picture clearly. There is little time left to thrive.

Ultimately, our external desires are overly specific, cheap substitutes for what we really want: bliss. When we learn to let go of them, we open ourselves to the fullness of the moment. Rather than needing that one specific thing to make us happy or feel complete, we are naturally happy *all* the time, regardless of our external world. We are always complete. Anything and everything we experience in every moment is a source of total fulfillment.

The other irony is, as Gemma discovered, that by releasing a specific need or desire and all the worrying, forcing, and unnatural pressing that comes with it, we now allow things to unfold naturally. We are in a state of grace and flow. Suddenly we find that in that fullness, we are given everything—and much more—than we ever even knew we wanted.

The Experiment:
A Small Experiment in Releasing Desire

In addition to all the other practices we've learned that indirectly help us shed desire, it's helpful to cultivate a direct awareness of our desires: to learn to notice and understand them as they arise, gain distance from them, and ultimately transmute them not only through indirect practices but also by directly and consciously releasing their grip on us. Here's a practice, with two variations, that takes direct aim at our desires.

Part A: Watching and Waiting

1. Pick a small desire: say, a hunger pang when you know your body doesn't need the calories at the moment, or some item you want to purchase but know in your heart that you don't strictly need. Or it can be a desire to have sex with someone or, really, any desire of your choosing.

2. Now, do nothing. Don't act on it. Make a vow to wait it out as long as possible and just observe what happens. Notice if there are different stages of progression and dissipation. Looking back, did you really need to have it after all? Do you miss it? Are you a worse person, or do you feel worse, for having skipped it? How quickly did you forget that you even craved it? How difficult was it to fend it off? Did it dissolve of its own accord? If so, what might this mean? Were you surprised that you had the ability to override that desire? What else did you notice?

Part B: Skillful Transmutation

If we choose, we can actively intervene in our formation of desires, lessening or redirecting them. Here's how:

1. Take a moment to become aware of all the desires floating in your mind right now. There may be several or only a few. Select a small one.

2. Examine the emotions you've formed around this desire. What are you feeling when you think of it? Why do you want it? What fulfillment will it bring? Can you see it not as a thing worth having but as a signal to continue your journey toward bliss?

3. Can you think of ways to release, use, or transmute this desire? See it as an opportunity to practice one or more of the skills you're practicing: perhaps to develop awareness, release the past, forgive others, set a good habit, reframe the negative, practice optimism, feel gratitude, see the underlying vibration of things rather than their surface, develop your capacity for compassion, selflessly serve others, practice unconditional love, or meditate on its nature. Is there a more positive substitution available? What would happen if you just ignored it? Examine all aspects of what it might mean or what responses you might have in relation to conducting a Bliss Experiment.

4. If you cannot think of any way to directly use or transmute the desire for bliss, do this instead: allow yourself to attain and experience the desire. However, as you do so, visualize experiencing it not in your senses, organs, or body but instead uplifting the experience into your spiritual eye, the point between the eyebrows. Visualize that you are experiencing it only through this third eye and not any other part of the body. Does this change the quality of the experience?

5. Practice consciously releasing your desires in this way as often as you remember or feel to, gradually working your way to larger and stronger desires.

Online

Additional videos and resources for this chapter are available at www.theblissexperiment.com.

PART 6

Completing the Journey

Now that we've understood and at least made some direct contact with bliss, it's helpful to explore some of the broader ramifications of our practice. Does bliss have wider import or impact? What does a blissful being look like in society? What's more, how we can move forward with our exploration and practice in the best possible way, ensuring our own successful journey while being emissaries of bliss and positive examples for others?

CHAPTER 27

Planetary Consequences

All of humanity's problems stem from man's inability to sit quietly in a room alone.

—Blaise Pascal, French mathematician,
inventor, physicist, writer, and philosopher (1623–62)

Bliss has positive ramifications far beyond personal fulfillment. Imagine if this world were filled with bliss seekers: people committed to happiness, meaning, and truth for all of humankind. Without a doubt, it would be better in every conceivable way.

Not only is seeking bliss not self-indulgent, it is the most effective, all encompassing, and enduring solution for our global challenges. As Albert Einstein explained, "Problems cannot be solved at the same level of awareness that created them." Bliss is the ultimate expansion of our awareness.

The blissful being is not interested in *any* of the things that generate evil, dissension, disharmony, and discord. Such a person sees no gain in hurting, stealing, controlling, humiliating, or degrading either our environment or our fellow human beings. Bliss by its very nature creates a more ethical, harmonious, tolerant, peaceful society. The bliss seeker consumes fewer resources, is dedicated to humanity, and spreads kindness, compassion, and unconditional love wherever possible.

Above all, the bliss seeker helps to share and spread inner peace and lasting joy with as many people as possible, doing whatever he can to uplift humanity. As we will see, both positive and negative emotions actually spread like contagious diseases through networks of people. One of the *best* antidotes to the misery we see around us is for each of us to become emissaries of bliss and then share that bliss with others. One of the *worst* things we can do is to hold others down by bombarding them with our unhappiness. If we care at all about the suffering of our fellow human beings, we have a moral imperative to discover the hidden bliss within and then transmit it as far and wide as possible.

The best news of all is that noticeable improvement doesn't require all, or even the majority, of our fellow human beings to become bliss seekers. Because of the way in which bliss and its attendant qualities spread through the network of humanity, large gains can be realized even if only a minority of people commit to discovering the bliss within.

The Story

Nathan, now in his late fifties, grew up in a wealthy family in affluent Chevy Chase, Maryland. He went to Yale as an undergraduate and the Wharton School of Business for his master's degree in business administration. After graduating, he worked at a Wall Street investment firm, then for a Fortune 500 company. His goal was to one day become CEO of a major corporation—a goal he finally attained around his fiftieth birthday.

The company he directed was an international conglomerate that had divisions ranging from medical supplies, to military contracts, to financial products for consumers. They contracted with factories in several developing countries. Like most CEOs, Nathan saw it as his sworn duty to maximize corporate profits above all else. Though his personal values tended toward the liberal, he completely removed such considerations from his business decisions. He freely admitted that it was his job to find every legal way to externalize costs and maximize profits. He felt absolutely no responsibility to anyone but his shareholders. He argued passionately that this was what made capitalism so great.

Nathan got married while still climbing the ladder. He had three kids. He sat on the board of directors of several major corporations and nonprofit organizations. He donated large amounts of money to a variety of charities.

For most of his adult life, Nathan didn't think much about religion or spirituality. He came from a secular Jewish family that put great emphasis on the social aspects of Judaism but virtually none on the religious. He felt little motivation to do so, as he had a nice family, was wealthy, philanthropic, and respected in his community.

Slowly, his personal life unraveled. After nearly fifteen years of marriage, Nathan got divorced. He quickly remarried a woman he met through work, but that marriage lasted only two years. He was estranged from his children, in part because they blamed him for the divorce. He had few friends and no social skills. He was a naturally suspicious person, a trait heightened by his wealth and community notoriety. He treated people poorly, acting as if others were there to serve him. He wasn't kind. Nathan knew that he wasn't happy, although he had little insight as to why—or even if it mattered.

During this difficult time, one of his few friends gave him a book written by a Buddhist monk. It struck a chord, although Nathan didn't feel a kinship with Buddhism. It did, however, get him to participate in his local synagogue. He started attending lectures and events. One of the guest speakers was influential in the Jewish Renewal movement, which heavily incorporates meditative and mystical practices. Nathan began practicing meditation. He began having intensely positive spiritual experiences. One night he found himself sobbing uncontrollably, his tears partly of sorrow, partly of joy. The sorrow came because he felt he had wasted so much of his life, made too many mistakes, lost track of his soul. The joy was that feeling of reconnection, of knowing that it was not too late to make radical changes, that he could become an agent of change for this world. Where once he had been part of the problem, he could now be part of the solution.

After taking a long, hard look at his life, Nathan decided to make drastic changes. He retired from his corporate job and began simplifying his life. He sold his mansion (which was ridiculous for one person anyway), got rid of both of his personal assistants, didn't renew his membership with a fractional jet ownership company, and traded in his Bentley for a Prius. For Nathan, ditching the personal assistants was a major decision, as he had used them to create a barrier between himself and the world. Even his own children interacted more with the assistants (who took care of all kinds of personal family business) than their own father.

He began volunteering with two different nonprofit organizations. For the first time, Nathan didn't just write checks, he participated. Working with one environmental organization, he even joined one of its sit-in campaigns, where demonstrators nonviolently protested the destruction of a local ecosystem.

Most important, he repaired his relationship with his children, spending as much time with them as they wanted. He had a completely unexpected reconciliation with his first wife, who had never remarried. By Nathan's own admission, he's a very different person now: warmer and friendlier, more trusting, less suspicious. His friendships are natural and based on mutual interest and his personality, not his status or resources.

Nathan is active in helping others, far less self-centered, and consumes far less material goods. He practices a Jewish form of meditation every day and leads one of the weekly group meditations at the center he now attends regularly. On a personal level, his life is far simpler, but globally, it is far more vibrant and connected. He is happier than he's ever been and is deeply committed to being a real mensch: a person of integrity and honor. And in Nathan's case: authentic joy.

The Science

As the English poet John Donne observed in the seventeenth century, "No man is an island." This isn't mere poetic sentiment but objective, scientifically verifiable fact. A large body of research shows that our feelings and emotions, both positive and negative, are highly contagious. Whatever we are feeling, we pass along to others—just as we absorb what others are feeling. Both our misery and our happiness greatly affect others.

A study conducted by James Fowler of the University of California at San Diego and Nicholas Christakis of Harvard University demonstrates this conclusively. Working from the data recorded by following nearly five thousand people over the course of twenty years, they concluded, "People's happiness depends on the happiness of others with whom they are connected. This provides further justification for seeing happiness, like health, as a collective phenomenon." Happiness, they wrote, *spreads up to three degrees removed from the initial source.* That is to say we transfer our happiness to both people with whom we interact directly *and to people we haven't met.* When we feel happy, chances are that a friend of a friend of ours will feel happier too.

This study is no fluke. Several unrelated studies have shown that emotional states, including negative ones, are passed easily from person to person. For instance, students randomly assigned to a depressed roommate became increasingly depressed themselves, while a study in the *Journal of Nonverbal Behavior* found that a huge range of emotions—both positive and negative—are contagious across vast networks of people.

Even more interestingly, there is compelling evidence that a small number of people making positive choices can have an outsized effect on the world around us, completely altering the behavior dynamics of the larger population. A 2011 study conducted at Rensselaer Polytechnic Institute used computational and analytical methods to discover the tipping point where a minority belief becomes the majority opinion. According to the scientists, when *just 10 percent of the population holds an unshakable belief that they are committed to spreading, over sufficient time their belief will* always *be adopted by the majority of the society.*

An astounding study published in the mainstream journal *Social Indicators Research* measured the effect that a small group of meditators had on the crime rate for the entire city of Washington, DC—an area with one of the highest rates of violent crime in the United States. During the summer of 1993, researchers enticed four thousand experienced meditators to move to the DC area for eight weeks. During that time, participants meditated as much as possible and consciously tried to project feelings of peace and calmness into the surrounding population. A twenty-seven-member project review board composed of independent scientists and leading citizens approved the research protocol and monitored the research process. Weekly crime data were derived from records provided by the District of Columbia Metropolitan Police Department, which are used in the FBI's annual *Uniform Crime Report.* Statistical analysis considered the effect of weather variables, daylight, historical crime trends, and annual patterns in the District of Columbia, as well as trends in neighboring cities.

Researchers found that after controlling for known variables, crime rates dropped by as much as 23 percent during the course of the study. In other words, it appears that a small group of meditators, by doing nothing more than meditating—not actively intervening in the community—created an atmosphere of peacefulness that was enough to cause crime rates to plummet. It took a concentration of only four thousand people (plus however many other meditators already lived in DC) to positively influence the behaviors of a population of more than five hundred thousand.

This is *not* at a unique result, with at least a half dozen other studies confirming it. Two studies conducted in Great Britain are worth highlighting. The first, published in another mainstream journal, *Psychology, Crime & Law*, was conducted in a way similar to the DC study, except that it focused on the population of Merseyside County, England. The same degree of crime reduction was found once a small threshold of the population practiced meditation.

A larger study enrolled twenty-six thousand people throughout Great Britain. Participants were asked to perform a variety of happiness practices, including gratitude, smiling more, performing acts of kindness, and so forth. It goes without saying that those who participated reported a boost in their happiness levels. More interesting is that both before and after people did the practices, the researchers randomly surveyed thousands of British across the country who did *not* perform happiness practices themselves and asked them to report on their well-being. These nonparticipants reported a 7 percent boost in their happiness, although they didn't know why. The authors of the study posited that the twenty-six thousand citizens who actively practiced happiness were able to lift the overall happiness level of the entire population of Great Britain.

It should also be noted that bliss practices such as meditation have also been scientifically proven to reduce aggression and violent behavior among convicted criminals, as well as reduce recidivism rates and helps convicted criminals improve their postprison lives.

That's not all. Studies have found that happy people engage in more prosocial behaviors than unhappy people do. Compared to unhappy people, happy people are:

- more altruistic and serviceful,
- less likely to commit crime,
- more ethical,

* less racist and race conscious,
* more open minded,
* less likely to abuse illegal drugs,
* more productive workers, and
* more creative and demonstrate better problem-solving skills.

Finally, it should be noted that happier people are more functional and emotionally resilient in times of crisis. When things are going very badly—in a given family, in a group, in society at large—happier people are more likely to respond better to adversity.

The Spirit

The opening sentence of the constitution for the United Nations Educational, Scientific and Cultural Organizations (UNESCO) declares, "That since wars begin in the minds of men, it is in the minds of men that the defenses of peace must be constructed."

It's not only war that begins in our mind, it's every form of ignorance and evil: greed, inhumanity, environmental degradation, materialism, sectarian hatred, racial discrimination, and, indeed, all kinds of aggression and intolerance.

Ultimately, the highest and most enduring solution to the world's problems isn't external rules, treaties, laws, prisons, punishments, and force. Admittedly, these are essential short-term solutions and necessary subcomponents for restraining ignorance, self-centeredness, and outright evil. But these are largely ways of treating the *symptoms* of lower consciousness; they are not a cure.

Let's look at just one example: racism in the United States. We've already seen a scientific study showing that happy people are less racist than unhappy ones. Now imagine the understanding of those who owned slaves and advocated slavery. They couldn't be reasoned out of their position. In fact, many argued that slavery was part of the natural order of things, even their divine right.

What happened when the North wanted to abolish slavery? Southerners didn't go along willingly. Instead they seceded from the Union and began the most violent and bloody war in America's history. Even after the Emancipation Proclamation, the North's victory, and a constitutional amendment to abolish slavery, what changed? In many respects, very little. The vanquished simply replaced slavery with Jim Crow laws. Just as badly, they continued to treat African-Americans as inferior. Laws alone—including the highest law itself, our Constitution—didn't change people's hearts, or even many of their actions.

Decades later, after Jim Crow laws were finally abolished, what was the immediate aftermath? Again, little changed. Most of the South refused to obey the anti-Jim Crow laws. Eventually they were compelled to, against their will, by a variety of external pressures. But this didn't end racism. It just took ever-subtler forms. That's one of the key reasons we needed to implement affirmative action programs. At no point in this sad, slow progression did the change in laws themselves do much to change the hearts and minds of racists.

Are these painfully slow advances better than nothing? Absolutely. But is this the *best* possible solution we can imagine? Absolutely not. No person of conscience should be satisfied with merely enacting a series of laws that compels people, often against their will, to behave in a certain way. It would be so much better if instead of sneaky, quiet, subversive hatred, we felt genuine oneness, compassion, unity, and love for one another. If we didn't feel the need to belittle or act superior to someone else just to feel better about ourselves. That's the *real* way to abolish racism in a lasting way, one that trickles into every detail, every interaction, and every moment of our relationships with one another.

So it is with all that ails humanity. Is it okay for greed, sexism, religious sectarianism, hatred, bigotry, naked aggression, sadism, materialism, narcissism, and the like to dwell in our hearts and minds so long as there are laws and armies restraining us? I don't think it's fine at all. Yes, having laws, penal systems, and militaries is certainly better than nothing. But it's not enough. We shouldn't be content with only this. Far better for us all if these attitudes were extinguished from our consciousness.

The only genuinely curative solutions—those that are thoroughgoing, complete, and lasting—are to transform the consciousness of humanity so that we no longer confuse ourselves into believing that self-centered or evil actions are beneficial either to ourselves or to those we claim to represent.

This is, of course, precisely what bliss is and does. It's the most intensive, comprehensive, and all-embracing way to alter our consciousness positively. We needn't even fully attain it. The very act of committing to it and beginning the practices goes a long way in solving most of our global challenges. Put simply: the higher the percentage of bliss consciousness we have, the less we do negative things to one another or our world. It's a clear, direct causation.

We can't permanently fix war, poverty, racism, environmental destruction, and the like by hitting them at the same level we created them. We must rise above them to a transcendent level of consciousness. In that moment, our troubles are no longer merely contained, they vanish.

Distributing the Cure

Unlike many diseases, we've already discovered the cure to what ails humanity: bliss consciousness. That alone is half the battle. What remains is the question of implementation and distribution. Like any cure, it takes awareness, time, and resources for it to reach every point on the globe. No cure takes immediate hold. Even diseases such as polio, measles, leprosy, and the plague, for which we've long had cures, have not yet been fully eradicated. But that doesn't mean that we don't try—or that there aren't good reasons for hope.

Actually, bliss has a striking advantage over the cures for physical disease: it is a self-sustaining, self-replicating *idea*. It doesn't require huge financial resources, government approval or oversight, manufacturing skill, import/export licenses, or physical transmission. Ideas can move at lightning speed through vast networks of people, now more than ever in our interconnected and amplified culture: from Internet social networks such as Facebook and Twitter, to mass media such as television, radio, and print, to word of mouth. A few can transmit to millions.

We need only have the right attitude and orientation. It's usually the case that pioneers and early adopters of new ideas—especially those who challenge the status quo—are derided as crazy, dreamers, or fools. In relatively recent times alone—never mind antiquity—automobiles, airplanes, roads, rockets, landing on the moon, trains, X-rays, radio, steam power, nuclear power, telegraphs, alternating current, personal computers, telephones, television, oil exploration, submarines, germ theory, brain surgery, and countless other innovations have been declared impossible, infeasible, or of no practical value.

As some of the above studies suggest—and common sense confirms—bliss needs only a healthy minority of adherents to have an outsized effect on humanity. Bliss spreads dynamically in networks of people, like a *good* virus. Every bliss-seeking person affects a whole slew of people, including countless folks we don't know and have never met. Small groups of people routinely exert significant effects on the world. Democracy, now a global force, began with just a relatively few people in the ancient Greek city-state of Athens. The entire Renaissance of Western civilization and culture began with just a handful of people in Florence, Italy. The progenitors of the scientific revolution could be listed on one piece of paper. The American Revolution was started and carried by only a tiny fraction of the population. A small group of meditators in the midst of a violent city lowered crime rates in just eight weeks.

Most important, happiness and bliss are self-reinforcing feedback loops. The more we have them, the more we spread them to others, the more our surrounding environment is happier, the more that reinforces our own happiness, the more people are touched by it. Bliss isn't necessarily linear. It can accelerate over time. What starts slowly will gain in speed by the very nature of bliss consciousness itself. When we access or attain higher levels of consciousness, we gain the ability to sow the seeds of inner peace, love, and bliss far beyond the limited scope of our physical bodies. We literally project vibrations of peace, love, and bliss into our environments.

It only seems difficult, far away, or far-fetched because we're at the beginning of the bliss-consciousness revolution. Real, noticeable results are achievable in a relatively short period. As every day goes by, and more and more people understand and practice these concepts, the impact grows exponentially.

Happiness, Bliss, and Suffering

A common objection to happiness, let alone bliss (at least in the philosophical circles that I used to frequent), is that it is "unseemly" to be happy in the face of so much suffering and misery in this world. In this view, happiness is selfish, self-centered, and perhaps even cruel. A few go even further: they are heroic in their choice to suffer.

This couldn't be more wrong. It is precisely this attitude that perpetuates, even worsens, human suffering. Genuine happiness and bliss require self-transcendence. Blissful people are the opposite of self-centered. They are engaged, forgiving, filled with compassion and kindness, innately interested in serving humanity, more ethical, and less superficial. Believing that we defer happiness until the world is more just, poverty is eradicated, and suffering eliminated is to promulgate exactly the wrong understanding about what genuine happiness is. It's to define happiness largely as something external and material. To convince others that happiness is unavailable to them because of their material conditions is to denigrate their spirit and trap them in unnecessary suffering. We become transmitters of the very suffering we claim to abhor.

We have a moral duty to pursue bliss and demonstrate to others that happiness is not primarily material or external. We must lead by example; by doing the work ourselves and then showing and helping others what they can do for themselves. The more we wallow in misery and allow others to do so, the more we invite the consequences of suffering into this world: hatred, intolerance, selfishness, and aggression.

If we truly want to help others, to make their lives better, it's essential that we work on ourselves. We can't give to others what we don't have. If we are miserable, no matter our superficial "good works," we will spread that misery, undoing a great deal of the benefits of our surface actions.

The Experiment: Contagious Happiness

1. Today make a conscious, concerted effort to spread happiness to others.
2. This means that we must feel that happiness ourselves. If for some reason, you don't feel you can conjure that right now, wait to do this

exercise until you can put yourself into a genuinely happy place or skip to step 6.

3. As you interact with people, visualize transmitting happiness to them. Think of it as spreading a "happy virus."

4. Try to notice the effect you are having on others. Are you helping them to feel happy, uplifting their mood? Can you confirm that happiness is indeed contagious?

5. Notice, too, the effect your positive mood is having on *you*. Do you feel more willing to help others, offer assistance, do a favor, or make an extra effort?

6. Alternative practice: since negative emotions are also contagious, if you cannot summon happiness, make a conscious effort to notice the effect that your *un*happiness is having on those around you. Furthermore, do you feel less inclined to help others right now?

Online

Additional videos and resources for this chapter are available at www.theblissexperiment.com.

CHAPTER 28

Bliss Is Yours

Life is a pilgrimage. The wise man does not rest by the roadside inns. He marches direct to the illimitable domain of eternal bliss, his ultimate destination.

—*Swami Sivananda (1887–1963)*

Bliss is our highest calling and potential. When we scrape away the false layers of sensory pleasures, worldly attainments, and the delusions of our mind, we discover it quietly dwelling inside us. All along, it has been with us, the solution to every problem and the answer to every question.

That we've always had it inside ourselves, even as we ceaselessly, restlessly explore our external world, is one of life's great paradoxes. In Hindu mythology, the entire universe is seen as a dream of God; a game that She plays by herself, like a cosmic game of hide-and-seek. God, in its infinite, transcendent, unmanifest form, screens off a part of itself to create the physical universe. The universe itself is nothing but vibrations of god-stuff crystallized into matter, much as vapor can become water, then ice.

To keep the game interesting, God creates *maya*, the force of cosmic delusion. Maya is the veil that we wear—or that comes over us—shielding us from immediately seeing the nature of the cosmic game. She wills her creation to forget temporarily that every atom is nothing but god-stuff. Without maya, there can be no game, as we would all instantly know the truth of our existence and melt immediately into blissful union. Maya is what allows the journey to exist, the cosmic game to seem real. We are nothing but that god-stuff, temporarily forgetting our true essence so that the Great Game can be played.

Like all games, there are winning and losing strategies. In the cosmic game of hide-and-seek, the only winning strategy is to look within and realize the depthless, eternal bliss that constitutes our very essence. At the moment this happens, we instantly realize all happiness, meaning, and truth. The game is over, and we blissfully merge back into the Source.

Like all myths, this is a metaphor designed to help us understand our existence. We needn't believe it literally. Anything spelled out in words and language is always lacking in some way. Language is just another tool, just as the mind is a tool. Language has its uses and applications, as well as areas it was never intended to serve. All language, even mythic language, can only help orient and point us in the right direction; even nudge us along on our journey. No amount of words can ever adequately explain the ineffable superconscious bliss to which it points.

Practical Bliss

Because bliss is the winning strategy to the game of life, it's the most practical course we can choose. Ignoring it, then, is among the most impractical, least grounded decisions we can make. To pursue bliss is the very opposite of being dreamy or pie in the sky. Bliss-filled lives function better than most. These people have greater chances at succeeding in whatever they pursue. Their powers of concentration are better, they are open to opportunities, they see more clearly, and they aren't hamstrung or undercut by their own negativity, anxiety, low self-esteem, or depression. They are confident, magnetic, ethical, and trustworthy.

Above all, the bliss-centric person is deeply engaged in this world. We don't need to drop out of society to pursue bliss. It's not an alternate lifestyle. It's a goal and state of consciousness that we bring *into* our world— into our work, relationships, families, and service. To feel bliss is to feel connected with everyone. There is no obsession with personal gain or loss. The bliss seeker works for the benefit of others, sometimes at her own expense, sometimes for the benefit of herself and others, but *never* solely for her own gain. We acknowledge our duties and responsibilities because we see in them the opportunity for self-transcendence.

Finding Balance, Avoiding Hypocrisy

As central as bliss is to our human essence and experience, it's important to avoid fanaticism. This is never the right approach to anything. To be fanatical is to give up all semblance of balance, self-forgiveness, and, well, reality. Life is seldom either/or, on/off, or yes/no. Recall the Happiness Scale. Few of us live entirely on the bliss end of the Happiness Scale—nor is that even our short-term goal. First we must discover that the bliss end of the scale exists. Next comes the commitment to slowly slide our lives toward bliss as much as possible. This is a journey that takes time. Like every journey, there are often setbacks and relapses, challenges and disappointments.

Each of us has our own journey, challenges, and circumstances. These affect the details and contours of our path. It may not—*will not*—look quite like anyone else's. It is vitally important that we not compare ourselves to others. Comparison is another external way of living. We must move forward relative to ourselves, based on what works for us as individuals. What works for others may not work for us.

It's usually helpful to avoid extremes. As the Buddha counseled, the middle course of moderation is usually the safest and most effective. Like all advice, this too is relative. What is extreme for one person is the middle course for another. Five hours of training per day for a young professional athlete is average—perhaps even too little. But five hours of daily exercise for an overweight sixty-year-old might be a death sentence.

We must step back and look at the long rhythms of our journey. As long as we're generally moving toward bliss, toward the attitudes and practices outlined in this book, all is well. Forward progress, even slow progress, leads to certain victory. We need always to be realistic, gentle, and compassionate with ourselves. Remember all that research on forgiveness and compassion? That applies to us every bit as much as to others. Fanaticism is the absence of empathy and compassion not only for others but ourselves.

On the other hand, it's crucial that we never become hypocrites. Sad to say, I've met more than a few. Hypocrisy is demanding of others what we don't demand of ourselves. It's the ultimate external, when we only *pretend* to believe or practice these things when, in reality, we don't believe it, don't practice it, and have no intention of doing so.

Hypocrisy, however, is not the same as merely falling short of our genuine goals. Imperfection is not hypocrisy. Almost all of us fall short of pure, unadulterated bliss. Most of us are still somewhere in the beginning or middle of our journey. We have not yet reached the final destination. Nor is self-honesty the same as hypocrisy. Certain things may be out of our grasp for the moment. Being okay with where we are on our journey is essential to a humane approach. Our internal motivations are more important than how things look to others.

It's best to keep focused on us, not on what others are (or are not) doing. Judging others is a fatal error. So, too is assuming that we are different or better than others. Worst of all is the belief that we are exempt from the same laws and truths that govern all of humanity. We must remain humble and ever vigilant against believing that what applies to others doesn't apply to us. That we can do and get away with things that others can't—that we are somehow special or different. This may well be the fastest possible route to spiritual disaster.

Bliss Is Yours

The awareness and experience of bliss is our highest priority. It is the only genuine solution to personal and planetary suffering.

Eventually the external world grows wearisome for us all. The endless highs and lows become tedious. The only true, lasting, and genuinely thrilling frontier left to explore is our inner realm. Undertaking this journey is our reason for being. Bliss is always there, quietly beckoning us to discover the secret of lasting happiness, enduring meaning, and eternal truth within.

Our only real choice is to decide how long we wish to continue playing the game of cosmic hide and seek. How long we wish to continue our cycle of suffering? How long do we wish to dawdle? How long do we want to stay in delusion? How much suffering do we want to heap upon our loved ones, our world, and ourselves?

The sooner we get there, the better. The only reason to delay is because we think that there is something equally or more interesting for us to find along the way. This is the cosmic delusion of maya whispering in our ear, beckoning us down false pathways and prodding us to look for happiness in all the wrong places.

Ultimately, there are only three obstacles to bliss. The first is not realizing it exists. The second is not having the tools or understanding to excavate it. The third is refusing to commit to the journey.

If we didn't know before that bliss exists, we do now. If we knew or suspected it existed but didn't quite know how to get there, now we know much more clearly. We have all the understanding, attitudes, and tools necessary to undertake the journey. The map is in our grasp.

There is only one thing missing: our conscious, willing choice to take the journey. We must choose, wholeheartedly, to embrace the path to bliss. We must make the most sacred of all vows to ourselves: to uncover the shining, pure diamond of bliss within.

The wonderful thing to remember always about the journey to bliss: it gets easier, lighter, more fun, and more filled with joy as we go. That's very different from how most journeys unfold. Usually we think that the longer the journey, the more grueling. Think of the last few miles of running a marathon or trying to reach the summit of Mount Everest. But bliss is always the inverse of what we experience in the external world: it gets easier with every step, every attitude adjustment, every practice, every conscious decision we make. The joy of bliss is that the journey becomes self-sustaining and self-reinforcing. The single hardest part, then, is to make the initial commitment to take those *first* steps. If we can do that, our life gets better with each passing day.

Right now, in this very moment, is the time to make the commitment. The only way to prove the truth of *The Bliss Experiment* is to take the journey, to make our lives the living proof of its eternal truth.

Bliss is here with us right now, in this very moment; lurking just beneath the surface, quietly calling to us, wanting to give you every fulfillment and satisfaction you have ever imagined. Bliss can be yours. Bliss *is* yours. You need only turn within and embrace it.

The Experiment: Expansion of Bliss

Every time a feeling of bliss—however small and potentially fleeting—appears in your consciousness, make it your priority to hold onto it and expand it. It doesn't matter what created it—whether something internal or external, trivial or important. Whatever its source, take the time to notice and enjoy it.

Try to see below the surface, the ostensible cause, and instead feel it as a thing in itself, something that is always there, always waiting to be triggered by anything and everything. Feel that it is bubbling up from an eternal reservoir of bliss hiding just beneath the surface of your regular, everyday consciousness.

Visualize the happiness or bliss you feel as a bubble of light, one that you can mentally expand at will. Paramhansa Yogananda said that bliss has no boundaries; it is "center everywhere, circumference nowhere." Dwell on this essential joy within your own being, continuing to expand your consciousness until you feel bliss pouring out from you and infusing the world. Feel yourself becoming that bliss itself. You are eternal bliss!

Online

Scan the Microsoft Tag above to view a brief video, "Final Thoughts and Quick Tips," or go to youtube.com/seanmeshorer.

ACKNOWLEDGMENTS

As anyone who has written a book knows, it's a profoundly collaborative process, even if only one person's name is on the cover. So many people helped to make this book, there isn't enough space to name them all or detail the help they proffered. But of course one can try.

Let me start by thanking all the dedicated professionals—and now friends—who made this happen. The process began with the help of my agents, Priscilla Gilman and Tina Bennett, certainly the very best in the business. They have been invaluable in too many ways to possibly list. One that I can list is hooking me up with Richard Prud'homme, who was an early reader of this manuscript and who gave invaluable feedback in every way, large and small.

There's a huge team of people at Atria who have helped shape this book. First and foremost, my editor, Johanna Castillo, who believed in me, took a big risk, and has worked tirelessly from the start. The very shape, structure, and direction of this book is very much her doing. Not to mention her enthusiastic and supporting championing of this project, spearheading the team at Atria. Amy Tannenbaum, who assisted and is a fine editor in her own right—and even found one of the key studies presented herein. Also at Atria: publicist Lisa Sciambra, Chris Lloreda, the crack sales team, plus Anne Gardner, Lisa Keim, and the whole Atria team, most especially of all, publisher Judith Curr, who is a visionary in every way.

Sandi Mendelson has been more than a publicist, she's been a mentor and guide. And all the great people on her team, including her partner Judy Hilsinger, with special appreciation to Iris Blasi and Deborah Jensen. Publicist Jacqueline Clark has been indispensable in her uncommon area of expertise in the mind/body/spirit world. The fine folks at Joonam

Productions, led by Bayan and his team who conjured immensely creative videos on not much of a budget. Jen Marcum created the companion website to this book.

There are so many people who've meant so much to me over the years, I can't thank them all. But of course I'd get in serious trouble if I didn't begin with my mother, Judith Meshorer. She couldn't have been more supportive of this project in every way. But mostly, she deserves thanks for putting up with years of life decisions that made absolutely no sense to her—but she stuck it out and never kicked me out. With what I put her through, not all mothers would do the same, I can assure you. To Peter Linsey, for helping to keep my mother sane and probably from disowning me long ago.

Also to my deceased father, Marc, the original writer in the family, with whom I never felt closer than while I wrote this. My sister Danielle (and her husband Gregg) for so many things, I don't know where to start. To Marilyn and Marshall Bedol for your love and support—plus years of crazy letters and care packages (Marshall your next one is overdue). To Michael Friedman, to whom I would never have made it this far if I hadn't stumbled into his help and guidance over twenty years ago. To Irv and Beryl Moore, who played an essential cameo at a key moment in my life, one of those small moments that meant a whole lot to me, though it wouldn't surprise me if you can't even remember it.

And of course to Brook, who has stuck by me through some unbelievably dark and gruesome times that came much too early-on, before we even finished the honeymoon phase of our relationship. Yet, she's still here. Keeping me light and out of my head as much as possible. She's been with me every step and every day through this journey.

And finally to all my friends, family, *gurubhais*, students, and congregants, who are far, far, far too numerous to list—a sign of a very blessed life. Each and every one of you has been immensely meaningful to me in your own unique way. Together, you've not only contributed to this book but helped make me who I am today.

A NOTE ON THE BIBLIOGRAPHY

Due to the extraordinary length of the bibliography, which contains citations for more than five hundred mainstream scientific studies, it's not possible to include it here in this book.

Instead, I have published the complete bibliography on the companion website for this book, www.theblissexperiment.com.

Not only does this permit me to show you the complete range of sources used for The Science sections of this book but it also means that I can continually update and add new studies as they are published. And of course, if you are aware of any important studies that I'm missing, please do let me know. I would love to include them.

ABOUT THE AUTHOR

SEAN MESHORER is a spiritual teacher and New Thought minister based in Los Angeles, as well as spiritual director of a nonprofit organization. He graduated from Stanford in 1993 with a degree in philosophy and religious studies. He spent fifteen years meditating, studying, practicing, and living in an ashram and spiritual community in Northern California. For more information about him, visit www.seanmeshorer.com.

Join Sean at www.theblissexperiment.com, which is a complete interactive community. Read *The Bliss Experiment* blog, watch the companion videos for this book, share your own bliss stories, ask questions, participate in discussions, meet other like-minded people, and practice The Experiments.

Sean speaks at events, workshops, religious organizations, businesses, conferences, retreats, and other places throughout the year.

To share your own experiences or invite Sean to speak, you can contact him at:

sean@seanmeshorer.com
310-876-2392

You can also follow him on social media:

Facebook.com/seanmeshorer
Twitter: @seanmeshorer
YouTube.com/seanmeshorer